THE ALCHEMY OF THOUGHT

THE ALCHEMY OF THOUGHT

BY

L. P. JACKS, M.A.

Essay Index Reprint Series

BOOKS FOR LIBRARIES PRESS
FREEPORT, NEW YORK

First Published 1910
Reprinted 1968

LIBRARY OF CONGRESS CATALOG CARD NUMBER:

68-8473

PRINTED IN THE UNITED STATES OF AMERICA

PREFACE

THE following essays deal with the belief that logical system is only one among countless forms in the self-expression of the universe. I have endeavoured to do justice to the claims of system; at the same time I have resisted these claims in so far as they threaten to usurp the whole field of human experience.

To say that the universe is a Rational Whole appears to me true. But to treat this as an adequate account of Reality appears to me false. I am equally averse to regarding the rationality of the universe as the fundamental or all-inclusive or even the dominant form of its self-expression.

What does form a Rational Whole and is adequately described by this term is the movement of thought throughout the ages—in a word, the History of Philosophy. To equate this movement with the universe to which it refers, to make the History of Philosophy into a History of Reality, appears to me an error.

We are constantly tempted to make this equation, and constantly prevented from seeing its falsity, by the habit of treating speculative thought as a form of *ours* into which all experience must manage to fit itself. An important step towards liberation from this habit was taken by Spinoza, who treated Thought as one among the infinite and eternal forms of the self-expression of Substance—as one and one only. The benefits of this liberty, which relieve the mind from a very great burden, were largely sacrificed in the subsequent developments of Spinoza's doctrine.

In much that follows I have repeated what is now common doctrine among Pluralists. But Pluralism has lost much of the strength it would otherwise have by denying, or seeming to deny, that the universe does express itself as a Rational Whole. This denial, however, is by no means involved in the affirmation that Reality expresses itself in many ways other than those which fit into the forms of conceptual logic. It is certainly true, as the Pluralists contend, that if the universe were *nothing but* a Rational Whole—taking rational in its strict sense—the richness and variety of life would vanish and freedom would be impossible. On the other hand, if the universe were not rational, and were incapable of expressing itself in that form— if, that is, Reality were forbidden by its inner constitution from taking that one among all the forms of a possible self-expression—it is equally plain that the world would be no place for beings constituted as we are.

It will be said, no doubt, that this last statement is itself an appeal to rationality. This rejoinder, common as it has now become, merely serves to remind us once more of the saying that logic is a "dodge." As James has pointed out, the word "rational" is a multidimensional term, and the constant effort of rationalism to confute all critics out of their own mouths appears to succeed only because rationalists expand the meaning of the term "rational" with every step in the progress of their opponents' argument, and thus make it serve the changing purpose of their own. The rule that "thought cannot go behind its own principles" is of great importance, so long as we are dealing with experience exclusively as a Problem-to-be-solved, and I have not hesitated to make full use of it in the essay on "Self-defeating Theories" and elsewhere. But when the rule is strained into meaning that experience must be taken as a Problem-to-be-solved, and as that alone, it appears to me unfair and inadmissible; in fact, neither more nor less than a logical "dodge." When once we have fallen into this trap there is, of course, no escape; all issues are foreclosed. If it be said that the very process by which we avoid the trap is itself a rational process, and only a more roundabout way of entering the toils, I must again protest against this fast-and-loose usage of the term "rational"; for the "reason" which avoids the trap is by no means the same "reason" which laid it in the first instance.

I confess it is only after some hesitation that I venture to include in this volume the allegorical piece which I have called "Devil's Island and the Isles of Omniscience." If any trained student of philosophy should read my book I trust he will not take implacable offence at this somewhat unusual method of exposition. My object in that piece is to express the dissatisfaction and rebelliousness which every attempt to fix experience into the form of a logical system provokes in the total personality. I found myself quite unable to effect my purpose by the method of direct exposition. That I have succeeded by indirection I am far from certain; but I shall be well content if the piece calls attention to certain by-products of philosophical teaching which are too little regarded.

The essays entitled respectively "The Universe as Philosopher," "The Alchemy of Thought," "The Moral Supremacy of Christendom," "Religion," have appeared in substance in *The Hibbert Journal.* Into the first two I have introduced some modifications, due to changes, or, as one always ventures to hope, to the growth of thought.

I owe a debt of gratitude to Professor Henry Jones and to the Rev. Charles B. Upton for their help in revising the proofs. The criticisms of Professor Jones have been all the more valuable because of his radical dissent from some of my main positions. My gratitude to Mr Upton is deepened by the circumstance that I owe to him my first interest in philosophical studies. I should be proud to think that he may recognise in these pages some trace of his own influence, as well as of that of his master, who was also my own teacher, James Martineau.

L. P. JACKS.

Manchester College,
Oxford, 1910.

CONTENTS

THE ALCHEMY OF THOUGHT

I.—THE BITTER CRY OF THE PLAIN MAN

AN APPEAL TO PHILOSOPHERS

" The best philosopher is the man who can think most *simply*."
JOHN GROTE.

PHILOSOPHY, like Religion, has to endure opposition
from a law in the members which wars against the law
of the mind. But as the rock-climber, with his foot
planted on a three-inch ledge, owes his safety to the
same gravitation which draws to the abyss, so it may
be said that without the law in our members the
law of the mind could neither get nor keep its hold.
The ultimate relation between these two is one of peace.
Nevertheless, for Philosophy as for Religion there are
moments of dizziness when destruction seems imminent.
Firmly planted on the truths of its highest experience,
the soul presently falls into a mood of scepticism or
indifference when all that was so sure an hour ago
seems incredible, impossible, absurd.

Religious men have never scrupled to make a clean
breast of this matter. They have rather taken pains
to describe the cunning assaults of doubt, that others
similarly tempted may be forewarned and forearmed.

1

When we turn from Religion to Philosophy (which, I venture to think, is at bottom rather an Experience or Life than a set of doctrines cut and dried), we find that philosophers have less to tell us about their misgivings. Perhaps they do well to keep silence, for their work is to exhibit the Truth as true. There is, at all events, a sharp contrast between the religious man, on the one hand, who confesses his weakness, acknowledges the difficulty of keeping the faith, and prays to heaven for strength to subdue the treachery of his heart, and, on the other hand, the philosophic man with his frequent air of having settled the question. Judging philosophers from the atmosphere of their works, we should scarcely suspect that they were subject to grave misgivings and sinkings of the heart, when they feel their systems turning hollow, their arguments losing relevance, and the very meaning of their work on the point of vanishing into thinnest air.

And yet, were philosophers to write their Confessions, as St Augustine wrote his, I doubt not that abundant witness would be borne to these misgivings. We have all known philosophers in what are called their lighter moments, though I am inclined to think that these are sometimes the most serious moments of their lives. We know that between the philosopher as exhibited in his works and the philosopher as we encounter him elsewhere there is a difference: sometimes a difference which we welcome and sometimes a difference which we deplore. And having observed the contrast we can hardly doubt that for him, as for the religious man, there are times of eclipse, times when his philosophy slips from his grasp and fades away, times when it is only by the greatest effort of mind that he can apply his philosophic insight to his present condition. Nor does he show any reluctance when questioned to acknowledge that this is even so. " My philosophy," he will say, " did ultimately help me on the occasions to which you refer ; but it was only after a very severe struggle with my unphilosophic self."

Now this unphilosophic self of the philosopher does occasionally put in an appearance in the pages of the profoundest thinkers, though he does so, if I may be pardoned for saying it, in a somewhat mythological shape. He appears, that is to say, as a person with whom our author has a purely external or bowing acquaintance, and the name given him is " the Plain Man." We are left to suppose that the Plain Man is some person whom the writer, as he looks up from his desk, sees passing in the street; or he is the casual acquaintance of a railway journey ; or he is some butcher, baker, or candlestick-maker, who receives and executes the orders of the Herr Professor or the Frau Professorin. We are left, I say, to suppose this; but the supposition is seldom true. Nine times out of ten the Plain Man is just the philosopher himself in one of those not infrequent moments when he is overtaken by an eclipse of his philosophic faith. The Plain Man is a living protest, originating in the heart of the philosopher, against the over-rigidity or the over-refinement of his system. He is, in fact, the unphilosophic self; a person with whom our author has a far more intimate acquaintance than he is always willing to confess; and his utterances, his illusions, his obstinacy, instead of being remote and external phenomena observed from the philosophic watch-tower, are the autobiographical confessions of some metaphysician who, to all seeming, would utterly conceal his human personality from the reader and write as though he were animated by the spirit of Pure Reason alone.

The present writer has, in what follows, endeavoured to make the Plain Man speak in this character. Throughout his studies of philosophy and his successive conversions to this school and to that, he has been conscious that there existed in his mind an unconverted residuum, which constantly criticised and challenged the converted part of him to give an account of itself. This unconverted residuum is here introduced as the Plain Man. We may think of him as playing a part like that of the chorus in a Greek tragedy. His station is within the soul; and he accompanies the successive phases of the mind's drama, not as a participant but as a spectator, and yet a spectator whose comments are not without their influence on the action of the main characters. Whether the Plain Man, considered as the next individual who passes my window, will recognise any resemblance between himself and the personage here presented, I do not know, and I do not ask. Some may even think that the Plain Man of the following pages does not deserve the name he bears; that possibly he would be more correctly designated as " The Tempter " to whom *retro Satanas* is the fitting word; but the justification for retaining the former name is that, so far as I understand him, he is identically the same individual as he who is called the Plain Man in accredited works of philosophy. He is, in short, the philosopher himself, with his pallium laid aside.

It may be said that any person who hears the Plain Man pleading within him as he pleads in the sequel thereby makes confession of his own failure to attain philosophic insight. Is it not the business of philosophy to reconcile a man with himself, and does it not follow therefore that an unconverted residuum is the sure sign of a dabbler or a neophyte?

This, I must admit, is a tenable supposition. For the present, however, its point may be turned aside by reiterating what has already been said, viz. that moments do occur, even to illustrious thinkers whose philosophy reconciles them with themselves, when the reconciliation somehow fails to work and the old conflict breaks out anew. Moreover, an occasional uprush of the Plain Man into the philosophic consciousness is no more remarkable than the existence of plain men, in the usual sense of the term, in the world at large. We cannot understand how it comes to pass that in the midst of that complete experience which we ascribe to the Unitary Soul of things, and forming, as it were, an integral part of the consciousness of that Being, there exist a multitude of individuals like ourselves whose experience is admittedly incomplete—just plain men. If the truth of Divine Immanence is to be taken seriously we must suppose that the protests, the pleadings, the bitter cries of millions of plain men surge up continually in the Unitary Mind and constitute a part of its experience. Now no one would think of describing God as a dabbler or a neophyte because the constitution of the universe involved this continual presence in the Divine Consciousness of the Plain Man's limitations and difficulties. The philosopher, therefore, has nothing to be ashamed of if on reflection he is forced to confess that voices from a world where insight is clouded occasionally make themselves heard in the heaven of his loftiest vision; nor will he, being who he is, cast about for hard names to throw at humbler persons who make this confession without any shame at all—much as these persons deserve contempt on other grounds. If it is a misfortune to have to hear the importunities of the unphilosophic self delivered in one's own heart, it is a misfortune we share with the universe at large, or with whatever Soul the universe may express. God, if one may use that term, seems to be wonderfully patient with the plain men who live in His bosom, making His sun to rise on the butcher, baker, or candlestick-maker as well as upon Plato, Spinoza, or Kant. Is it too much to ask philosophers to grant a small measure of that patience to the Plain Man who is now to speak?

THE APPEAL

"Gentlemen, there is some misunderstanding between you and us which we, no less than you, would fain remove. There have been faults on both sides, and the greater fault has been with us. That you have an indictment against us we all know. Our petulance, our obstinacy, our suspicion, deserve your rebuke; our stupidity deserves your pity. On your side, however, there has been some aloofness; you have made it difficult for us to get at you, while at the same time you have claimed the right to descend upon us from your great castles and harry our defenceless fields at your will. And may we not also plead that there has been some want of perspective in the judgments you have passed upon us? Justly conscious of the great gulf between our easy ignorance and your hard-won wisdom, you have not truly measured the greater gulf between your wisdom and that of God. Viewed from that end, are not you also plain men like ourselves? Does not all the trouble, indeed, arise from this—that neither party is plain enough? Let us endeavour at least to be plain with one another. Then we shall surely discover enough philosophy in the Plain Man, and enough plainness in the philosopher, to make us the best of friends.

"Do not believe the evil tongues which say the Plain Man has no dealings with the Philosopher. Our interest in your work is great—greater than you are wont to imagine. Many of us have done our best to understand you, clinging to our plainness the while with perhaps excessive zeal. We have tried to raise ourselves to your level, not doubting that you had won further on the upward way of life than we. Nor are we

ungrateful for the friendly hands so often extended by
you to help our feeble effort to rise.   We acknowledge
our debt to the Great Masters.   In their faces always, and
in their books sometimes, we perceive a genuine concern
for the troubles of the poor Plain Man.   They have seen
the frequent tragedy of his life; and their own lives have
been freely given that they might find him a key to the
mysteries of his being.   Often, indeed, when asking for
bread they have given him a stone; but the stone was
all they had to give, and the winning of it had cost
them dear.   And a strange thing would sometimes
come to pass.   The spirit of their giving would enter
into the gift, and, working there like a powerful alchemy,
would turn that stone into the Plain Man's bread!   Oh,
we have seen it, and our hearts have overflowed with
gratitude to the giver who gave so much better than he
knew!   Gentlemen, among all your critics it is often
the Plain Man who understands you best.   Baffled by
the hardness of your written words, he falls into a habit
of reading you between the lines.   He gives you credit
for the things you leave unsaid, because you cannot say
them.   Is it not, then, a matter for infinite regret that
you and we should meet so often as strangers?   There
ought to be more in common between us.   There ought
to be more interchange of thought.

" Yes, *interchange* of thought.   For perhaps you have
not realised as fully as you might have done that we,
too, are thinkers of a sort.   By some of you, indeed,
our thinking has not been overlooked; it has been
treated with even more respect than it deserves.   But,
broadly speaking, you have been too unwilling to let
the Plain Man speak for himself.   You have insisted on
speaking for him, and many of the words you put into

his mouth do scant justice to his thoughts. He has a richer life than that for which you give him credit; and because his life is richer, his troubles also are deeper than you imagine. Gentlemen, the thirst of the Plain Man is great; it craves abundance of water. You must dig your wells deeper if you are to satisfy him. Both you and he must become far plainer men!

"Your books are often crabbed, but the kindly faces among you embolden us to speak. We are thinking of the great ones, or rather of the greatest. If there are any of your followers who would drive us from the doors with sticks and with stones, you will forbid them. We are come to speak with the Masters of the House. Of such we have known several among the living, and never once have we seen them frown upon the poor Plain Man. We have met them also among the mighty dead; for of these too we know something, thanks to the excellent books which you have written especially for us. We open a little treatise on Spinoza; we see before us the portrait of the sage, and as we look into his wise and gentle eyes we say to ourselves, 'Here is one to whom the Plain Man might confess himself without shame.' Confident that there are many among you on whom that spirit has fallen, we shall use great boldness of speech. There are many; would that there were more! For often, alas, there comes into your councils another spirit which strikes the Plain Man dumb. Something forced in your manner, something hard on your faces, something strident in your speech, warns us to hold our peace. Then it is that we would rather suffer you to speak wrongly on our behalf than say one single word for ourselves. For the Plain Man has a sensitive soul, and goes away sorrowful from all assemblies where the fingers of cavil are playing on the harp-strings of life.

"Gentlemen, we are going to make a full confession, hoping thereby to ease ourselves of a perilous load that weighs upon the heart. There shall be faithful dealing on our side. Knowing your good-will towards us, we will tell you plainly wherein you have failed to help us hitherto. You shall feel our minds reacting on your own doctrines, and if they react with some bitterness we shall try to make you feel it none the less. Not of our wants alone, nor of our difficulties, shall we speak, but also of our disappointment, it may be of our anger, and of any secret grudge we harbour against yourselves. We have declared our gratitude already, and by nothing that follows shall the declaration be unsaid; but gratitude is obstructed and mixed with other emotions, and these also shall be revealed. Will you not be patient while we make a clean breast of it all? If we have hard things to say, you, who are wise, will bear with us; you will listen and discriminate and answer us, not by rude words of contempt, but by showing us a better way. It is a hard thing to ask, a high thing to expect; but we remember to whom we speak. Such is our confidence in your wisdom that we are even content to become fools for your sakes.

"We doubt whether you, as a body, have ever been deeply desirous of our conversion; for we cannot but observe that with rare but splendid exceptions your efforts to convert us have been short-lived, intermittent, and ill-conceived. Too many of you, seated in the high places of Zion, have waited for the Gentiles to come to the light, and when they came not, have betrayed an aristocratic indifference to their salvation. You have taken no pains to acquire their language that you might speak to them in a tongue they can understand, but have required them to learn yours, a condition which you must know they cannot fulfil.

"Are you content with this estrangement between you and us? Shall we not try to understand each other? Will you not deign to listen to the stammering tongue of the Plain Man and bear with him while he lays his trouble before you?

"In the first place, then, we ask you to consider that things have a language of *their own* which is richly eloquent to the Plain Man. Beyond the information needed for his present purpose, in which the Plain Man is ever thankful for your help, things go on speaking to him about matters which have nothing to do with any purpose of his, and which, though perfectly clear, are not translatable into the language of purpose, but must remain for ever embedded in the more musical speech in which they are first spoken. There are tongues in trees and sermons in stones; but in order to hear them you must take the tree at its own valuation, the stone on its own terms, and not try to make either stone or tree speak any language of yours. Set the stone upright with a black coat on the back of it and it will preach no more of the sermons we love to hear. Cut down the tree and make it into an image of your god and the divine tongue that is within it falls dumb. Leave it, we beseech you, to tell some part of its story in its own way.

"For it is precisely this part of the message of things which most interests the Plain Man and gives him the joy of life. Whether that other part of this message which you translate for him into the language of his purpose has anything to do with this infinitely vaster part which so often escapes you, is precisely one of those points on which the Plain Man will be grateful for further information. But leaving that aside, please attend, gentlemen, to the outstanding fact; which is, that what the Plain Man loves most and values highest in the world is the untranslated part of the world's message. Though untranslated he finds it, as we said, eloquent and precious; so much so indeed that he responds to it with a degree of welcome, of enthusiasm, of delight, which he can only express by lifting up his head and smoothing the wrinkles out of his ape-like brow, by clothing himself in gorgeous apparel, by making music, by carving statues of the gods, or even by laying down his life as a ransom for many. Nay, more. Were it not for that part of the world's message which he cannot and does not wish to translate, there are times when that other part which you interpret would become intolerable, would overwhelm him with despair, and he would snatch at a bare bodkin and end his life.

"Of this vast comfort, of this abiding joy, of this heavenly refuge from the storm, the Plain Man often feels himself bereft in your presence. You will not allow the world to speak that language of its own which, so long as it remains in the original, is the Word of Life to the Plain Man. All that, you insist, is misrepresentation; the world left to itself to tell its own story in its own way cannot do other than mislead. And you propose to rectify the distorted lines of the universe by forcing them into the straight moulds of your philosophy. Instead of the universe you give us your system, your science, your book. 'This system,' you say, 'is the tongue of the world; this book is the message of things; this Science is the speech of the

Real. Here are published the sermons of the stones;
here are written down the language of the stars and
the true voices of the running brook.' Oh, gentlemen,
it is a poor exchange !

"And now, what happens next? Well, you are not
all alike; but the Plain Man is no chooser; he takes
the first guidance that offers, and, alas, it is seldom the
best. He opens your book as you bid him; and lo,
his gorgeous palaces, his towers of defence, fade like an
unsubstantial pageant and leave not a wrack behind.
His world is spoilt, the voices he loved are silenced.
The ineffable poetry of things is reduced to crabbed
prose. The breath of life is stifled. The world has
become all that the Plain Man loved it for not being.
He loved it because it ever seemed to say to him precisely what it meant. You have made it equivocal
and obscure. He loved it because it was disingenuous;
you have made it a conundrum. 'The Riddle of the
Universe'! What kind of a universe is that which
addresses the soul as nothing but a Riddle ? A devil's
universe through and through. What kind of a Reality
is that which for ever seems to be what it is not ? A
nightmare horror, a hideous dream, a thing in whose
presence our souls take up a lamentation like that of
Rachel, weeping for children that are no more.[1]

"And what of the Plain Man's God? Gentlemen,
the Plain Man knows just as well as you do that his
conception of God is a most unphilosophical affair.
But what you seldom understand is that the Plain Man
loves his God, worships his God, tries to serve his God
just so far as He transcends the bounds of your systems.

---

[1] "Dialectic is the universal and irresistible power before which
nothing can stay." Hegel, *Smaller Logic*, tr. Wallace, p. 128.

Made philosophical, as some of you would make it, the Object of the Plain Man's devotion would lose every attribute which he recognises as Divine. Do you realise what you are doing?

"You have told us many times that we are a poor anthropomorphic lot of heathens, and you have quoted the old saw about the religious lions whose gods are bigger lions than themselves. It is true. And yet we have often thought that there is no class of men in this world, certainly not the class of plain men, who confirm that saw more neatly than some of you. For what are you—and what is your God? Is it not the business of many of you to rack your brains in the contriving of hard questions that you may put the trembling neophyte to the test? And what kind of a Person is God when we think of Him as these say we ought? Gentlemen, their God is an Examiner like themselves. Their God, we repeat, with his Riddle of a Universe, is a Magnified Examiner made in their own image, a Being who has no dealings with his creatures save such as he may express under the form of questions, problems, conundrums, which the creature must answer aright at great pain and peril to himself. 'Life,' said one who addressed us not long ago, 'life is the passing or the failing to pass of a continual examination'; and in so saying he disclosed, if we mistake not, the innermost nerve of his thought. What, according to such an one, is a *fact*? Something whose sole reason for being is the need to get itself explained; problematic in essence, interesting only so far as understood. His facts when they come before us do not say, 'We are what we seem'; they say rather, 'We are not what we pretend to be; find out therefore what we are, and

beware of the consequences if you fail.' Thus experience is converted into an interminable Examination
Paper, and God is the author of it. The universe, of
whose intelligibility you are so anxious that we should
be convinced, is intelligible only in the same sense as
the questions are which these, with deliberate and sometimes sinister cunning, contrive as a sore trial for the
sons of men. ' I Am That I Am ' is no more ; ' What
Am I ? ' has usurped his place. Not for one instant
does ' What Am I ? ' leave us alone. Written and *viva
voce*, graven in the rocks, traced in vast letters on the
midnight sky, volleyed in the thunder, whispered in the
breeze, hummed by the beating heart, sibilating in
lovers' sighs—the awful interrogation pursues its course,
and the Inexorable Examiner, seated on a throne more
terrible than that of any king or judge, looks out upon
the poor examinees with the cold eyes of a Perfect
Rationality, abiding the answer. Such is their God.

" Is it surprising, then, that many of us have come to
think of you with some bitterness of heart ? For to
you, we often think, is owing much of the sorrow that
afflicts us in these modern days. First and foremost,
there is the burden of all this weary, unintelligible world.
We deny it not. We see it waiting for every man at
his appointed hour. But who has tied it upon our
backs for ever as a thing from which there is no escape ?
Who has brought it to pass that the weary weight
never leaves us ? Who has put a question in the
mouth of every fact and plied us with riddles till we
reel and stagger and are at our wits' end ? Gentlemen,
you have overdone all this. You have forced your
riddles in season and out ; and not content with those the
world will furnish, you have invented others of your

own. It is you who hold us to the question night and day. Have you not dealt too hardly with the Plain Man? Is it none of your doing that this bad dream never leaves us—the dream that we carry on our backs the weary weight of an unintelligible world? Have you not made of life a blacker mystery than you need?

"There is a mystery in life; but is there not something else? By your showing the mystery seems omnipresent, pervasive, essential; in the real scheme of things it is occasional, and attached as it were to only one point on the ever-turning wheel of life. Again, there is a puzzle in the world; we know it well. By your showing the world holds it like a pistol at the reluctant head of man; in the real scheme of things, however, it is mercifully hidden until the appointed hour draws nigh. Yes, there are ten thousand matters of negotiation between us and the world which we can carry through from start to finish with no thought given to your Sphinx-riddles. Oh, leave them in their place! Sufficient unto the day is the evil thereof!

"Your business, you tell us, is to solve problems, and we have no right to complain of you for trying to solve them. 'If you don't like us,' you say, 'leave us. We will attend to our business and you to yours. No one compels you to read our books. Keep to religion or poetry, or whatever else may give you satisfaction, and leave the problems alone. The remedy is in your own hands.'

"Gentlemen, the advice is good, but the trouble is that you will not suffer us to follow it. We go away, as you suggest; we leave you, as we think, to yourselves: we go to the church or to some other place where a Plain Man may find comfort—and lo, you are there before us, waiting, as it were, at the very doors. We would fain say our prayers, but who is this at our elbow who whispers 'Answer,' 'Understand,' 'Solve'? Barely have we time to cry the name of God before we are bidden to define our terms and explain what we mean. Did we not go to church the other day and lift up our hearts in a song of gratitude to the All-wise, and did not one of your number thereupon go up into the pulpit and entertain us, for fifty minutes, with an apology for his God? Oh, it was not wisely done! Alas, there is no getting away from you. What avails it that we forsake your dwellings and betake ourselves to religion, if you are there before us with the 'Problem of Religion' in your hands?

"Is there not something artificial about all this, some thing forced, something overdone? Do you not often compel us to take our Experience in the form of a Problem when there is no need? Are you not less merciful, or less wisely reticent, than the universe you would fain interpret? Ah, how pale, how sicklied o'er, the world would be had it nothing to offer us, nothing to say to us, save what can be offered as Problem-and-answer, save what can be said in the language of your systems, your science, and your books! Do you not realise how the constant forcing of Experience into that mould wears down the spirits of the Plain Man and puts him at odds with his life? Will you not try to understand, Gnostics and Agnostics alike, that to him the world is neither a riddle with an answer, nor a riddle without one, but just no riddle at all! To him the world is the world and there's the end! Often it seems to him that he can live his life all the better for having

2

no 'Theory of the Universe' to hamper him.   For
those who want such things they are perhaps to be had,
and when they get them they will find, no doubt, that
the theoretical side of things is neatly covered by the
theory.   But here the Plain Man remembers what wiser
persons are apt to forget.   He remembers that Experience has something to offer us all which is not theoretical.   Deeply were we touched by a remark once made
to us by the plainest man we ever knew.   'I would not
insult the universe,' said he, 'by pretending to understand it.'   Was he condemned out of his own mouth?
Did he proclaim by his words that already he understood the universe after a fashion?   Perhaps so, gentlemen; but his fashion was not yours.

"And now let us try to explain how the difficulties and perplexities of our life are apt to become
greater and not less when we try to follow you in your
'interpretation' of our experience.   In the first place,
we cannot escape the conclusion that if you are right in
these interpretations, we, on our side, are the victims of
some strange illusions.   We know that some of you
deny this and speak words of comfort to our wounded
amour propre.   But when all is said it still seems to us
that, on your showing, we plain men have got things
topsy-turvy and turned them inside out.   And our first
difficulty is to understand the source of our own error.

"Opposite our window we see a rose-bush.   One of
you informs us that the rose-bush is 'a construction of
the mind'; another that it is 'a group of sense impressions'; another that it is 'a projected idea.'   Now, if
any such-like 'interpretation' of the rose-bush is true,
it seems certain that the rose-bush is playing us

a trick. We take the rose-bush for just what it declares itself to be, and this does not bear the slightest resemblance to ' a construction of the mind ' or to anything of that kind.

" Well, we plain men may be wrong when we take that rose-bush on its own terms and refuse to accept it on yours. But if so, we cannot help wondering what it was that first started us on the wrong road and kept us on the wrong road up to the present moment. If the bush really *is* and always has been what you say, then how came it to pass that any son of man ever took it for something else? Being a construction of the mind (or what not) one would expect that everyone from the first would take it as such. But nobody took it in that way till you came on the scene. Why should the human mind start thus on the wrong road when there was nothing to prevent it starting on the right ? What Deceiver thus beguiled us ?

" Or again. If, as some of you profess, there is no Reality but Thought, or Process, or Experience, what can have started the notion common to all plain men that there are many realities besides Thought, Process, or Experience ? If all we can think is Thought, then nobody would ever have been able to think of something else which isn't Thought. But we plain men have always been able to think of something else which isn't Thought. How did we first manage to do that, and how do we manage to keep it up or carry it on ? Who, once more, is the Deceiver ?

" Granted, then, that our error is great, you must admit that the origin of such an error is extremely perplexing. There seems no reason for it. It appears to us that if your interpretation of the world be true, there would be no plain men, and our view of things could never have arisen. But it has arisen. The Plain Man with all his errors is as much a fact as anything else. So that, were he to accept your solution of other mysteries, his doing so would involve him in a greater mystery than all the rest which you have removed— the mystery, namely, of his own appearance on a scene where he, with his gratuitous errors, is obviously superfluous.

" Then, again, you can hardly fail to have observed that all this language about one thing 'manifesting itself' as *something else* is a sore trouble to plain men. We can't make it out; and the more we try to understand what you mean the more you bewilder us. For are we not right in supposing that a thing can *manifest* itself only by coming out in its *true* colours? If it comes out in false colours, and shows itself as something *other* than it is, then the proper name for the process is not manifestation but masquerading, or (pardon our plain language) lying. Now, broadly speaking, all things are liars, as thus presented; they wear false colours.

" You tell us, for example, that the Permanent manifests itself as the Changing, the Universal as the Particular, the One as the Many. You are bold enough, some of you, to affirm that Freedom is revealed under the form of Necessity. Gentlemen, forgive a plain man for expressing his conviction that this kind of thing will never do. We are sorely puzzled to know by what right you call this 'manifestation.' We are given a universe in which everything puts on the mien and livery of something else and tries to pass itself off as this other thing whose mien it has copied and whose

clothes it has stolen. And this process is called 'manifestation.'   It is impossible for us to accept these
'manifestations' and at the same time retain our belief
in the sanity of things.   Why all this mendacity?
What end does it serve?   May we assume that the
universe *wants* us to understand it aright, that spirit
is averse to be mistaken for flesh, that the heavenly
wishes us not to confuse it with the earthly? Why,
then, should the heavenly consistently present itself
in a most ingenious earthly disguise; why should spirit
masquerade as flesh; why should a 'construction
of mind' put on the air of a rose-bush? You have
assumed that the universe is intelligible; which is as
much as to say that things deal with us intelligibly.
But in the universe as interpreted by you, everything
is sailing under false colours. Nothing deals with us
intelligibly.   It is a world of mistaken identities, so
constructed that every excuse is provided for mistaking
them. If the heavenly always appears as the earthly,
who is to blame for denying that there is a heavenly
and asserting that the earthly is all in all? If the One
is manifested as a Many, who can help thinking that it
is Many and not One?   If the spiritual reveals itself as
the material, then the spiritual has itself to blame if we
take it at its own valuation and accept it in the form it
has chosen to assume. Thus we are introduced to what
seems a mad world. Under the term 'manifestation'
we are asked to accept a universal system of disguise,
impersonation, and masquerade, which is not only
purposeless but opposed to the purpose we cannot help
ascribing to an intelligible world—the purpose, namely,
of getting itself understood. It is only by reversing
our supposition and ascribing to the world the purpose

of getting itself *misunderstood* that we are able to see any sense in these arrangements. If the One *wants* us to mistake its nature, how could it effect the purpose better than by appearing as the Many?

"So, then, it comes to this. In much that is written about Appearance and Reality you seem to us plain men to be engaged not so much in solving a problem as in unmasking a meaningless fraud. We cannot understand why Reality, anxious to get itself recognised for what it is, should adopt the method of presenting itself as the Unreal. Gentlemen, the situation is infinitely perplexing, and all your fine words cannot make it anything else.

"We were taught as children that when God chose to reveal Himself to man He wrote a Book, or caused a Book to be written. Whatever we may think of this now, one is bound to admit that here, at all events, the word 'revelation' is honestly used. Compare the strange performances of the philosopher's Absolute! Being Real it reveals itself as Phenomenal; being out of Time and Space it reveals itself as in Time and Space; being Absolute it reveals itself as Relative; being Spiritual it reveals itself as Material; being One it reveals itself as Many. But then the philosophers appear—and everything is set right. The Absolute having 'revealed' itself as what it is not, now produces the philosopher who, by introducing another 'not' into the revelations, brings them back to the original truth. The Real negates itself, and then by negating the negation comes once more to its own. Well, there is no accounting for tastes, and if this is how the Real proclaims its reality we must put up with it as best we can. We cannot complain that Reality is kept under lock and key, but may be thankful

that, having locked itself in the darkness, it thrusts the
key under the door, so that when philosophers come
that way they may let it out again into the light.[1]   But
how much simpler it would have been to leave the door
open from the start !

" This Moment of Negation, as you call it, is, indeed,
a most superfluous moment to plain men.   To us it
appears a needless pause in the process of being, a
bewildering back-eddy in the process of thought,
whereby a result is delayed for the sole purpose of
giving a certain piquancy to its arrival, as when Jack
jumps out of his box.

" We often wonder if you have realised the dreadful
sinking of the heart which is produced in some of us
when we stand face to face with the philosopher's
Absolute and consider its ways.   Do not condemn us
too harshly if we make our confession particularly frank
at this point.   Our dominant feeling in presence of this
Absolute is a kind of regret that we have made its
acquaintance, coupled with a wish that the Absolute
were other than it is.   And it is for you to consider
whether you can claim to have explained Experience
when this is the result of your explanations.   When
with the Moment of Negation, or what not, the world is
made to rest on principles which no Plain Man in his
senses would ever dream of making the principles of
his own conduct, when you have left him in the
presence of something so bizarre and unintelligible in
its intelligibility, so odd and weird and round-about
and perverse in its mode of attaining the simplest
objects, that he can only stand aghast—can you, I say,
on these conditions, honestly profess to have explained

[1] See the quotations from Hegel's *Logic* on p. 29.

anything to that man ? When he asks you to explain
his experience, he hopes that the result of your labours
will make him feel at home in the world. What is thus
given him makes him feel not at home. The more
thoroughly he agrees with you, the greater becomes
the cleft between his intelligence and the rest of his
life. It is not true that you 'reconcile' this man
either with himself or with the world. You put him
at odds with the world and with himself. You make
him feel, in his deeper consciousness, a stranger in a
strange land.

" Consider the following passage written by a distinguished representative of your order :

" ' Negation is not to be regarded as a positive substantive
moment in the objective dialectic, but as implicit in the moment
of affirmation or " determining-so "—the idea. The " idea " which
seeks to fulfil itself as " end " fulfils itself as a concrete, we said,
in terms of the sense-categories, and as fulfilled it is " determinate "
or " actual." It is in the moment of End, fulfilled as a phenomenal
determinate, that the positive idea as essence and the negation
that gives individuality meet. Thus we say that the individual
is a synthesis of affirmation or idea and of negation. The negation
is thus a constitutive principle contained in the affirmation and
enters into the method of the universe' (Laurie, *Synthetica*, vol. ii.
p. 415).

" Now, gentlemen, far be it from us plain men to
speak slightingly of this passage, for we recognise it as
earnest and pathetic. Far be it from us to criticise its
statements ; for we scarcely understand what they mean.
But after trying our best to understand them the conclusion we come to is this : that if the truths most
important to man explain themselves in this manner,
then our lot in this world is dismal in the extreme.
The Truth which requires this passage for its expression,

whatever that Truth may be, is unlovely and not to be
desired by the heart of man.   That is how we feel about
the matter.   That is our emotional reaction as we close
the book.   We do not pretend to be logical; we cannot
justify our attitude by any argument; but neither can
we help or overcome the unutterable repugnance with
which we look forth on a world which hides its message
from us under the garb it is here made to assume.   It is
not that we are afraid of hard things.   As plain men
we meet hardness, and endure gainsaying, and stand
up to opposition every hour.   But this is worse than
hard; it is supremely forbidding.   Nor are we merely
affrighted from want of courage, like men whose hearts
fail them at the crossing of some precarious bridge
thrown over the boiling waters of Death.   The thing
before us, though intended as a bridge, would serve
better as a trap, for it is so contrived that whoever
trusts himself to its support must inevitably fall in.
Our suspicions are aroused.   Were the truth of things
friendly, we think it would not cloak itself in this disguise; were it desirous to get itself recognised, as friendly
truth assuredly would be, it would not stake the recognition on the chance of our being able to rightly emphasise
each several word in such a passage as this.   It appals
us to think we are living in a world which opens its
mouth in parables like these.   Thus addressed we
recoil, we shiver, we cry out in alarm; our blood
turns to water.   And the world we once welcomed,
and in whose presence we were wont to rejoice as
before a living thing, seems to die under this treatment of it; and it dies no decent death, but resents
the dying, and gnashes its teeth at the slayer and
yields up the ghost with convulsions and groans of

agony, like a stricken monster twisting and splashing in its blood.

"Is it beneath you, gentlemen, to attend to these by-products of your work, to study the effect of your potions not only on some isolated nerve of the intellect, but as affecting the vital pulse of the human heart? Are not some of you like those physicians who purchase the relief of a single member by poisoning the whole man? What though your logic dispels for a moment some local doubt, some problem on the periphery of the mind, if all within us that lives, not by the chopped straw of logic, but by God's light and air, sickens under the drug and dies?

Doubtless some of you will say that in all this bitter cry we have revealed ourselves not as good specimens of the Plain Man but as bad specimens of the philosopher. Our difficulties proceed from our misunderstanding of your doctrine and from our attempts to meddle with things beyond our powers. The Plain Man, you will add, is a very worthy fellow; but the Plain Man who dabbles in philosophy is a hopeless fool. So be it. But remember, gentlemen, that in the last resort you, as well as ourselves, are plain men. May we not, then, ask you to study, more thoroughly than you have yet done, the reaction on our mind of the teaching you are continually offering to those of us who cannot forget our plainness? Or is philosophy by its very nature a mission to the converted? Are you content to address your brother professors in the pages of *Mind*? Is your calling esoteric? We are sure that you will answer these questions in the negative. You cannot leave us altogether out of the account. Benighted as we are, you yet desire that we, as occasion permits, shall look into what you are doing and try to pick up a crumb here and a crumb there. Well, all we ask of you is that you should hear our story. We only beg to tell you how the crumb tastes which we have picked up. And we say it tastes bitter.

" Gentlemen, you are the helpers of the world ; you prepare the harvests which feed mankind. Plough not the hungry sand, we beseech you. Give us bread, not husks, to eat, and we will come to your tables. Cleanse your threshing-floors from the chaff of past harvests. And look to your storehouses, for there is famine in the land."

II.—ART AND EXPERIENCE

WHATEVER philosophical "attitude" or point of view the mind may take in regard to the world, whether that of the Monist or the Pluralist, will be found to involve that the world, on its part, has an answering "attitude" towards the mind. It is always well to remember this reciprocity and to ask ourselves, when our own "attitude" is taken, what corresponds or answers to this from the side of the world. Are they the same or different? Is the world indifferent in the matter, in the sense that a lump of iron is indifferent while a metallurgist is expounding its properties; or is it an intelligent accomplice, a sympathetic partner, aiding and abetting the mind's efforts to understand its structure and to define its laws?

It will probably be admitted that the world-process as expounded by the idealists, and notably by Hegel, is something more than the *corpus vile* of a philosophical process. It cannot be treated as indifferent to its own interpretation. It has an interest in the result, and is an active accomplice in the production of the Idealist Cosmology. Its "attitude" in the matter is analogous to that of a person who has a meaning to impart to others and is taking the necessary steps to get his meaning recognised. Using plain language, we may say that the Hegelian universe *wants* to be understood as a consistent or rational whole. It makes no difference whether it would so comprehend itself or be so comprehended by another. It *tries* to make itself known in its true character. Indeed, the Hegelian dialectic is meaningless unless we assume the world to be controlled by a purpose—the purpose being to attain that reflection, recognition, or knowledge of its own process which constitutes the Hegelian insight or consciousness. When the Hegelian consciousness appears the goal is reached, the end is fulfilled, and the world may be imagined to say, for the moment at least, " actum est." On our side there is the satisfaction that we have solved the riddle of the universe; from the side of the universe this means the satisfaction of having, in our success, accomplished its own design, by making itself intelligible, by getting its process recognised for what it truly is.

The purpose of the world, then, being to attain consciousness of itself as a rational or consistent whole, is it not a little strange that the first step, so to speak, taken by the world for the attainment of this end is that of presenting itself *in the form of contradictory experience*? " In the course of its process," says Hegel, " the Idea makes itself that illusion, by setting an antithesis to confront it, and its action consists in getting rid of the illusion which it has created."[1] And elsewhere: " The true knowledge of God begins when we know that things as they immediately are have no truth."[2] Recurring, now, to our analogy of a person who desires us to recognise his consistency, would it not greatly

[1] *Logic*, tr. Wallace, p. 181. Quoted by James, *A Pluralistic Universe*, p. 51.
[2] *Ibid.*, p. 304.

surprise us if the person in question began the process
by presenting himself as inconsistent or by delivering an
illusory account of his own character ? So long as we
think of the world, or of this person, as indifferent to
whether we understand him or no, the fact that he addresses us by way of contradiction or illusion will create
no surprise ; but the moment we remember that he *wants*
us to understand him, that he is *trying* to make himself
known, that this is the purpose of his communications,
the strangeness of the proceeding will start into view.
There is certainly something piquant in this mode of
revealing consistency ; and if piquancy is the object,
well and good ; but short of this the method of " revelation by puzzle " is extremely *bizarre* and very difficult
to take seriously.

To make this clear let us reverse the supposition
by crediting the world with the purpose of concealing
its consistency or of leading on to the belief that it is
not a rational whole, or of creating that " pluralistic "
consciousness of itself which turns up, for example, in
Professor William James.   What mode of address
would such a world adopt ?   Under what form of experience would it present itself to the mind ?   Can we
hesitate to answer that a contradictory form of experience would be admirably adapted for the purpose ?   In
short, from a world bent on baffling our quest for unity,
should we not expect just such an endless series of
antinomies as we actually find in the life of Pure
Reason ?

We shall be told, of course, that our minds seek
unity and cannot rest in anything else.   But we are
now looking at the matter not from *our* point of view,
but from that of the world ; we are asking not what *we*

seek, but what the world seeks; we are considering how
the world would proceed on the assumption that it
wants us to recognise it as this or that. And we affirm
that the admitted contradictions of experience are
exactly what one would expect from a world which
desired us to rest in the Many rather than the One.
On the one hand, it may be true that if *we* want unity
we can get it only by solving contradictions, and that
therefore a contradictory experience must be provided
for the purpose; on the other hand, a contradictory
experience is exactly what would be provided by a
world whose attitude is supposed to be hostile, or
indifferent, to those efforts after unity which the mind
is making.

For ourselves we are equally averse to the adoption
of either hypothesis. Admitting, as we do, the contradictions of experience; admitting also that metaphysic
arises in the attempt to solve them, we are yet unable
to see in the world-process any design, intention, or
deliberate challenge in virtue of which we are *bound* to
make that attempt. Nor are we sure, in spite of some
prima facie likelihood, that the universe intends us to
leave its contradictions alone. We can only say, and
we say it with some confidence, that either course
derives an equal warrant from the facts. So far as the
intentions of the world-process are manifest, there is no
condemnation for the man who refuses to regard the
solution of the world's antinomies as the primary business of his mind. We infer that the world-process is
quite content with that man who finds for himself forms
of commerce with Reality other than that which consists
in solving the intellectual contradictions of experience.
Though we fully concede that a world-process which

aimed at the reconciliation of opposites would have to provide us with opposites to reconcile, yet we are by no means willing to convert this proposition by affirming that the actual provision of the opposites proves their reconciliation to be the aim of the world-process. This illegitimate conversion appears to us to vitiate some conclusions of the Hegelian Logic. The actual existence of contradictions in experience—which of course is not denied—is a fact of doubtful meaning; it is compatible with more than one hypothesis. To read it as a challenge enforcing the quest for unity upon every reasonable being, to read it as this and this only, is dogmatism. It may be read, with equal justice, in other ways. Thus we are prepared to say, for example, that the contradictions of experience, far from tying us down to the solitary task of their solution, may be read as an eloquent hint warning us not to make the quest for unity the *exclusive* business of the mind. The metaphysician must not be too hasty in claiming the whole universe as *his* and no other's. After all, his " licence to trade " extends no further than the province of the metaphysical purpose, which is by no means co-extensive with the whole field of self-conscious life. He is a little too apt to assume that the appeal of experience is exclusively for that kind of response which metaphysical science alone can give—an appeal, namely, for " explanation " or even for " reconciliation." It is certain, for example, that a work of art does not ask us primarily to " explain " it. And the philosopher will find the question well worth asking, whether the world does not, in this respect, resemble a work of art. To this question we address ourselves in the following essay.

I

So far as the world is treated as an object of discussion we are bound to assume its rationality. No object can stand before the bar of thought and maintain the character of an unknowable. Were the object unknowable, thought could not apprehend it, could not single it out from other objects as the one to be examined, could not summon it into court to receive judgment. Whatever else Reality may be, it cannot be unknowable so long as we are able to call it up for discussion and to assure ourselves that we have, so to speak, "caught the right man,"—that the object before us is Reality and not the unreal. It is futile to discuss the nature of ultimates on any other basis, or in the hope of reaching any other conclusion. Were we fully instructed in the secret workings of our own thought we should probably discover that some of the ultimate conceptions we are dealing with have been constructed by the intelligence for its own purpose, the process of "understanding" them being no more than a taking to pieces by the mind of what the mind has already put together. Be that as it may, there is no going back from the rationality of a world whose nature we have undertaken to discuss. The undertaking itself is impossible on any other terms. As one cannot eat what is uneatable nor drink what is undrinkable, so he cannot discuss what is not discussible nor assign reasonable limits to the absurd.

All this is a truism, but a truism which is constantly being forgotten and needing to be revived. Nevertheless its application is limited; and it has become a source of error in the work of thinkers who have

3

pressed it beyond its limits and put upon it a strain that it will not bear.

Were our commerce with the world limited to the task of discussing its ultimate nature, then the assumption of its rationality would be the only assumption we should require; to that we should attend and to that alone. But our commerce with the world is of infinite variety; discussion of its nature is no more than one of a vast multitude of tasks which life lays on us; and the warrant of rationality, so indispensable in the sphere to which it belongs, does not run beyond.

A being, or race of beings, with no object in life save that of moving more or less rapidly through space and transporting objects from one position to another, would find in the assumption of universal mechanism all he required to attain his purpose. A mechanical universe would be all he would want, and all he would find. Or if we imagine a type of consciousness exclusively occupied in the enjoyment of those emotional raptures when thought is said to expire, the assumption of rationality would never so much as come within its ken, and would be as unnecessary as it was unknown. That assumption is needed, and needed only, by that man who, in addition to the other tasks with which Nature or choice has provided him, takes upon himself the burden of understanding the world. Nor can we conceive of any dogmatism more narrow or more groundless than that which seeks to make its own particular presupposition the sole basis of a self-conscious life. It would seem rather that the world is rich enough in its resources, not only to provide an infinite number of presuppositions other than this, suited to every variety of human purpose, but also to make room for the life which needs no conscious presupposition at all. Nor are these forms of living, each with or without its appropriate assumption, distributed among an equal number of individuals, one for you, another for him, a third for me. The same individual must live through many; and as he changes from this to that, so must the presupposition change on which he bases his life. The only man whom the world refuses to gratify with all the presuppositions he needs is fortunately a type which exists only in books—the abstract man who sets up the assumption of his own calling as the standard of intelligent life for everybody. For him—or for us (for who is wholly guiltless?)—there is no mercy. If we try to live exclusively in the light of any single presupposition, the world will assuredly break us.

A person who takes up the study of Philosophy is in perpetual danger of regarding himself as a being endowed with a purely theoretical consciousness. And the life whose mysteries he would pierce, or the universe whose secret he would discover, is apt to become, in its turn, something with a purely theoretical significance. For himself, the student thinks, there will be no rest till his theoretical consciousness is in possession of the theoretical secret. And there can be no doubt that, within the limits thus artificially laid down, he is right. As a mere student of cosmology or anthropology nothing but a solution of the world-riddle, nothing but a formula of life, will suit his purpose. But suppose these things attained—what then? The only purpose they serve is the purpose of a mind which, as we have said, regards itself as endowed for the time being with a purely theoretical

consciousness. As a mere student of philosophy, *i.e.*
as an abstraction, his life-formulæ may *satisfy* him ; but
they will not satisfy him as a *man*, which is as much
as to say that they will not satisfy *him* at all. No
doubt he has tried an important experiment, and it
will not be without influence on the very different,
but equally important, experiments which other men
are trying in other spheres. The problem he has set
himself to solve is this : " What can be made of the
world when taken as an object of theoretic study ? "
ignoring for the time being that the world is infinitely
more than this. Life, for him, shall be as a field in
which questions are sown and answers raised, and he
will find out what will grow, he will try his hand at
raising a crop. This is the experiment, but it decides
nothing outside the sphere to which it belongs. As the
farmer tries what he can make of the world for growing
wheat, the financier for making money, so the philosopher tries it as a field for raising systems of thought.
And all these are necessary ; and the work of each inter-
penetrates the work of the others. But none of them
is all-inclusive. The farmer's experiments do not solve
the problems of the philosopher. But neither do the
philosopher's solve the farmer's. Philosophy will
bake no man's bread—Hegel himself has told us so.
And yet bread has to be baked, as well as the world-
problem solved.

No man either is or can be a mere philosopher.
This, of course, nobody will deny. But the correlate
is more easily overlooked—namely, that the world, on
its side, is no mere philosopher's world, try as we
will to make it such. In his own personality the
philosopher combines many characters which he may

distinguish but cannot separate; lives many lives besides that whose business is to solve the riddles of the universe. He too must plant and sow, must earn his living, eat and drink, marry and give in marriage. He is farmer, financier, lover, animal, and philosopher all in one. And each of these functions has its own "presuppositions"; all of which have the same right to be considered valid and indispensable for the purposes they severally serve. Regarding himself as a mere theoretic consciousness, and arming himself only with such doctrines as are suitable to that character, the philosopher can neither till the land, nor earn his living, nor love his wife and children. As thinker, it is true, he cannot think without assuming the intelligibility of the object of thought; but as lover he must assume much more than this, or the beloved will never be won. To say, as may be truly said, that you cannot think about an unintelligible universe may be matched by saying that you cannot marry the Pons Asinorum. The assumption of intelligibility for intelligence, and of something else for love, stand on precisely the same footing—and so with all the rest. None of these can oust the others and set up a claim to be the sole, or the ultimate, formula of life. The philosopher must make one when he thinks; but with equal inevitableness he must make another, or many others, when he falls in love. To the mere thinker, if there were such a being, the rationality of the universe would be the central, the all-important, nay, the only truth; and to the mere lover, in the same sense, the presence of his mistress would be the central, the all-important, the only fact.

And just as the student of philosophy is always

in danger of regarding himself as a mere theoretic consciousness, and reducing the presuppositions of his many-sided life to the single form his theoretic consciousness demands, so we may say of every man that he is in danger of imposing his own life-purpose on the world. Indeed, philosophy is perhaps the only calling in which this danger is not recognised for what it is. When we encounter it in any other walk of life we know what we have to deal with. We call it bias; we amuse ourselves at its expense, for is it not the usual form in which men make themselves ridiculous? An auctioneer who had been to Iceland was asked to give his impressions. "I assure you, sir," he replied, "that the 'ole country, if put under my 'ammer, wouldn't fetch a 'alfpenny." Now this, to the auctioneer - consciousness, is "a fundamental characterisation" of Iceland. If one had no business with Iceland save that of selling it, then the sole presupposition of our dealings with that island would be that it was saleable, that it would fetch something, and the only question to decide would be, "*how much* will it fetch?"

If it may be said without irreverence, we are inclined to think that too much of our philosophical literature is pitched in the same key as the auctioneer's remark. The assumption too often is that we have nothing to do with the universe save to understand it, just as our auctioneer conceived himself as having nothing to do with Iceland for the time being save to put it under his hammer. Proceeding from this assumption, the thinker describes the universe as though it were a mere object of thought, and informs us that it is a rational whole. But in all this he is apt to ignore that our

dealings with the world consist only in part of thinking
about its ultimate nature, and that our demands on
experience go far beyond the desire to satisfy ourselves
of its rationality. As rational merely the world does
not respond to the satisfaction of self-conscious life,
and it is mere professional prejudice to pretend that it
does. As the wheels of experience revolve there is
one point in the circle, and one point only, at which
the truth of rationality arrests us; and that point on
the circumference, though related to all the others,
must not be made to do duty for the whole circle.
As we pass on to the other points we find ourselves
asking more of experience than an answer to rational
questions; we are seeking a response which can only
be given in terms of feeling, action, love, and never
in terms of rationality alone. Hence we may refuse
point-blank to treat experience as a mere subject of
discussion.[1] Nor need we measure the *value* of anything by the sole test of its intelligibility. There is
no direct proportion that we can find between the
worth of things and our powers of explaining them or
accounting for their existence. The world may be very
dear to us or very terrible even in those moments when
we are least conscious of what it is or what it means,
and least desirous of knowing. There are at least some
objects in the world of which this may be said without
hesitation—namely, works of art.

---

[1] Nowhere is this emphasised with greater force than in what
William James called the "vision" of Hegel. See, for example, the
preface to his *Philosophy of Right*, with the famous passage about the
owl of Minerva. Unfortunately, as it seems to the present writer,
the Dialectic of Hegel leads, not to the "vision" but in the opposite
direction.

II

Treated as the object of a theory the world can never rise to the greater dignity of a work of art. It is and must remain a work of science, *i.e.* an object which can be exhaustively interpreted in rational terms. In this respect there is no difference of principle between thinkers who take a strictly mechanical view of the universe and those, on the other hand, who, while opposed to mere mechanism, would lay experience under formulæ of another kind. So long as experience is treated as subject to categories, and so long as these categories are stated exhaustively and in rigid form, the distinction between "mechanical" and "spiritual" does not fundamentally affect the resultant type of thought. In either case the world comes out as a work of science. Mere differences of terminology must not be suffered to mislead us. The substitution of "process" for "motion," or of "growth" for "change," the addition of the adjective "spiritual" to any of the nouns used in this connection, may make important differences of another kind; but these changes of phrase leave the world with an essentially scientific structure and present us in the long-run with a system of the universe as rigidly determined as any mechanical system could be. Hegel, for instance, is reported to have revealed the Dynamics of Spirit; but, though something is gained by substituting Dynamics for Statics, Hegel's thought, just because it is a rigid system, is no more commensurate with Life, which is not a rigid system, than any other that might be named. The rigidity of the Hegelian Dialectic is apt to be disguised by the circumstance that it is expressed throughout in a *fluid*

terminology, of which the word " Dialectic " itself may
be taken as the chief example. But, while refusing
to join in the now popular outcry against Hegel, who
like all great thinkers builded better than he knew,
we find ourselves forced to the conclusion that a
" system " of fluid terms is itself a more perplexing
contradiction than any of those it is employed to solve.
The terms become equivocal under the use that is
made of them : to get their meaning they must wait
upon the process they profess to define. So far as the
thinking is systematic the terms lose their fluidity.
When the terms are fluid, the thinking ceases to be
systematic. Not even Hegel can have it both ways
at once. In a certain sense, therefore, and yet an
important sense, Hegel's thought is as mechanical as
that avowedly " mechanical " Philosophy which it is
commonly supposed to refute. Just as Newton laid down
laws of motion for a world conceived as made up of moving masses, so Hegel's Dialectic may be described as the
Law of Motion in a world conceived as the progressive
Manifestation of Idea. What is accomplished in the
long-run is neither more nor less than a rigid statement
of the way something works, or grows or becomes.
What this something may be, matter or spirit, here
concerns us not ; enough that it " works " in the way
assigned and cannot work otherwise. From this
circumstance alone it results that the world of Hegelian
Philosophy is a thinker's world ; adjusted from the first to
meet the demands of Pure Reason. And no thinker
has ever attacked that world with greater thoroughness.
Hegel seems to have completely disentangled, or pre-
cipitated, the thought-element of experience ; he may
be said to have exhausted that aspect of Being, at least

in principle, thereby accomplishing the work of philosophy along that particular line.   But the very
completeness of his work only serves to bring out its
insufficiency to meet the total demands of our nature.
So long as something remains yet to be done in
showing what thought can make of life, we may
cherish hope that complete satisfaction would arise
from the result.   But when the result appears, as it
seems to appear in Hegel, we realise at once that
the satisfaction extends no further than the original
purpose which inspired the work.   It may satisfy
thought, but it satisfies nothing else.   Thinkers as we
all *may be*, we *are* yet so much more than thinkers that
to "rest" in a rigid system which solves all problems is
as impossible as it would be to "rest" in one which
left half our problems unsolved.   Abandoned by Hegel
in a world which, after all, resembles so many others in
being a work of science, a thinker's world, we can only
cry, "This is not the world in which we *live*.   We have
other business in hand than to reconcile opposites and
effect a synthesis of all contradictions."

There is, however, an earlier thinker whose writings
seem to me, in spite of the current opinion to the contrary, to represent a much richer philosophical experience
than can be ascribed to Hegel.   I refer to Spinoza.

According to Spinoza, Substance, or, as we should
now say, Reality, enters into experience under a double
character—as extended, and as thinking.   How these
two aspects of Being are related to one another, with
many other similar questions familiar enough in this
connection, need not detain us here.   Enough if we note
the following points.

1. In allowing Reality to enter experience under a *twofold* character, Spinoza stands apart from all those thinkers who would reduce experience to a *single* formula, or even to formulæ of a single type. We have here the beginnings of Pluralism, the plural being represented by the modest number "two." Critics of Spinoza have indeed pointed out, with much truth, that he fails to maintain the strict parallelism of the two attributes, that the rights of the one are frequently merged, or taken up, in the rights of the other; but we can hardly doubt that by representing them as parallel he wishes us to understand that, though matched, they are otherwise independent, that each speaks a language of its own, that extension cannot be explained by thought, nor thought by extension. Hereby Spinoza would do full and equal justice to the mechanical and the spiritual aspects of the universe; and however he may stumble or fail in the accomplishment of this design, we must admit that the design, so far as it goes, reveals in this philosopher a catholicity of outlook and an effort to do justice to both sides of the question, for which we look in vain in some of his successors. It is rather by the irony of history than by his own intending that Spinoza has come to rank as the prophet of a "block universe" with a fixed unitary formula. In the whole literature of philosophy we know of nothing more genuinely catholic than the "Definition" of Substance with which the Ethic opens; of nothing better fitted to stand as the mind's charter of liberation from all attempts to tie it down to a single view of the world. For that "Definition," rightly understood, simply declares that the world cannot *be* defined or circumscribed by any view or formula whatsoever; that

nothing less than the universe is adequate to the explanation of the universe; that Reality, therefore, must be left to tell its own story in its own ways.

2. On the other hand, by limiting, or seeming to limit, our commerce with reality to *not more than two* of its attributes, Spinoza betrays the characteristic vice of all who would set bounds of ordnance and cry "thus far and no further" to experience. To Spinoza, as to any man who would circumscribe experience or exhaustively state its "conditions," we cannot refrain from saying, "Who art thou that the full compass of experience and the whole sum of its 'conditions' should have come within thy ken?" Why this perpetual insistence on the number two? Are there any "first principles of thought" by deduction from which such a limitation can be made good? There are not. Is, then, an *a posteriori* proof forthcoming? Can we establish by observation, or by introspection, or by any other such method, that our intercourse with the world does *de facto* assume one or other, or both, of these forms and no more? Surely no one is in a position to answer this question in the affirmative. Even were it proved inductively (as it never can be) that up to date the mind of man has broken out into no experience which lies beyond this double wall of extension and thought, one might yet hope that in other conditions we might be able to burst the boundaries and enter upon an inheritance richer than this. For though a world divided between *two* attributes is less barren and less appalling to contemplate than a world monopolised by *one*, yet the relief, after all, does not amount to much, and we feel ourselves recoiling from the first picture as from the second with a sense of infinite dissatisfac-

tion, and with an irresistible impulse to rebel. For, frankly, our experience does *de facto* overflow the boundaries here assigned to it, and goes on overflowing them undeterred by the threats of any formula whether of the double- or of the single-barrelled variety. Nay, the very presentation of this formula only seems to provoke our experience into breaking bounds and going further afield, according to the saying, " I had not known sin but for the law." May it not be, then, that this limitation to two " attributes," to two sides of existence, to two modes of approaching Reality, is an arbitrary and accidental affair due to the contingent fact that in modern times man's interests have been mainly confined to the world as a work of science, to the task of moving its masses and solving its problems ? Is there anything behind all this more august than the prejudice of an age and place ? And even now, under the power of this prejudice as we all are, may there not be less prominent types of experience which by no manner of means can be made to fit into the moulds of extension and thought ? When we enjoy anything that is beautiful, or pay homage to any ideal that is worthy, can it be said that " the twin attributes " cover our experience and exhaust our world ? Will the amorous youth of Schiller's poem[1] with the " namen-loses Sehnen " catching at his heart, or the child who moves in light that never was on sea or land, yield on analysis a confirmation of the doctrine that the world as thinking and extended is the only world in which we live ? We believe not.

3. But there is a feature in Spinoza's thought which redeems it from the hard-and-fast character it would

[1] See *infra*, " The Manipulation of Man."

otherwise have. What of those "infinite and eternal attributes" of Substance, other than extension and thought, of which after a bare introduction we hear so little and desire to hear so much? This is a matter which has not, perhaps, been weighed with the care it deserves, though Spinoza has himself to thank for the comparative neglect into which it has fallen. Here is pluralism, and pluralism with a vengeance. Here, too, is a matter which Spinoza did not, and indeed could not, explain. How comes it to pass that a Reality which is known to be capable of telling its own story in infinite ways is yet niggardly enough to restrict the actual telling to two of these and no more? Surely a mind whose experience is limited to the reading of those two stories would know nothing of the others, not even that they exist. Either, then, those infinite and eternal attributes, other than extension and thought, are not there at all, or else they reveal more of themselves than Spinoza's system would allow. For our part we incline to the latter alternative. Spinoza, it seems to us, here acknowledges a great truth in the presence of which every cut-and-dried system of the universe, his own in-cluded, becomes inadequate to its object. The world of our experience which thought has so long en-deavoured to tie down to a unitary or a dual character, and to define by a single or double formula, now appears as susceptible of infinite characterisation, as capable of sustaining an infinite number of parts no one of which, and no two of which, may be set up as including, as explaining, or even as dominating the rest. The reign of thought and extension, either or both, here comes to an end. They take their place among the others; they cease to stand above them.

The mere circumstance that these have names and the others have no names, or uncertain names, is no reason why the former should rule and the latter serve. For the theoretic consciousness thought and extension will continue to do their work, to serve their purpose. But conscious life in its fulness they can oppress no more. The world with its riches is free of access to all who would use it otherwise than a mass to be moved or a thing to be understood. "Be it unto thee even as thou *wilt.*" Do we want the world to be a problem? As a problem we can have it. Would we treat it as a work of science? As a work of science it waits to our hand. But do we want it to be something else? Who can say that we shall not be satisfied?

III

Divesting ourselves as best we may of professional prejudice and contemporary bias, is it not obvious to every man that what his life, his self-conscious being, demands, is neither the mere explanation of its objects nor the mere synthesis of its contradictions, but *the enrichment of its resources*? Science with its explanations, metaphysics with its reconciliation of opposites, are but two among a thousand streams whose waters, rich with the gathered rains of continental watersheds, have formed the mighty River of Life. Even here, no doubt, we are in danger of being misled by words, and may fall, if we are careless, into the trap of an abstract formula. Let the words, then, be taken as no hard-and-fast definition, and let them remain meaningless until their meaning is supplied by the inward meditation of those to whom they are addressed. Quickened by the sense of something within us which demands not to be explained only, but to be enriched by every contribution which experience can pour into our bosom, we open our eyes to see and our arms to receive whatsoever gifts are held in store for us by the inexhaustible riches of the universe. Then it is that the world begins to change its character and to address us in another language. We look no longer upon a scientific construct which asks to be understood; upon an instrument that waits to be employed; we are in the presence of a work of art which bids us receive.

To those lofty spirits who receive life as a gift *to be used* for ends beyond itself, ever ready to sacrifice the life that is their own for the life that is another's, the life that *is* for the life that *is to be*; to those, again, for whom experience is a school of moral discipline, an educational system for the training of a soul which when trained must be eternally trained anew—to all such, perhaps, our plea will seem a profane proposition. Nor may we expect a warmer welcome from that far more numerous class to whom life is an opportunity for "making good," and Nature a workshop well supplied with tools, machinery, motive power, and raw material, ready to the hand of him who can use them. All that is merely moral, all that is merely strenuous, all that is merely scientific, all that is merely hard-headed, all that is merely covetous, will find here nothing but profanity, moonshine, or irrelevance. "Call the world anything but *that*," they will say. "Call it a system, an organism, a school, a workshop, a battlefield, a mine, a scene, a background, a phantasm, a lie, or even a cemetery, and we know what you mean. But call it a work of art and you are using terms to which nothing in our experience can respond."

Nothing? Let us win more space for our thoughts, and then ask if that "nothing" holds good. Turning our eyes from the diagrams we have drawn on paper, let us look up at the stars. Let us pass out from the close atmosphere of our studies, or from the smoke of our battlefields, and stand on some high promontory where we can breathe the winds. Forsaking for once the unsavoury meat of straight line and flat surface, let us lay our hands on the concrete fact—the bread of angels, the food of gods.

When we analyse our experience—placing it under the microscope of thought, taking it to pieces that we may piece it together again and so understand "how it is made"—we never fail to discover sooner or later something *given*, and we call it a *datum*. This *datum* we characterise in many ways: if in one way, we become materialists; if in another, idealists; and so forth. Without the *datum* no type of reflective thought can do its work. Were it even to be contended that the experienced world is nothing but thought evolving under its own laws, we should still be compelled to take this thought and its laws for *granted*. They are the *data*, the given facts at which our analysis has come to a stop. They are the raw material by operating upon which philosophy repeats the construction of experience, the genesis and growth of the world. And in all this there is no suggestion, not even the faintest, that we are in the presence of a work of art. But there is a strong suggestion that we are dealing with something analogous to the mechanical work of our own hands. All that we should require for the building of a house, for the construction of a machine, for the manufacture of a useful article, is there—the raw

4

material to work upon, the rules of the process, the category-mechanism, the standards and tests by which the product is to be judged. All that essentially belongs to the creation of a work of art is absent—the abandonment to first impressions, the acknowledgment of a secret which defies analysis, the liberty of the workman to be a law unto himself. We are, as it were, in the atmosphere of a great industrial centre; we feel the pressure of economic arrangements; we study the division of labour; we hear the buzz of wheels—and above all we see the *datum*, the raw material, arriving at the depôt and carried in great waggons to the mill. We follow the history of this *datum*. We see it going in raw at one end of the process and emerging at the other a "constructed" experience, an "ordered" world.

But there are times, more frequent perhaps than most of us are aware of, when we are in another atmosphere; when instead of analysing our experience we see it steadily and see it whole. If experience is to mean what we actually do experience; if it is to be taken as concrete and not abstract, then it may be said that experience never *occurs* as the analysed process of the philosophic workshop, save at such moments as we for a set purpose compel it so to occur. It occurs, so to speak, *en masse* to the accompaniment of great emotional reactions of gratitude, satisfaction, anger, horror, love, of *tedium vitæ* or the *joie de vivre*, all of which emotions (if we must call them such) are as much a part of the experience as are the good dinners, the bad men, the beautiful women, the fair landscapes, the hard work, the ponderable masses and measurable forces by which they are severally evoked. So occurring, experience never comes with the

question " What can you make of me ? " It says simply
"*take me.*" All those characteristics which appear, and
appear only, when experience is passed on for analysis
to the psychological laboratory, are absent from its
normal occurrence as a vital, concrete fact. The full
contact of life is not with the *datum* of a raw material
waiting to be constructed, but with the *donum* of the
Artist's work. It is as receiving a *donum*, not merely as
manipulating a *datum*, that man, in the broad amplitude
of self-conscious life, confronts his world, reacts upon
his experience, and takes up his task. In their ultimate,
which is also their primary, appeal, things address themselves not to the question-haunted intellect but to the
receptive soul. Their language is the primitive speech
of experience, the mother-tongue of life, unique, un-
translatable into meanings borrowed from that which is
beyond themselves—*id quod in se est et per se concipitur;
hoc est id cuius conceptus non indiget conceptu alterius
rei a quo formari debeat.*

Now this is the language of Art. Art is a *donum* to
be taken on its own terms, or not taken at all. Let
those who would take it as a *datum* attempt their uttermost ; let them analyse it to the last atom of its pig-
ments, measure it to the last subtlety of its curves ; let
them write its history, criticise its achievements, educe
its meanings ; let them squeeze it as a sponge till everything has been said about it that the tongue can utter ;
and still it will abide their question—inviolate, untouched. In vain do we shackle it with rules, canons,
formulæ ; it stands outside them all, or if it enters for
a moment, it enters but to die. Would we reconstruct
experience, or reconstruct the world ? Let us try our
hand at reconstructing a Velasquez or a Turner, a

tragedy of Sophocles or an ode of Keats. No doubt the results of our reflection or our criticism may be imbedded in the *donum* and may enhance its value; but it is not they that make it what it is; nor can it, by their means, be re-made. Evermore we shall find that there is something that escapes us, something that is not "made" by any of the modes of "making" that we can specify or imagine; and this something is not accidental but essential,—it is the vital secret of the whole. To "reconstruct" the picture on paper is not to reconstruct *the picture* at all; it is to construct something else, which differs from the picture as the explanations on a concert programme differ from the actual music to which they refer. How much or how little we know about the picture matters not; *we can never make another or re-make the original by the aid of what we know.* If you doubt it, try! Take the original to pieces in any way you will, analyse it by aid of a pair of scissors, by chemical reagents, or a critical apparatus of what kind soever; then put it all together again and see what you get! You may take a work of art into your intellectual factory and subject it to every process of dissection and reconstruction the wit of man can devise; it goes in a work of art and it comes out—something else. Thus it is with all paper reconstructions of experience, with all "genetic" theories of the universe. It is experience that goes in; it is not experience that comes out. We begin with the world, and we end with the diagram.

Unquestionably the world can be "made" to speak the language of science, of philosophy, of categories— mechanical, logical, vital; and in like manner the

Sistine Madonna can be "made" to fit into our systems of æsthetic, and defined as the "expression of an intuition," or what not. But need it be said that whosoever receives the Madonna as the "expression of an intuition" and nothing more, does not receive it at all; that he misses the *gift* which the picture has to give? The "value" of the work, its "power," all that makes us welcome and rejoice in its presence, lie, not in that which falls within our formulæ, but in that which escapes and overflows them. So it is with the world when "made" to speak the language of our analytical, critical, reconstructive intelligence. In gaining the form our philosophy has imposed upon it, the world loses the form under which we know it *best*, respond to it most completely, and react upon it with the full tide of our conscious life. All that we can "make" it say is but the merest fragment, a scarcely noticeable grain of sand on the shores of being, compared to what it says when left to itself. Reduced to the diagram of thought, its values are expelled, its light quenched, its pulses stilled, its atmosphere lost, and the expression on its face turned into the fixed stare of an effigy in stone. This is not the world that we "experience." This is not the life that we live. Like a picture by a great artist, like a flower by the wayside, our life is given, our experience is found. The world stands in its own right; it waits for no passport from the intelligence. As, on the one hand, we have not earned it by a price paid down, neither, on the other, do we receive it on condition of our own ability to understand or explain it. It is a free gift, given like the picture, neither to be sold for money nor harnessed to a purpose of whatsoever kind, but to be received on its own terms. To treat life as a conundrum, to regard the world as a problem, to withhold our full acceptance of things till their why and wherefore has been made clear, to value any moment of experience only so far forth as we can make it pay in the markets of thought, or submit to the shackles of descriptive speech—this is to reject the *donum Dei*, and therewithal to deprive ourselves of everything that makes it good to live. Waiting till we can "make something" of the world, the life of the world passes us by; waiting till we can explain experience, we experience nothing; the music sounds and we, preoccupied with desire to say what it is, as though its value hung on the interpretation it will receive from us, miss the music no less completely than if we heard it not at all.

It is surely we ourselves, then, and not the world, who have tied upon our own backs that crushing burden of an unsolved mystery under which so many of us in these days labour miserably through life and not a few stumble disastrously into death. The world never asks us to take it exclusively thus. It is we who refuse to take it otherwise, because we are in bondage to the prejudice of our time and place. We have chosen to make contact with life at the solitary point when life is enigmatical, and with a strange perversity we have planned our commerce with the world along rivers where the ice never wholly melts, by ports which our own intelligence has so often blockaded in advance. Poverty-stricken indeed the universe would be could it not provide a sufficient crop of problems for those who gather such harvests. But why desire them exclusively? Why, with the whole land before us, well watered everywhere like the plain

of Jordan before the Lord rained fire on Sodom and
Gomorrah, why should we pitch our tents for ever on
this unpromising spot?

Life and the world are not alone in being mysterious.
There is an enigma, an insoluble problem, in every
work of art. There is something we cannot understand
nor explain in every perfect lyric, or in every masterpiece of whatsoever sort. Do we value it the less,
do we feel it "burdensome," on that account? Do we
groan in spirit before a play of Shakespeare, a ballade
of Chopin, a landscape of Turner, and say of these
things that they "are black as the pit from pole to
pole"? But we might say it, and *should* say it, if we
made our contact with them exclusively on that side.
Who, by choosing that line of approach, could not
prove that the Holy Child in Raphael's picture is
absolutely and for ever unknowable and to be ignored!
Had we no business with works of art save to understand them; did our intercourse with them withhold its
satisfaction until we could give a why and a wherefore
of all that they are, who would not clothe himself with
sackcloth and put ashes on his head and sit down on
the dunghill by the side of Job? Nay, is not their
value, which is their deeper meaning, strangely bound
up with our inability to explain them? Deprive the
song of all that by which it overflows intelligence and
escapes from formulæ, and who would sing it any more,
who would welcome it if sung? Why, then, when
confronted with experience as a whole do we force
ourselves into an attitude which in other connections
we recognise as cancelling experience in its richest
form? Why do we limit our intercourse with Reality
to channels in which the water of life runs thin and often

runs not at all ?   Is it because the others are not open ?
But who has authority to declare them closed ?

Every work of art is also a work of science, and may
be so treated, though never so as to exhaust its meaning.
And if Ruskin may be followed, it is a "moral order"
no less. By approaching the world as a work of art,
therefore, we by no means exclude its characteristics as
a scientific construct and a moral order. But the world
when approached exclusively on either or both of these
sides seems to us to withhold its essential values, to lay
a burden on the soul, and, be it added, to leave us with
the slenderest basis for religion. Unless the world is
more than this, then—disguise the matter as we may
by theological diction—there is nothing for it but to
accept the inevitable, to bend to the categorical imperative and go through life with the hope of its rewards
and the fear of its lash before our eyes. It is a poor
look-out !

Enough, and perhaps more than enough, has been
said in support of the contention that among the vital
needs of a self-conscious spirit the need of explanation
has received an artificial, exaggerated, and too exclusive
prominence. To avoid this exaggeration is, however,
no easy thing. It requires, in the first place, that we
rise above our professional prejudice as students of
philosophy. Stern candour will have to be practised,
and some cherished claims will have to be abandoned.
The bias of our age is also against us. Engaged,
as most men now are, in scientific constructions of
one kind or another, we are apt to treat the whole
world as though it were a scientific product, and to
live in it as though it were nothing else. Immersed
in the atmosphere of this limited, and perhaps

temporary, purpose, we *want* no other view. But were we to emerge suddenly into a state of society for which artistic creation had the absorbing interest of present mechanical activities, the scientific world-view would no longer appeal to us as satisfying, would no longer occlude the imagination nor present itself as the chief argument either for or against the existence of God. The relative importance of Freedom and Necessity would then be reversed; problem-solving would cease to be the central business of the mind, and instead of contemplating an "iron system of Law" we should stand in the presence of a free work of art, whose "infinite and eternal attributes" no science of ours could ever exhaust.

III.—THE USURPATIONS OF LANGUAGE

How can the Universe tell its own story save by making use of human speech; how convey its meanings to finite minds save by employing a thinker to declare them? So long as the story remains *unspoken, unwritten*, can we say it exists at all? Does not the significance of things become a story by the very process which ends in the movement of an intelligently guided pen over a sheet of paper, in the reading of printed types, in the utterance of recognised vocables; and until this process has been accomplished is not the "meaning" a mere promise or unrealised potency? Can we learn the history of the world, and of human life, otherwise than by reading, or hearing it spoken? How, then, can we receive it without the intermediation of a writer, a speaker?

If a story be defined in advance as the work of a tongue or pen, then it is plain that the story of the Universe cannot be told without the intervention of a human *raconteur*. But have we the right to enforce this definition? True, there is no story without form; but to treat language as the one and only form by which connected meaning can be expressed or conveyed is a preposterous assumption. Are there not many Arts which, though speechless, express their meanings with perfect adequacy, with satisfaction to the recipient, and serve at the same time as a medium of communication between soul and soul? Is not a drama a thing to be acted? Is speech, after all, anything more than one of a vast number of arts by which dramatic meaning is expressed and intercourse carried on, and does it hold any prerogative or special excellence which entitles it to supersede all the others and absorb their functions into itself? Or, looking at the matter from another point of view, is not every man familiar with situations in his own life, when the needs of self-expression cannot be satisfied by *saying* anything whatsoever—times and occasions when, to make his fellows understand what he means, he must straightway *do* something, or *be* something, and perhaps hold his tongue the while? And can we deny that the same holds good of the Universe? May not the world also express its meanings by *doing* and *being*; or must it confine its self-expression to that solitary form of verbal reproduction which we recognise as inadequate enough even on the narrow field of our own lives?

Let us press the point a little further. There are types of experience, familiar to all men, about which none of us, save the foolish, *want* to talk. Enough if we meet the glance of an answering eye or feel the pressure of a friendly hand. There are objects, there are presences in the world, before which speech would be a profanation. There are crises in life which can be indicated only by the barest hint or by some distant suggestion, and which, if characterised at length, would lose their inmost significance in the process. Two lines of Wordsworth:

"But she is in her grave, and, oh,
The difference to me!"

are a more adequate expression of human grief than all the funeral sermons ever preached. Are not the richest and most significant experiences of man precisely those which are the least patient of verbal reproduction? A book, a treatise, a discourse, is the very thing that cannot contain them— that can contain at most their lower elements, their less significant aspects. Who shall transfer them *to paper*, write them in ink, utter them in words? And yet, though inexpressible thus, these things crave expression, for they are full of meaning and must be expressed. They have a language of their own. Art can utter some of them, and Nature, perhaps, can interpret them all. They borrow her tongues, speaking in the winds, singing in the voice of moving waters, looking down upon us in the cold shining of the stars. What they mean, we, too, can express; but we express it, not by speaking there and then, but by all that we *become* through their influence, by all that we are led to *do*, through their compelling, till life shall end.

When we adduce these vast conceptions of "life" and the "universe," are we referring to that type of experience in which we can establish a perfect equation between speech and meaning; or, on the other hand, are these terms anything more than mere hints of an experience whose meaning can never be exhausted in verbal reproduction, mere pointers towards an object which speaks for ever in a tongue of its own, but is never to be adequately spoken of in ours?

Philosophy is not so high a thing, nor are philosophers hedged by a sanctity so awful, that we must needs forbear from trying them by the simple test,

"What do you want?" Does Philosophy, then, want only a verbal reproduction of experience? Is the object merely to get life copied in language, the Universe photographed in concepts? William James has pointed out that nothing is to be gained from such an undertaking. For the original will always remain more significant and more interesting than the copy, and it is to the original, and not to the copy, that we shall always refer when we want to know what life is or what the world is. And since the originals are always there for reference, the copy will be useless—at best a plaything, at worst an encumbrance and a superfluity. This, therefore, can hardly be what the philosopher "wants."

May we not assume that the true aim of the philosopher is something quite other than to furnish experience with a mounted photograph or a printed description of itself; that what he actually wants is to enlarge experience—to extend its boundaries, to enrich its contents, to reinforce its energies, to deepen its value?

This being so—and here we count on general consent —how comes it to pass that such a work as the philosopher's, namely, the enlargement of experience, should be needed in the world? Since the originals of experience are there for every man to consult, why should we want a philosopher to introduce them to us or us to them?

We want philosophers, among other reasons, because the world is full of false philosophy. The way of experience is beset on every hand by a multitude of verbal judgments, of empty phrases, of word-copies, which pass themselves off as the real thing, which pretend to do duty for concrete fact and, by force of their number and importunity, capture our attention and cause the true originals to be overlooked. If it is true that philosophy must perforce fight its battles with words, is it not equally true that words are the weapons against which it must everywhere contend? The philosopher bent on the enlargement of experience perceives at once that his work cannot be done, cannot even be commenced, until he has cleared away the heaps of verbal detritus under which the bedrocks of experience lie buried. And when that is done, what more remains to do? Enough that philosophy lays bare the ultimate fact and leaves it to speak for itself. But what a labour is this, and how little need the thinker fear that his task will soon be exhausted and his occupation gone! For the crusts of rubbish are very thick, hard-beaten by the traffic of ages. And when at last the solid rock is reached, a sandstorm from the desert or a flood from the mountains may cover it again in an hour. Hence the thinker who has cleared his object must labour on to keep it clear. For the human mind loves the bondage of words and is apt, when freed from one form of their tyranny, to set up another more oppressive than the last.

The highest function of philosophy is to enforce the attitude of meditation and therewithal restrain the excessive volubility of the tongue. To us it seems that the reflective thinker wins his greatest victories when by what he says he compels us to recognise the relative insignificance of anything he can say. His task is not to capture Reality, but to free it from captivity. For there are some things about which men disagree only because they have chosen to discuss them. The same yesterday, to-day, and for ever, they break out into a thousand differences the instant men try to say what they are. The originals of experience, the last objects of thought, are all of this kind. Enough that the thinker has brought them and us face to face. With them the thinker can do no more than to lift the veils in which language has shrouded them, that they may stand, not as suitors for explanation but as self-explained; to free them from all that " which the intellect perceives *as if* constituting their essence," and then leave them, not in the dark, but fully illuminated and illuminating by their own inward light.

Thus, in dealing with the last facts, the words best suited to the thinker's employment are the words which call least attention to themselves, inviting us not to look *at* them but to look *through* them, disarming our criticism by their allusiveness, and claiming no prominence in the total effect upon our minds. Among words of this class it is difficult to make a choice, and we could often be as well content with one as with another.

Philosophy resembles poetry in being an art for enforcing meditation, for driving the mind inwards until it sinks into its Object. Those who attempt the contrary, who would bring the Object into thought, who would reveal it by explaining it, are obviously working in a circle. For, unless the Object were in thought to begin with, we should never so much as know that there is an object. Hence there is no relevance in the criticism that such and such a philosopher fails to explain any concrete object or event unless you are sure that he means to explain them.[1] Things and events explain themselves, and the business of thought is to brush aside

---

[1] "So far as the terms they [Plato and Spinoza] employ are unambiguous . . . . they do not sufficiently explain any single concrete object or event." Professor R. B. Perry, *Hibbert Journal*, April 1910, p. 622.

the verbal and conceptual impediments which prevent them from doing so. Start with the notion that it is *you* who explain the Object, and not the Object that explains itself, and you are bound to end in explaining it away. It ceases to exist, its place being taken by a parcel of concepts, a string of symbols, a form of words, and you find yourself contemplating, not the thing, but your theory of the thing. The Kantian Theory of Knowledge is of this kind. It sets out to explain the object, and ends by the admission that the only real object is what it cannot explain, viz. the " thing-in-itself." Is not this inevitable? Get the thing *out of* itself, get it *into* your explanation, and obviously it ceases to be the *thing* at all ; it becomes your theory of the thing, which you, in desperation, make to do duty for its original.

Surely this attempt to make the thing intelligible by getting it out-of-itself, into an explanation, would never be undertaken were we not the victims of long-engrained habits of verbal slavery. We have confused the unsayable-by-us with the inexplicable-in-itself, and drawn the Agnostic's conclusion that things about which *we* can say nothing, can say nothing about themselves. It is only on that absurd assumption that any object can be classed as unknowable, or thrust beyond the boundaries of intelligent intercourse. Were we to reflect more deeply, we might discover that the true reason of *our* being able to say nothing about this or that object is that it tells its own story so completely as to leave us nothing to say, explains itself so adequately as to leave our powers of explanation with nothing to do. For that particular purpose the thing-in-itself does not *want* us (*non indiget*) ; it can get on very well without us, perhaps better than with us. But philosophy will find all the occupation it desires in saving us from the engrained vice of our minds in making concepts and their verbal equivalents do duty for the real originals to which they refer.

It is only after prolonged, and often painful, self-examination that any of us can realise the extent to which our minds are in bondage to words, to phrases, to formulæ. We are the children of an age which spends the best energies of its life in the discussion of life, in an atmosphere of deferred fulfilment, continually postponing the act of living to the work of mentally preparing to live. Preoccupied with these preparations, we become sceptical as to all that lies beyond ; and if for a moment we pass the boundary which separates the area of discussion from the fact discussed, our minds become troubled and amazed, and we conclude, strangely enough, that we are in a land of moonshine and of dreams. There are philosophies which may be not unjustly described as systems of everlasting preparation, and it is only when we begin to ask, as we must do in the long-run, " What is it all for ? " that we awake to the discovery that we are living in an artificial world. Many are the shocks to our *amour propre*, great are the sacrifices of vested interests in the realms of thought, before any of us can arrive at the point of candidly confessing his true condition. Our minds have gone a-whoring after their own inventions, and naturally the admission is one which it costs some effort to make, and which we desire to put off to the latest possible moment. And even when the admission is made, our difficulties have only begun. Habituated so long to the close and sickly atmosphere of an invented world, and

5

accustomed only to face such storms as the tongue can raise, we are apt to suffer great distress at the first taste of the air of heaven, at the first shock of the blast.   We want to go back to our docile abstractions—things which had no rights of their own and suffered us to handle them, to arrange them, to combine them at will.   We hanker after the flesh-pots of Egypt and the pleasant smell of the onion and the garlic.   What matters it that in the world of our invention there is not, and never can be, any room for God, Freedom, or Immortality ?   Yonder, at all events, we knew where we were, and were masters of the situation.   But these desert spaces bewilder us ; these wild winds make us afraid !

There can be no doubt that much scepticism has its roots in nothing deeper than an exaggerated estimate of the functions of speech.   We begin by equating the speech-universe with the fact-universe, and when an alleged fact is offered us which cannot be fitted without excess or defect into the forms of language, we promptly dismiss it as nothing to the purpose.   Capacity to reproduce itself in words becomes the test of reality, and the work of thought degenerates into a mere effort to find some verbal form in which facts shall repeat themselves, things re-appear, and experience be had over again.   Inability on our part to effect these reproductions is taken as indicating some fatal defect in that which it is sought to reproduce.

But there are some truths, as Plato reminds us, in contemplating which the mind is radiant with intelligence, but which are no sooner described in speech than we " fall into the twilight of becoming and perishing and have opinion only, and go blinking about, and are first of one opinion and then of another."   Indeed, that any concrete fact (or event) should be *put into* language, so that the language shall *contain* the fact, whether by description or explanation, is a manifest absurdity.

The fact " in words " is one thing : the fact is another. The first can never be made to do duty for the second ; can never replace it ; can never play the part of its *alter ego*. From confusing the two things—the fact and the fact-in-words—we are bound to go blinking about and be first of one opinion and then of another. For every fact can be " put into " a number of different verbal forms according to the different points of view from which we approach it and the varying purposes we entertain regarding it. Among the various forms thus provided we can never be certain which contains the fact ; we wander from one to the other crying " Lo here, lo there " ; we take up arms now in favour of this, now in favour of that ; and end by the discovery that the fact escapes from them all. Observing, moreover, that among the descriptions to which a thing lends itself some are the flat contradictory of others—that we can describe it in terms of " being " or " not being " at our pleasure—we straightway jump to the conclusion that the thing itself is contradictory. The object before us which was perfectly self-consistent till thought essayed to place it on the tongue, now with a strange perversity seems to be equally patient whether we make it say " I am " or " I am not." This indicates, we then think, that the object is unreal, imaginary, or fraudulent.

The whole trouble arises from our not perceiving that the thing we have been handling all along is not the fact, but the fact-put-into-words, the contradictions we ascribe to it arising solely from the opposite points of view from which we approach it, and from our using it for purposes which cannot be simultaneously fulfilled. Broadly speaking, so far as we have any purpose in regard to an object it can always be made to say of itself " I am," and so far as we have no purpose it can always be made to say " I am not." Again, if our purpose is A and not B, the thing can always be made to say " I am α and not β "; but if our purpose is B and not A, the thing will answer " I am β and not α." In all this we are in constant danger of confusing what we *make* the thing say with what the thing says of itself, this latter being always expressed in a form which is unique and for which therefore no equivalent translation or *alter ego* can be found in human speech. It is the familiar confusion between a theory of knowledge and a theory of being.

A good illustration may be found in current discussions about the nature of the will. Put the will into words and it will seem to break out at once into inconsistent duplicates of itself. We can reproduce the will with equal ease under two contradictory verbal forms. We can make it speak in the language of Necessity; and we can also make it speak in the language of Freedom. In both cases we are handling the will as an object to be studied; but a moment's reflection should convince us that in so handling it we have got hold of something which is not the will at all. The will is very much more, and other than an object-to-be studied. *What* it is we can find out only by willing and in willing. For when acts of will come up for study *they are already done*; that is, the will-element, which is the process of getting them done while yet undone, has, so to speak, gone out of them ;

they have become mere empty simulacra of themselves. These empty simulacra are all that the intellect can lay hold of; and all its characterisations of "free," "determined," and so forth apply in consequence, not to the will, but to *post-mortem* copies or records of what the will has done. Here the intellect is always too late to apprehend the fact, and must perforce content itself with the simulacrum or fact-in-words. About this fact-in-words contrary statements may be made according as we approach it from different points of view and for different purposes. If our purpose is scientific there is nothing for it but to use the categories of science, and these will not allow us to regard acts of the will as anything but determined; the idea of scientifically studying that which has no determinate character being, of course, absurd. If, on the other hand, our purpose be to get something done which is as yet undone, we are bound to describe the will as free; since the purpose to get it done would be vain were the will already determined to do it or to leave it undone. But neither of these descriptions will express *the will*. This can be done by self-conscious action and by that alone—in other words, by willing. Accept a verbal interpretation in place of this, treat the will simply and solely as an object-to-be-studied, and that object inevitably becomes a mystery and a contradiction; and little by little we drift into the sceptical conclusion *that the will is nothing*.

Another illustration, which if fully discussed would lead us further afield than we intend to travel, is to be found in the perennial problem of Permanence and Change, the One and the Many. Philosophy has been called the search for the Permanent amid the changing.

With this account of philosophy there is no need to quarrel. But having accepted it, a distinction remains to be observed, a distinction of capital importance, which we are in constant danger of forgetting. It is one thing to find the Permanent; it is another thing to find a form of words in which the Permanent shall stand *permanently expressed.* It is one thing to experience something fixed and changeless; it is another thing to fix this something by a changeless definition. The first may be possible, while the second remains impossible for ever. It may be said that *de facto* no permanence has been displayed by any verbal reproduction of the Permanent that has been attempted up to date. This is as much as to say that the Permanent has never been *reproduced*; and we are prone to think that from the nature of the case it never can be. For a copy which proves itself transient—as all verbal copies must ultimately do; a copy, that is, which duplicates all the characters of the Permanent except its permanence—is not a reproduction at all. Are we, then, to condemn the Permanent as unreal because the verbal copies of it turn out to be transient? Some thinkers have done so; but only because they have failed to draw the distinction noted above—that it is one thing to *discover* fixity in experience, and quite another thing to *confer* fixity in experience by a form of words. The former, we repeat, may succeed; the latter must always fail. But the failure of *this* must never be taken as involving the failure of *that*.

Suppose, however, that some thinker, undeterred by this distinction, sets out not only to discover the Permanent, but to deliver it, when found, under the form of a verbal expression to his fellow-men, so that they for all time may share with him in the benefit of his discovery. What condition may we lay down in advance as indispensable for the success of his undertaking? He is going to catch the Permanent in a formula, a definition, an expression, which shall fix its identity beyond the risk of cavil and save us henceforth from the danger of confusing it with the changing. Plainly the outstanding condition of his success is *that he shall find a perfectly unambiguous formula.* If the attempted reproduction is going to change its meaning, if it is liable to read differently, to convey various impressions to the minds of different men or different ages, then the formula itself will fall over the line into the ranks of those changing things from confusion with which it was to deliver us. To succeed only in presenting a changing expression of the changeless, an ambiguous reproduction of the unambiguous, is to fail altogether. Certainly you can fix nothing in a fluctuating medium. And since the medium here employed is language, it is an absolutely indispensable condition that our thinker shall find for his purpose some language, or fragment of language, altogether exempt from change.

This we say, and say confidently, cannot be done.

For of all the media of expression employed by man (and let us never forget that they are many) none are so unstable, none so quick to change their meaning, as words. Even sculpture, architecture, painting, in their noblest works, speak differently under different conditions; but these arts are relatively immortal compared with speech. Words which are the spears of one age may be the pruning-hooks of the next; phrases which are the ploughshares of the Greek may be the swords of the Goth. Nor are the words of science, of philosophy, exempt. Just as no modern audience can ever receive from a performance of the Antigone the same impression it made in Athens, so there is no man living to-day who can read Plato with the eyes and mind of Aristotle. And as it is, so it will be. A thousand years hence the works of Darwin, the theories of Kelvin, will be seen in another light, connected with another experience, evaluated on another scale, taken up and transformed in the relationships of a larger whole. Even the truths of mathematics enter the flux. Standards of universality in one age, august things to which philosophers take off their caps, they become in another mere pragmatic expedients with none so poor to do them reverence. Every meaning conveyed by words is relative to the total experience into which it falls; it changes, therefore, with every change of the world. The laws of motion, the truths of the multiplication table, fall ultimately, though more slowly, under the same fate as the maxims of politics or the canons of literary taste; they change their values with every new purpose for which they are used. It is indeed surprising, and yet richly instructive, to observe the extraordinary modifications of meaning which pass over the most carefully framed scientific definitions, through some slight shifting of the point of view, or through a change in the atmosphere into which they are introduced, or even in the tone of voice with which they are spoken. Indeed we may conclude, not without reason, that of all the works of man's self-expression—and again let us remember they are of many kinds—his word-utterances are precisely those which fall most completely and soonest under the law of change. And yet it is by means of these ephemeral, winged things that some of us would reproduce Permanence, copy the unchanging, fix the secret of life. To those, therefore, whose object is not merely to *find* something permanent *in* the Universe, but to *say* something permanent *about* the Universe—and most of us have confused the two aims—to all such may we not say that their labour is utterly vain?

One has only to contemplate for a moment any possible characterisation of the Permanent and its instability becomes immediately apparent. Let us call it, for example, "the Good." Not only is the meaning of this term unfixed, not only does it vary with every change in the moral atmosphere; it may be said to even forbid us to think of fixity. For the good is that which becomes better. The good which has arrived at the end of its resources, which cannot transform itself into a better, is the good-for-nothing; in other words, the bad. A more inadequate term to *reproduce* the Permanent could not be found. What this definition intends is probably the converse state-ment — that the Good is permanent, that its gains are gains for all time; but this is a very different thing from the definition — "the Permanent is the Good."

That the Permanent can be expressed in a large variety of verbal forms—as A, as B, as C—should merely serve to remind us that it cannot be verbally expressed at all. For if it were expressed in any one of them it would not need the others. By exhibiting a group of such forms we indicate, not the permanence of the Object, but its change, its instability under any one form, its tendency to seek expression in another.

" Implicit " and " explicit " do not help us ; they merely point to varying degrees in which given attributes appear—in other words, to " change." The more we add to and vary our devices for exhibiting the Changeless, the more surely we defeat ourselves by making it plain that the object of discourse is changing under our very hands.

Here, perhaps, we may appeal for light to the critics of the Fine Arts. The various arts, they tell us, differ in the degree of adequacy with which they severally render the "permanent" or universal interests, emotions, aspirations of humanity. Architecture is here more successful than Sculpture, Sculpture than Painting, Painting than Music. Regarding speech, then, as only one among the arts of expression employed by man, what place does it occupy as a vehicle for the conveyance of this particular aspect of the world or life? Can we hesitate to place it very low—perhaps the lowest of all? As between a Greek temple, on the one hand, and a Platonic Dialogue on the other, which leaves the soul in fuller possession of, in nearer contact with, the thing that changes not? As arts of expressing the changeless, which is the more adequate to its object? The temple may be in ruins, but, even so, it *speaks* of Permanence with a directness of appeal which no verbal dialectic, however carefully framed, can even approach. Among the arts of expression one is suited to this purpose, another to that. It is hard to express movement in stone or rest in music. It is harder still to express permanence in speech.

But speech itself has many varieties, and some may be less adequate than others. Prose and Poetry have different functions in this respect; and their respective values as vehicles of expression vary according to the point of view from which the object is approached. If we are considering an object as something to be used for a given purpose, the prose of a scientific definition will express the thing's nature, in that respect, to our perfect satisfaction. But if we would approach the thing as what it *is* in its wholeness, seeking its permanent values, attending to its reality and disregarding its uses, then the poet is a better guide. Wordsworth does not " define " the mountains nor analyse them ; but it is from him and not from the geologist that we learn most deeply what the mountains *are*. To the man who would mine the mountains for gold Wordsworth says nothing, science says everything. It is true we cannot turn this statement round. Though science makes no use for poetry, poetry is enriched by science. Poetry "takes up" the scientific vision and re-expresses its truths, but always in forms which compel us to look beyond them to the total object which is telling its own story and standing in its own rights. In this the poet and the philosopher are one. Using language as the lever, they lift thought above the levels where words perplex and retard its flight, and leave it, at last, standing face to face with the object which reveals itself.

The objection will perhaps be raised that what has been said about language destroys its value as a medium of communication between mind and mind, and leaves every man without the means of escaping from his private consciousness and tapping the resources of his neighbours. Such a view, therefore, carries its own condemnation.

To this it may be answered that whoever defines

language as a medium of communication between mind
and mind makes a statement than which no better could
be found for illustrating the inadequacy of words to
express any fact of the self-conscious life. For the
statement implies that something is now passing from
you to me—let us say, ideas; that between us a
medium is interposed, namely, audible or written
words; that only by passing through this medium
does that which was an idea in you become the same
idea in me. Need one do more than say simply that
all this is the crudest of metaphors which, if literally
construed, wholly misrepresents what is taking place?

Again: assuming a Reality which can explain itself
to everybody, would this Reality become less interesting
or important in the event of our being totally unable to
explain it to one another? Is the value of a fact to be
measured by the degree in which it offers itself as a
theme of human eloquence, submits to the limitations
of language, and suffers itself to be bandied about from
mind to mind? Are things *no good* until we begin to
talk about them?

And, lastly, would not all we mean by " communication between mind and mind " be provided for if we suppose that common knowledge comes about, not from
our explaining things to one another, but from things
explaining themselves in the same terms to us all?
Accepting the object as its own interpreter, as its own
" medium of communication," do we not begin to
understand what is utterly dark on any other view,
how it comes to pass that the resulting knowledge is a
common possession? "

Here, once more, our best witnesses are the poets.
Poetry is the true *lingua franca* of the world. Far

more richly than prose it stores up the record of human experience; it is the strongest link between the ages. It is no paradox that in poetry there is less ambiguity than in prose, and far more of what all races and ages have, and know, in common. Shakespeare, after all, is more intelligible than Bacon. Our minds " communicate" with Greece more richly through the verse of Homer than through the wisdom of Socrates. For the poet takes us straight into the presence of things. Not by explanation, but by indication; not by exhausting its qualities, but by suggesting its value he gives us the object, raising it from the mire where it lies trodden by the concepts of the understanding, freeing it from the entanglements of all that " the intellect perceives as if constituting its essence." Thus exhibited, the object itself becomes the meeting-ground of the ages, a centre where millions of minds can enter together into possession of the common secret. It is true that language is here the instrument with which the fetters of language are broken. Words are the shifting detritus of the ages; and as glass is made out of the sand, so the poet makes windows for the soul out of the very substance by which it has been blinded and oppressed. In all great poetry there is a kind of " kenosis " of the understanding, a self-emptying of the tongue. Here language points away from itself to something greater than itself. " Lo," it seems to say, " there cometh one after me the latchet of whose shoes I am not worthy to stoop down and unloose."

We thus return to our first position, that the work of philosophy is to enforce the attitude of meditation. Reflective thought ends in the discovery that we do not experience any object until, like the poet, we " fade away" with it into the silent forest, far from the strife of tongues. Thus philosophy ends in the wonder with which it began. But wonder is no name for a calf-like astonishment at the ways of the world. It is the state of a mind which prefers to attend rather than to speak; which listens, and listens with great and ever-changing emotions, to the deep voice of the world. There is no nescience in wonder; at the same time there is no loquacity. Wonder reads all languages, though it is eager to speak in none. It reads the language of Art by which many things are said which the tongue cannot say; it reads the truths which require whole personalities to express them and cannot be rendered by anything less; it reads all words that have been made flesh; it reads the actions by which alone the truths of morality can be made articulate; it reads the fact-language of the Universe. Wonder is also a patient student of philosophy, but looks narrowly between the lines and weighs the things that are left unsaid. But with all this acquisitiveness it remains to the end the most silent of all the children of the gods. For it has discovered that speech is insufficient to utter the last things; and this troubles it not, because the last things may be heard speaking for themselves. At last, after long delay the wondering soul gives form to that which is stirring within it and produces its works—art and song and mighty deeds.

" If a man were to inquire of Nature the reason of her creative activity, and if she were willing to give ear and answer, she would say—' Ask me not, but understand in silence even as I am silent and am not wont to speak.'"[1]

---

[1] Plotinus. Motto prefixed to Bergson's *Time and Experience* (English translation) by my lamented friend F. L. Pogson.

IV.—THE UNIVERSE AS PHILOSOPHER.

In all that has been said in the preceding essays we have been endeavouring to break free from the habit of mind which regards the world as an object which we must either interpret exclusively in the forms of our conceptual logic or, in the alternative, treat as outside the bounds of human concern. This habit appears to us a prejudice having its roots in the purpose which dominates the life of man for the time being—a purpose for which scientific explanation is the paramount need. Thinking conducted under this prejudice seems to us to be incommensurate with experience: it fails to do justice to the inexhaustible riches of the Universe. This is shown by the fact that experience instantly bursts and overflows every logical dam by which the intellect seeks to confine it. Using another figure, we may say that experience is always new and the metaphysical bottles are always old.

In place of this habit, which, so to say, allows us no rest until we have forced our words into the mouth of the Universe, and restrains it from speaking any language but our own, we have tried to substitute a more catholic temper. We credit Reality with infinite modes of self-expression besides that which becomes articulate in the forms of our conceptual logic. And we differ from the Agnostic in holding that man, as self-conscious, has as much concern with these unnamed and nameless "attributes" of Being as with the one or two which lend themselves to expression by Science, whether of the positive or the metaphysical kind. We are not referring to "mystical" states of consciousness. The actual and normal experience of the Plain Man is a reservoir of Life, containing much that neither seeks the explanations of science nor sustains them. Man is something more than a mere "interpreter" of the world. He is the recipient of the Cosmic Address—of what we have ventured to call the *donum*; which address is conveyed to him in countless forms other, and perhaps richer in their expressiveness, than the concepts of the understanding or their corresponding verbal counterparts.

In this, of course, there is nothing new. In the opening pages of his *Ethics* Spinoza announces the essential truth for which we are contending, namely, that Reality must be left to tell its own story in its own way. We hold no brief for Spinoza. He seems to have fallen at last into the toils of an intellectualism from which he had promised to set us free, and to offer a "view" of the world, or rather of man's relation to the world, which falls far below the depth and catholicity of his original insight. From him, nevertheless, better perhaps than from any other, may be learnt the secret of deliverance from that "bondage" of mind which has its roots in the exaggerated claims of the intellect. A similar lesson is being taught us by what has recently been written about "the subconscious," though we are prevented in this case from grasping the full importance of the doctrine by the extraordinary confusion of psychological metaphors in

which it is presented.   The doctrine of the subconscious
appears to us a hopeful attempt to assert a place in
experience for those " infinite and eternal attributes "
other than Extension and Thought, by reference to
which Spinoza warned us off from every attempt to
limit the self-expression of the Whole.

The world is like an actor who plays many parts,
and the " intellectual " part is undoubtedly *one* of them.
Philosophy, in other words, is one of the forms of the
Cosmic Address, just as Extension or Thought is one
of the " infinite and eternal attributes " of God.   If it
should seem that in what has been said we have been
denying the rights of Philosophy, our reply would be
that the only way to effectively assert those rights is
to keep them in their proper place, which is what we
have been endeavouring to do.   A Universe which
addresses us in the language of metaphysics and in
that alone is, indeed, the *ne plus ultra* of absurdity.
A Reality whose every language needed translation
into the language of problem - and - answer before
evoking our response would be a Reality to which
we could not respond at all.   But while we challenge
this monopoly of the intellect, this attempt of conceptual
logic to lay hands on the whole field of human experience,
we are willing to concede everything that can be
claimed for the rational order as one among the
many self-expressions of the Real.   The world does
speak to us in the language of Extension and Thought.
At certain moments, perhaps, it addresses us pre-
dominantly, though not exclusively, in that form ;
and no doubt we are intended to listen.   We may go
even further.   That man alone can receive philosophy
aright to whom it is throughout a speech *of the*

6

universe, and not a speech of his own to be imposed by him on the infinite other things the Universe has to say.

So regarded, philosophy becomes not less but vastly more important than it is when seeking to empty the world of all values save such as itself can express. So long as that claim is made, or even seems to be made, Philosophy may count upon the permanent rebellion of the human heart. It is only when the problems of life are set in the context of an experience which as a whole is not problematic that we can measure the importance attaching to their solution. Hence the advantage of making our first approach to the Object of Experience, not as a scientific construct appealing only for an intellectual response, but as clothed with those infinite and eternal attributes which belong to a Work of Art.

The further elaboration of this will be attempted in the two following essays.

If Nature produces all things, we cannot escape the conclusion that our theories of their production are themselves natural products. Philosophy must not be treated as a mere *addendum* to the Universe it professes to interpret, itself having no intelligible place in the world. On the contrary, among the facts of which any complete view of things must take cognisance, the view itself surely counts for one.

The theme of the present essay is that the mere concept of the world remains incomplete until it includes the interpretation of the world as an element of the world-constitution. The philosopher who, like Mr Herbert Spencer and many others, professes to give an intelligent synthesis of all the facts accessible to observation, must not forget to include among them his own occupation at the moment. I shall plead that this occupation of the philosopher, as he forges the master-keys of truth, so far from being a fact of no importance, is one of the facts which vitally affects the significance of the rest. The effect of its inclusion, by any scheme of thought which has hitherto excluded it, is revolutionary.

In a sense, the question before us is the old one of the relation of subject and object—an admission, it is to be feared, not likely to engage the interest of the reader. I propose, however, to vary the dull exercise by making it specific and concrete. We shall not trouble ourselves with the abstract question of how mind is related to matter, but we shall enter the controversy at a higher point, and ask how Philosophy (as a special manifestation of mind) is related to *its* object, if it have one. We shall turn reflection on its own process and results; we shall ask the philosopher to consider his own act in putting forth any theory of the All-of-Things, and to tell us what place in the All-of-Things that act and that theory hold. Have they any place, or none? If any, what? If none, why not?

From yet another point of view our study may be said to refer to the general context of philosophical investigation. How comes the Universe to provide room, not for intelligence in general, but for philosophic intelligence and for the philosopher's point of view? What kind of a Universe is that which contains, as this Universe undoubtedly does contain, Mr Herbert Spencer's Synthetic Philosophy? How is our conception of Nature affected if we are to admit that Haeckel,

T. H. Green, James Martineau, with all their speculations, are natural products? Or when Huxley discovers
that Nature is indifferent to the moral needs of man,
what is that in Huxley which makes the discovery, and
what is the discovery itself? Do these fall outside
Nature or inside? If inside, what shall we think of a
Nature which in the fulness of time is able to produce
a brilliant essay on her own shortcomings, and advise
men how best to bear themselves in consequence? If,
on the other hand, Huxley and his works fall outside
Nature and have nothing to do with her, then to what
or to whom do they belong? Were Huxley to admit,
as probably he would have done, that after all, the
Romanes Lecture is Nature's doing, then, we must
ask, is she also responsible for the very different view
of herself put forward in Martineau's *Study of Religion*,
and, in addition to that, for the attempt to reconcile
these contradictions which we call Hegelian? Are
Huxley, Martineau, Hegel (or the Hegelian) mere
spectators of a pageant in which they themselves as
philosophers have no acting part? Is the exhibition
of their respective doctrines to be treated as something
wholly severed from the pageant itself? Must we
think of these great men as seated on the kind of throne
once occupied by the God of Deism, neither of the
world nor in it, but employed in that very work of
ab extra criticism and unrelated vigilance which each
of them has taught us to dissociate from the name of
God? And if these questions are answered in the
negative, and the whole situation thrown back into
the arms of Nature, is not the reader immediately
aware that a new element has appeared on the
scene? Does not the fact that Nature can, at one

and the same time, confess her moral indifference by
Huxley, proclaim her moral concern by Martineau,
and strive to harmonise the discord by Hegel—does
not this fact radically transform the conception of
Nature from which the inquiry began? And if, again
—the reader must be patient,—it be said that we are
now showing symptoms of a "tender mind," all the
more must leave be given for a final question, namely
this: Whether the pragmatic doctrine itself, pragmatically appraised according to its own rules, would
not be pragmatically valueless if Kant and his tender-
minded "crew" had not appeared on the scene? For
if Kant had never set us wrong, it is hard to see what
"difference would be made" by James setting us right;
and whatever makes no difference is, according to
Pragmatism, nothing. No tender mind, no tough:
no Kant, no James. Pragmatism itself compels us
to think that tender minds and tough are necessary
correlates in an organic whole. They are like quarrel-
some twins, each of whom finds it difficult to get on
with the other, but impossible to get on without him.

In short, philosophy needs to consider her context.
We ask the philosopher, who explains how all things
come in, not to forget to explain how he happens to
come in himself, and what in the total production is
the significance of his part. The secret of the Universe
being, for instance, matter and force, is it a fact of no
significance that the Universe has somehow managed
to find out and publish its own secret, and to grow
hilarious, contented, pessimistic, or heroically defiant,
as the case may be, over the discovery? This consideration, which becomes the more weighty as we
ponder it, has been curiously overlooked. There are

not many thinkers who have learned Fichte's lesson of catching themselves in the act of thinking out their own metaphysics, and asking whether the metaphysics so thought out are wide enough to embrace their own significance. If the reader will subtract from the sum total of modern philosophy all that which, while explaining all else, leaves itself unexplained, as a mere surd in things, he will find but a scanty remnant left on his hand. The type of thinker too commonly met with to-day is one who violently seizes a point of view outside the problem he is seeking to answer, and builds for himself a crow's-nest of observation on territory and out of material secretly filched from the object of his inquiry. I have in mind three schools of philosophy — Dualism, Naturalism, Pragmatism — claiming gifted exponents and a wide currency of which it is strictly true that they either beg, borrow, or steal a point of view clear outside the Universe before they can tell you anything about it. There, in their crow's-nests of observation, they stand and speculate, as truly apart from the object as the soul seated in the pineal gland was apart from the body it was thought to control, and stubbornly negligent of the fact that all the difficulties of that long-exploded theory are suggested in aggravated form by their own attitude to the business they have in hand. In all these cases there is a suppressed factor—the philosopher himself,— and though this may look at first sight like a piece of self - abnegation on his part, it turns out on nearer view to be mere defective logic. It is a lame sort of synthesis which omits the synthetising intelligence : *Hamlet* with Hamlet left out is complete in comparison. Had we not other business in hand, it would be easy to fill the rest of this essay with modern instances of speculative theories which appear to " work " only so long as they and their authors are regarded as existing in two absolutely separate and unrelated worlds, but which lose even the semblance of truth the moment you try to establish a relation between the two.[1] Give the philosopher a free charter to deal as he will with " his own " intelligence, so that he may introduce it into the universe and withdraw it without notice, and any conceivable interpretation of the world becomes equally possible with any other. He will prove to you, according to his bias or yours, that the world belongs to God, or to the devil, or to himself, or to nobody. Let him withdraw his intelligence from Nature, and he will show, for instance, that Nature can never produce the human conscience. Nature then becomes a mere machine, and is capable only of the works of a machine. Let him surreptitiously introduce his intelligence into that machine, as Haeckel does, and he will doubtless be able to persuade you that machines can say their prayers, play chess, and indulge in repartee. Such a charter has, indeed, never been given, but it has been assumed by many philosophers; and it is in virtue of this stolen right

[1] An instance of this, taken from the work of one of our finest thinkers, which I cannot forbear adducing, will be found in Ward's *Naturalism and Agnosticism* (vol. ii. p. 171), in the famous passage dealing with the ten men and the ten suns. If the reader will carefully consider how the ten men, each perceiving his own sun, come at last to agree among themselves that it is one and the same sun they all perceive, he will find that they do so only because an eleventh man is surreptitiously introduced, viz. Professor Ward himself, who, unknown to himself or any of the ten, pulls the strings of the whole operation.

that not a few of our recent guides, deceiving themselves as well as their followers, have been able to account for the wonderful tricks the Universe is able to play.

Between the mental habits of the age and its moral tendencies action and reaction are incessant. The logic which governs great systems of thought inevitably reproduces the principles underlying the daily life of the communities in which they are born; and, on the other hand, practical tendencies gather a new strength from this reproduction. The correspondence is often as clear in details as it is on the grand scale, and many a trick of thought turns out to be the reflex of thoughtless tampering with the ends of life. In what immediately follows I shall suggest that this holds true of that false conception of the relation between interpretation and the Universe interpreted which enters and remains unnoticed in so many current forms of speculation. It remains either unnoticed, or, if noticed, condoned, for this reason: that this is only one more instance of a divided mode of thought to which a divided mode of life gives perpetual encouragement. It repeats in a particular case, and in a less explored region, a conception of man's relation to his environment which, in many other ways, sets the one over against the other as unrelated and mutually exclusive terms.

Of the many forms of this divorce the characteristic example may be found in current ideas of private ownership. Here pluralism reigns supreme and needs no advocate. Here the ego is accepted without question as the starting-point of the whole adventure; and, since the adventures are many, the word, which was obstinately singular for the tongue that coined it, is endowed with a plural for British use, and we speak of the "various egos of various men." Society is the sum total of these "egos," round each of whom possessions gather, as rubbish gathers round a stake fixed in the midst of a swirling stream. The relation which binds the ego to his goods is an external attachment only; like the stake aforesaid, he has them as long as he can hold them, and in no other sense; and the condition of their belonging to him is that they shall not belong to anyone else. The egos of this pluralistic society have for environment a world which is conveniently plural also; for it is divided into a sufficient number of small lots, and as you get the lots by dividing the world, so you get the world by adding the lots. Each lot is of a mixed character: it comprises cash and other values of all sorts — money, health, mind, morals, religion, and a number of other things as well. As the egos are many, the lots are many also; each ego has its own lot; and thus a picture is constituted, of which it cannot be said that the interest of variety is lacking.

This is the pluralism of the natural man: what mischief it has wrought in the field of social ethics no serious observer needs to be told. I suggest, however, that the same mode of thought, disguised under other names, has invaded the innermost citadels of speculation. Thought also is treated as the property of thinkers; and the thinkers are merely "egos" of a special sort. Philosophy itself becomes a kingdom of small holdings. Its harvests are portioned out into a miscellaneous assemblage of "little systems," each of which is assigned to its little day and to its particular philosopher, who, like a pedlar, hawks it round the world in his pack. These little systems are exhibited as emphatically "ours"—and the truth remains unperceived that not only their littleness but their insignificance is often due to that very fact.

The idea of possession might be claimed with some plausibility as an ultimate category of thought. The question, "To whom does this belong?" or "Whose is it?" occurs as inevitably to the philosopher criticising a new system as to the child who has captured a stray kitten. As a popular type of what is unthinkable, a thing which belongs to nobody would serve as well as an event without a cause. If the thing does not belong to man it must belong to God. Taking the prevalence and force of mental habit as a test of truth, it might be claimed that the concept of possession is exempt from criticism.

Let the reader at the outset measure for himself the extent of the tyranny which ideas of private ownership exercise in the thinking of the West. The thought of the East, or rather of India, here stands out in sharp contrast to our own, and perhaps the subject is best approached in the light of that contrast. What makes Indian thought unintelligible, or at least unattractive, to many whose thinking has been fashioned in the British temper, is that it does its work without employing the category of possession. When Indian philosophy is discussing the nature of experience, or the self, no reference is made to what for the British mind is an essential feature of the case, viz. that "somebody" must be implied to whom this experience or self appertains as a freehold.[1] There is no point, I imagine, on which it is harder for East and West to understand each other. The philosophy which emanates from the well-furnished studies of Britain, and proclaims at the outset that experience also is "my own," must be a sore perplexity to those whose fee-simple in the world extends only to a loin-cloth and a beggar's bowl. Here we may find an interesting illustration of the influence of social conditions on mental habit. In the civilisation of the East possession, as the end of life, has not acquired the dominance it exercises in the West, where it may be said without exaggeration to control the structure of society, and to pass thence and return thither from the structure of our thought. The differences between feudalism and democracy, between individualism and collectivism, are reducible to different methods, theories, or ideals of possession. Industrial society, so far as it is merely industrial, is motived from the same source. And we often find ourselves unable to *think* save in terms of proprietorship. This concept is, for example, the centre of gravity of our legal system, and out of it we weave our theories of the rights of man. It is the basis of the most effective half of our moral distinctions and the characteristic notion of the West. We treat the whole Universe as a thing to be

[1] For an example take the following :—" But as the idealist *does* set forth from experience, we are forced to inquire from *whose* experience the start is made. . . . We must surely start from someone's experience. From whose experience, then, do we start? Each, we say, must start from his own experience or from the sympathetically imagined experience of another. But another's experience *qua* imagined is still one's own experience. Each, therefore, must start from his own experience."—Mr Boyce Gibson, " A Peace Policy for Idealists," *Hibbert Journal,* January 1907, p. 417.

exploited in somebody's interest, and build our doctrine of reality on a metaphor of cash-values. The rich man's difficulty in entering the kingdom of God is ours in an aggravated form ; for riches are not so much the means of our forgetting God, as the form under which we try to remember Him. God is the proprietor of the world. Even Milton, in times when the fever of possession was a milder thing than it is to-day, traced the history of the world, and the whole scheme of man's redemption, from an attempt to *dispossess* the Almighty of His own. Thoroughly native to the Gothic mind, and strongly reinforced by what the Goth has borrowed from the Jew, the concept of possession has laid its moulding hand on the entire history of Christian theology, and was never more potent than it is to-day. Not so long ago the present writer followed an argument for the existence of God based on the necessity of postulating an *owner* for the world. Was it conceivable that a property so vast and so eligible *belonged to nobody*? Surely the earth was the *Lord's*, and the fulness thereof. Whether there was or was not a First Cause, who could say? But the necessity of a First Owner was self-evident. Such an argument, whatever be its defects, may at least be praised for taking advantage of the weak spot in the heart of a property-loving age. When possession is treated as nine-tenths of the Law and the whole of the Gospel, it is not wonderful that men should ascribe proprietorship to God.

It is, however, in connection with an idea of man rather than of God that the category of possession is most unsparingly applied. Passing over the question of the rights of property, in the technical sense, let us consider how the matter stands in the realms of

psychology and metaphysics.   Here we are at once
confronted with a doubt whether the philosophers of
the West have ever taken heed that the verb "to
have" which they use so freely in the psychical sphere
must be given a totally different sense from what it
bears in the purely objective or physical.   When we
say a man *has* five senses, reason, will, conscience, soul,
we are surely speaking of a different relation from that
implied when we say he *has* five children, a grand
piano, a medical adviser, and a balance at the bank.
You *have* your character (an Intuitionist will emphasise
this) ; you *have* also, let us say, a testimonial from your
last employer ; but "having" in the first case denotes
the exercise of an essential function of your being ; in
the second, a purely accidental circumstance.   Conceive
then the confusion which results, when even in approved works of psychology the mechanical category is
transferred into the spiritual world, and we are asked
to do our thinking as though this category meant the
same thing in the one as in the other.   Man *has* a body
and he *has* a *soul* ; but who is the man claiming these
assets if he be not the assets he claims ?   Or perhaps
the soul is the owner of the body.   Is the body, then,
a *corpse* ?

But these are crude examples taken from children's
primers and such like : let us consult the philosophers.
According to them, man *has* a place in Nature ; he *has*
a relation to the Universe and God ; he *has* duties to
his neighbour and to himself ; he *has* an end to accomplish ; he *has* experience in all its varieties ; he *has*
right impulses and wrong ; he *has* individuality which
he is told to guard lest it be taken from him ; he *has*
virtues of which hostile powers would "rob" him ; he

has vices which he had better get rid of; he *has* an ego
which is his very own; he *has* a soul which he may
sell—and so on through a veritable auctioneer's cata-
logue of man's effects. But who is the owner of these
job-lots? He is behind the scenes; but if you seek
him there you will not find him. When you think you
have got him, he turns instantly into one of his own
possessions. It helps not a whit to refer us to a *higher*
self: for this higher self also turns out to be something
man *has*. Who, then, is Man? Is he the selfless
owner of himself? We flounder in a realm of nonsense, trying once more to cook the hare we cannot
catch.

In regard to Philosophy itself we are apt to set up
the same dualism, and again to think of the relation
between philosopher and system under the category of
ownership. Noteworthy here is the impersonal character of the great systems of Indian thought. We of
the West, although on occasion we can adopt impersonal language, are yet inclined to allow an importance to persons, in this connection, which is foreign to
the philosophic temper both of India and of Greece,
and which, I venture to think, has done much to darken
the outlook of Western thought in the higher realms of
speculation. The question, " Whose is it ? " disturbs
the significance of any interpretation of the Universe
we may happen to consider. It is Plato's; it is
Spinoza's; it is Kant's; it is Haeckel's. We cannot
rid ourselves of the obsession of the possessive case.
The truths of thought, like Mr Boyce Gibson's
"experience," must belong to someone, and the shadow
of this someone—often, alas! his speaking substance
as well—is only too apt to dominate our interest in

the controversy. If truth is to be told, we must confess that no small part of the current output of philosophy is concerned with the rights of famous thinkers to possess their own. Standards are raised; parties formed; raids planned on the reputation of great names. There can be no doubt that this feature of the case has added something to the zest of philosophical controversy in the West, and won to it the interest of many persons who might otherwise have concluded that philosophy provides nothing worth fighting about. How much the higher thought owes to this kind of belligerency is not an easy question; but I am not one for overestimating the debt. Nor would I rate more highly the services of another set of individuals whose method, though a seeming antithesis to that just described, is but an exaggerated expression of the same spirit. Not least among the chastisements of that plague of egos wherewith our sins have afflicted us is the apparition of superior persons who, under the proud title of "independent thinkers," glory in the shame of being no man's disciples. Owing everything to the leaders they are so anxious to repudiate, and smiting them with weapons stolen from their armouries, they contribute nothing to thought save an illustration of the utter blindness that overtakes it when ingratitude and vanity are allowed to enter in. To capture any portion of the kingdom of truth and to keep it for one's very own, is not only forbidden by the nature of truth, but is an ambition unworthy of the thinker. The example of Plato might be studied with good effect. Advancing far beyond the teaching of his Master he nevertheless placed his own thoughts on that Master's lips and himself passed out of sight.

Certain it is that the temper in which these lofty studies are pursued is too often identical with that which prompts an Englishman to proclaim his house as his castle or to form a syndicate for buying up a promising concern. To *have* a philosophy is dear to the heart of an enlightened Western, and he "has" it in the same sense that he "has" an edition of Plato in his library, a Morris paper in his drawing-room, and an ornamental knocker on his front door. It is the captive of his bow and spear. If you attack his views he will treat you as threatening his property. You shall not "rob" him of his faith; you shall not dispossess him of his point of view. It is remarkable that the sphere in which this temper is most active is that of Philosophy and Theology. "My philosophy" will always pass current; "my religion" is condoned; but "my science" is admittedly absurd. The field of scientific inquiry, alas! is not free from the curse of personal claims, but we should be startled to hear the ether described as Lord Kelvin's, or a treatise on iron introduced by the statement that the iron in question belonged to "somebody." The subject of science may safely be trusted to walk abroad by itself; but metaphysical entities must always be accompanied by the owner and led by a string. Why is this?

The foregoing discussion is intended to suggest that we are dealing with no casual metaphor but with a deeply rooted intellectual habit continuous in character with the ethical conditions of the age. We have now to examine the actual effects of this habit in the field of philosophical inquiry. Briefly, the effects may be summed up as the introduction of an unsuspected

dualism into the centre of the Monistic camp. Thanks
to the power of the possessive case—a power equalled
only by that of " juxtaposition "—philosophy has been
detached from its fitting context in the All-of-Things
and made the property of a set of persons, namely
philosophers, whose business is to stand apart from the
Universe and take copies of its underlying principles.
Here stands the philosopher, ready to begin ; there lies
the Universe, the *corpus vile* of the experiment, a poor,
passive, long-suffering object, waiting to receive a
character and be clothed upon by any rag of a theory
which philosophy may cast upon its nakedness. The
inquiry proceeds, and, "facts" having been duly
examined and the victim graciously permitted to give
evidence on its own behalf, sentence is pronounced for
the One or the Many, for Chance or Design. The
philosopher has given *his* award and the spectators may
now disperse, leaving the Universe in its rational clothes
and with the judge's label pinned on its back. That
professed dualists should conceive the matter in this
way need occasion no surprise, though to them one
might commend the criticism of Mr James, and remind
them that it "makes no difference" to the Universe
whether it is thus "copied" or not. But that any thinker
who goes the length of asserting the essential unity of
the world should thus desert his principles every time
he enters his own front door is, I venture to think, a
very remarkable and perplexing phenomenon. Such
combinations of fidelity abroad with treachery at home
are by no means uncommon.

    To one who professes Monism in any of its forms
this may be commended as self-evident truth: that
every interpretation of the Universe is itself an element

                                                    7

in the Universe to be interpreted; whence it follows that no interpretation is valid which fails to account for its own presence as an organic factor in the All-of-Things. If we take two philosophers, one of whom habitually speaks of the Universe as containing his own interpretation of it, and the other as not containing this, it is clear that they are not speaking of the same Universe. The conception of the latter is obviously incomplete, for there is something which *that* Universe does not include, viz. the interpretation given, in consequence of which exclusion it cannot claim to be the *All*-of-Things. Even Mr James seems to regard the world as containing the pluralistic hypothesis, perhaps as one of its unaccountable elements, and as owing not a little of its interest to that circumstance. The reader who is candid with himself will, I believe, have to confess that whenever he *thinks* of the world he must needs think of it with his own interpretation superadded, and cannot indeed think of it in any other way. The mere fact that he calls it "a world" shows that he has already found a meaning *in* it.

Let us, then, suppose a formula to be discovered which should enable us to give a rational explanation of the Universe throughout the entire range of its physical and psychical phenomena. The formula might be Spirit, or the Idea of the Good, or One Substance with infinite attributes, or Matter and Force: the content is quite irrelevant. What we have now to ask is, Does the formula cover its own presence among the facts to be interpreted? Is it self-explanatory? Has Plato's Universe a place for Plato and his Republic, Spinoza's Substance for Spinoza and the Ethic, Haeckel's for Haeckel and his Riddle? Or does the formula fail at that precise point where the arrival of the philosopher is the feature of absorbing interest? Would the interpretation embrace every conceivable fact and problem save only the seeming detail that someone is interpreting all things in that precise and particular way? If the exception be allowed, let the reader carefully consider what follows—which is nothing less than the downfall of Monism. We are left with a Monistic formula on this side and a Monistic Universe on that: but the formula and the Universe are as separate from one another, as distinct in being, as mind and matter were in the Dualism of the Middle Ages. An explanation which explains the Universe, but which the Universe itself cannot explain in return, leaves us still groping among the beggarly elements of common sense: it fails to bring the controversy one hairsbreadth nearer to solution.

The point at issue is obscured by the abstract form in which the problems of philosophy are usually stated. Thus we are asked to consider the relation of mind to matter. Can matter account for mind? can mind account for matter? Well, let us suppose that either could be done. You have, say, a theory of the Universe which sufficiently accounts for mind as the necessary consequence of some primordial arrangement of matter and force. But that is not the last question at issue. It is nothing to the purpose when you tell me how matter accounts for mind: what I want to know is, how it accounts for mind *as manifested in the very act of putting this interpretation on matter's potencies and powers*. For if your Universe is really one, this is what it ought to do. It must show itself capable of producing, not mind in the abstract, but those concrete operations

of mind which Spinoza's or Haeckel's answer to the
riddle exhibits. If it is only Spinoza or Haeckel who
provides the answer, and not the Universe itself, then
you are no Monist, but a Dualist, the Universe standing
on this side and Spinoza and Haeckel with their keys
on that; but how the keys came to fit the lock will
give rise to a new riddle several degrees harder than the
old. If, on the other hand, you scorn such incon-
sistencies and boldly profess your willingness to regard
Haeckel and his works as facts, organically related with
all other facts to one another and to the whole, qualifying
by their presence the meaning of everything else and
being qualified in return, then there is no escaping the
conclusion that it is the Universe itself by means of
Haeckel, and not Haeckel apart from the Universe,
which answers its own riddles in the systematic and
intelligent, manner of the German biologist. And that
discovery will send you further than Haeckel in search
of light. For, as we have said, what precisely we want
to know is not in general how matter can evolve intelligence but how the Universe comes, first, to present
itself as *this* riddle and then to evolve *this* answer. In
other words, Haeckel will not explain the Universe until
he has shown how the Universe explains him.

To say so much is but to repeat a doctrine with
which every student of the first chapter of St John's
Gospel is familiar. The Monist, of whatever com-
plexion, who, consistently with his principles, casts
his own philosophy back into the arms of the Universe
he claims to interpret, is a confessor of the Eternal
Word. It is the Logos which speaks through him:
and he is a revealer of the truth just in so far as he
is also an element in the truth to be revealed. What

he says about the Whole would be a meaningless story were it not read in the light of what the Whole says about *him* : save as himself explained by the system he would explain he is nothing, and his point of view is nowhere. At first he seems to himself to be looking *out*, from his private window, upon the All-of-Things, a mere spectator of the scene before him : but it is the light of the All streaming *in* through the window that renders his speculation possible and reminds him that he knows only because he is known. At this point philosophy begins. The philosophic ego, severed from his context, and claiming in that severance to interpret the context from which he is torn, is now seen to be a pure abstraction, ineffectual as any ghost. It is of the essence of mind that it embraces itself within the sphere of its own inquiries, and if the cost of admitting this is to introduce a paradox into every philosophical problem, the penalty of neglecting it is to render philosophy dumb.

Indeed, the above doctrine, far from being novel,[1] can claim a witness wherever Religion and reflective Conscience have found a voice. " Thus saith *the Lord* " is ever the word of the Prophet : " Thus thinks the Whole " is but the deeper implication of the Prophet's cry. " Our wills are ours to make them Thine " ; and Thought is ours for no other end.[2] Were the second

---

[1] Students of Schelling, and of the transition to Hegel, are not likely to think it novel.

[2] O Light that followest all my way,
 I yield my flickering torch to Thee ;
 My heart restores its borrowed ray,
 That in Thy sunshine's blaze its day
 May brighter, fairer be.
 Scottish Hymnal.

false, the first could not be true. Thought, like
morality, must lose in order to find; and in surrendering
her insight to the All-of-Things, she achieves on lighter
terms a victory won in other spheres at the cost of
agony and bloody sweat. We are not here straining
after far-fetched and unheard-of things ; we are repeating our daily confessions and moving among our most
familiar thoughts. With impeded utterance and with
a slightly foreign accent, philosophy is here speaking
the language which ever flows from the lips of Religion
with the easy music of a mother-tongue. What is far
stranger than this doctrine is the spectacle of devout
thinkers fiercely contending for subjective interests
from which Christian men seek deliverance every time
they repeat the Lord's Prayer. For the meaning of
things is no more *my* discovery than the moral order
is *my* creation, and the philosopher who discerns this
and proclaims it deserves no harder name than the
saint who cries " *Thy* will be done."

The habitual neglect of these considerations by
Monistic thinkers is probably due to a one-sided
tendency in the Western mind to assert the Right
of Private Judgment—a right specially dear to the
Goths and supported by the whole group of powerful
instincts which gather round the concept of possession. But if the foregoing exposition is sound, the
first duty of a consistent Monist is to abandon the
assertion of this right in its exclusive form. He
must, from the outset, surrender the claim that
his thoughts, views, or beliefs are exclusively his
own. If they are *his*, that is only because they are
also Another's. This in general he is ready enough to
do ; but the full significance of his surrender will not

dawn upon him until he has learnt to include within it, not his thought in the abstract, but that particular thought of his which achieves this final interpretation of the world—in brief, the Monistic philosophy itself. By hypothesis he has no status, as a being apart, from which to form an outside opinion of the Whole. His views of the Whole are also the Whole's views of itself. It follows that every form of Monism implies that the Universe is self-conscious. No ultimate distinction can be drawn between what you, the philosopher, think of the world and what the world through you thinks of itself. In no wise do you escape this conclusion by holding "mechanical" or "materialistic views" of Nature: for, if your Monism is consistent, the assertion on your part " *It is* a machine," is just the assertion on its part, " *I am* a machine." Whatever *you* say " It is," *it* says " I am." Your only escape is to constitute yourself an outsider, or, which is the same thing, an unrelated part of the Whole—in other words, abandon your Monism altogether. Spinoza proclaimed this over and over again : in the deepest sense it is the theme of the *Ethic*. " The intellectual love of the mind towards God is the very love wherewith God loves Himself." [1] The principle underlying this statement compels the Monist to translate every doctrine of reality from the form " It is " into the form " I am." [2]

To every Monist, one would suppose, the most

---

[1] *Ethic*, pt. 5, prop. xxxvi.

[2] Religion also, it may be added, has but a secondary concern with the proposition " It (or he) is " : its main concern is with " *Thou* art." A demonstration of the existence of God, in the third person, would have no value for *religion* unless it were susceptible of translation into the second.

thought-compelling fact of the Universe is the continual
effort it seems to be making to get its own nature
expressed. This effort he will see reflected in every
system of philosophy the wide world over. So far as
these systems are true he will regard them as the self-
confessions of Reality. But here a sore difficulty
awaits him, for these self-confessions of Reality seem
to be exceedingly various as to their import, inconsistent, and even contradictory. If some are true, it
would appear that others cannot be free from error.
And precisely the same line of argument which makes
the Universe responsible for the true makes it responsible also for the false. No serious Monist needs to be
reminded that the gravest difficulties the system has to
encounter are precisely those which gather round the
origin of error. These difficulties come to a head when
we remember that among the errors for which the
All-of-Things is accountable, are those which attach
to its own most intimate self-confessions in the form
of philosophy. If certain systems, regarded as true,
represent the effort of the Whole to explain itself, how
can we resist the conclusion that other systems regarded
as false reveal the Whole in the act of belying its own
character ?

It may be said that to speak of " true " and " false "
in this connection is to evince a *parti pris*. Let us be
content, then, with the fact that the Universe, monisti-
cally regarded, gives birth to a series of differing
interpretations of its own nature. It would surely
be hard to find any single fact which at first sight
gives greater encouragement to a pluralistic view of
Reality, and one is surprised that Pluralists have not
made better use of its support. The co-presence *in*

Reality of differing interpretations *of* Reality would seem to be fatal to the hypothesis that Reality is the expression of Unitary Mind. If Nature is one, she surely cannot be simultaneously in two, or twenty, minds about her own constitution. How is it possible to read the Monism of Spinoza, the Dualism of Martineau, the Pluralism of James, as the self-confessions of a Single Being?

The consideration of this difficulty will form the subject of the next essay.

V.—THE ALCHEMY OF THOUGHT

THE previous essay concluded with an undertaking, perhaps rashly given, to entertain a problem the statement of which is prophetic of difficulty. The argument professed to lead up to the conception of philosophy as one among the many Self-confessions of the Whole. Now, the least we can demand of a world which tells its own story is that the story shall be consistent with itself. The voice that contradicts itself cannot, it would seem, be the voice of God ; the philosophy that says and unsays, that affirms and denies the same thing, is no part of a Divine Revelation. This, however, is precisely what philosophy appears to do. One philosopher grounds existence on matter, another on spirit ; one exhibits evolution as the progressive realisation of a moral ideal, another finds evolution unmoral ; one proclaims unity, another treats unity as a meaningless term. In the face of such contrariety, how shall we treat the assertion that philosophy is a Self-revelation of Unitary Being ?

The work of philosophy, like that of its kindred[1] occupation charity, begins — and ends — at home. Whatever *ultimate* truth or law the philosopher may discover, it is obvious that the process of discovery is itself subject to the law or truth discovered. The

[1] See Fichte, *The Way of the Blessed Life.*

denial of this means that the law or truth is not ultimate. Thus Mr Joachim has written an extremely able defence of the "coherence" theory of Truth. Does Mr Joachim's defence of the theory itself conform to the theory defended? I am far from saying it does not: I suggest only that, when "Truth" is the subject, conformity to the theory defended is essential to the validity of the defence. Again, in the field of speculative ethics there are theories of the Moral End (one need not name them) in the construction of which the philosopher shows no sign of being himself subject to any moral end whatsoever. There are others which, in the endeavour to give morality an assured scientific basis, let so many dangerous secrets out of the bag as to completely demoralise any person who accepts their final results. No department of his business can vie with that of ethics in the number of temptations it offers the philosopher to detach himself from the moral order he is considering, and to evoke a set of ethical principles to which his own manual or treatise can only be regarded as one flagrant act of disobedience. And in general, any system of thought which fails to illustrate its own principles in the very process by which those principles are reached stands self-condemned. The philosophy which merely legislates for its "other" is worth little: that alone will stand secure which submits to be tested by its own standards and bows its neck under the yoke itself has set up. The consciousness of subjection to its own results is the breath of the nostrils of speculative thought. Nowhere else is the rule of "Practise what you preach" so stringent; and nowhere else is that rule treated with more disdain. How great the

temptation is to lay down a law which one violates in
the very act of laying it down, few persons who climb
the slippery heights of speculation can long remain
unaware. Here, for example, is a system which proclaims the rule of universals, and itself remains a
particular outside their sway. Here is one which places
an everlasting gulf between subject and object, but in
so doing bridges the gulf with its own arms, and is
itself that very unity which it declares to be impossible.
Here is one which teaches that man is free, on the
ground that he is compelled to take that view, and
therefore not free to take any other. Here is one which
announces determination, but pauses not to consider
that determination loses its sting where it has thus been
found out. Here is one which gives the Will priority
over Reason, but does so by a process which is
apparently an attempt to reason, and not to will, us
out of the opposite opinion.

To interpret experience is to change it. Of all the
errors which have been suffered to creep in through the
back-doors of the towers of speculation, I give the place
of chief malignancy to the notion that experience is a
kind of tailor's block, which, having already displayed
a hundred different suits in the shop window, remains
on hand for the display of as many more. To suppose
that any physical or psychical object remains passive
under our effort to understand it, and is the same
when understood that it was before, is as though one
were to say that the bacon which a man eats for his
breakfast is still bacon when it has been digested and
used up in the nourishment of his brain. An interpretation is a kind of alchemy which, when applied to
any object, transforms its character as a thing to be

understood. The object *grows* in and with our knowledge of it; and this growth of the object is no
mechanical addition of moments, no mere loading of
the tailor's block with successive overcoats each a size
bigger than its predecessor, but an organic process as
genuinely such as the growth of an animal body. The
results of each stage become the raw material of the
stage following, not to be lost there nor destroyed,
but to suffer a process of transubstantiation. A fact
understood bears the same relation to the fact not
understood, both as to its sameness and difference, as
the man bears to the boy.

This, I imagine, will not be seriously disputed.
Philosophers are ready enough to proclaim it—in
regard to everybody's business but their own. In the
walks of physical science illustrative instances might be
gathered by the handful. When, however, we enter
those realms of speculative philosophy where this
truth was born, and whence it has been announced,
we encounter an order of " facts " to which it has
seldom been applied. The most striking examples
are, as I have said, in the field of ethical thought.
It is surprising that John Mill, for instance, having
explained the love of virtue as the love of pleasure in
disguise, does not seem to have realised the effect of
such a theory upon any person who should happen to
close with it. Mill seems to have assumed that the
love of virtue, confronted by this explanation of itself,
would remain passive under the operation, and retain
the place and character it had before. Plainly it would
do no such thing. The moment I understand that
what I am really aiming at is not virtue, as I previously supposed, but pleasure, all my delusions about

the supereminence of virtue will vanish, and the love of virtue will, if I am true to my convictions, give place to an entirely different order of desire. I dreamt that I was in a palace : you have now awakened me to the truth that I am in a stye ; and being awake you cannot expect me, as a rational being, to play at believing that my acorns are pearls and my wash the nectar of the gods. Assuming Mill's explanation of the love of virtue to be true, my only chance of retaining that love is to remain in total ignorance of the explanation. Similarly, Mr Sidgwick bases a loftier theory on the "reasonableness of Egoism." But a little reflection will disclose the interesting fact that (again assuming Mr Sidgwick's system to be true) the only egoists whose egoism would be reasonable are those who know nothing and suspect nothing of the conclusions to which Mr Sidgwick is leading them. No sooner do these unfortunate egoists close with Mr Sidgwick's conclusion, and look upon themselves under the searchlight of his Rational Utilitarianism, than they discover that nothing is more unreasonable than egoism : whereupon the basis of the theory will vanish entire. It is certainly reasonable to be an egoist provided you know no better ; but such blissful ignorance the *Methods of Ethics* has rendered impossible ; so that now the position of the reasonable egoist becomes embarrassing to the last degree. He must either give up his egoism, and so leave Mr Sidgwick without a base of operations ; or he must stick to his egoism and defy Mr Sidgwick.[1]

Yet another instance is afforded by the controversy about the Freedom of the Will. The process of

[1] Other instances are given in the essay on "Self-defeating Theories."

proving the Will to be free is itself an instance of the exercise of Will. On the theory of the organic unity of Reason and Will, which no competent psychologist will deny, it is obvious that the activity of a philosopher constructing a theory of moral freedom is as plain an instance of the operations of Will as that afforded by any kind of human activity whatsoever—as plain or perhaps plainer. To those who have made the attempt it will be evident enough that the realm of such inquiries is a realm of effort through and through, and of effort under law. Hence, whatever theory of moral responsibility you set up for conscious activity in general must apply to your own activity in setting up the theory, unless you would maintain the convenient but absurd proposition that as a philosopher you are exempt from the rule to which you are subject as a man.

Now if a man's views as to the nature of the Will are determined for him by logical necessities over which he has no control; if, that is to say, he can allege that Truth *compels* him to hold either this theory or that, then it must be remembered that this plea of compulsion by Truth is open equally to the honest fatalist as to the honest libertarian ; and it is certain that the Truth which has compelled the man to adopt the one theory, say fatalism, cannot condemn him for conducting his life accordingly, nor hold him responsible for not conducting it as those other men do whom Truth has equally compelled to believe in free-will. Fatalism and free-will do not represent two ways of dealing with the same moral situation, which remains passive and unaffected whether we interpret it in one way or the other: they represent two entirely different moral situations, each of which becomes what it is precisely because we understand it in this way rather than that. My theory of the Will profoundly influences my moral world. It follows that the construction of a theory of responsibility itself represents the supreme responsibility the human agent is capable of incurring, inasmuch as the nature of such a theory inevitably determines the attitude of all who accept it to all responsibilities whatsoever. A doctrine of freedom, therefore, which proves me morally free in regard to other activities, but cannot prove me free, in the same sense, in regard to each and all the steps by which I have reached that conclusion, has failed of its purpose. But how many of the apologies for free-will will stand that test?

It is not, however, in regard to such special problems as those noticed above that the constitutive function of interpretation is most fully operative. The function is seen at its maximum activity when we pass to that final view of things which metaphysic attempts. Now, the work of metaphysic is that of building a universe *for thought*. Whosoever offers me a final philosophy offers me a world. To accept the view, for instance, that the world is the manifestation of a good Spirit, or again of an unconscious Will, is to accept a principle according to which the whole length and breadth of my thinking must henceforth be constituted and to which it must be conformed. The function of such a principle is essentially creative: whatsoever concept it touches, in the realm of psychology or of morals or elsewhere, is changed as if by magic to a new thing. Nothing is left as it was before. The broad fact of the world becomes just such a fact as the principle makes it, and every one of my relations to that fact becomes charged with a corresponding meaning.

To me, holding either one of these doctrines, nothing is
what it would be if I held the other.   Neither the stars
in their courses, nor the moral law in the heart; neither
God, my neighbour, nor myself retains the meaning
under the second which each holds under the first.   All
are transformed; and in so far as I may forsake either
of these philosophies for the other or for a third or a
hundredth, the possibility of a fresh transfiguration of
the whole world of thought is ever before me.

So long, therefore, as thought is growing, all meanings
grow with it.   And as there is no such thing as fixed,
static, and final thought, so from the bare attempt to
find a fixed formula we learn that there is no such thing
as a static and final world.   The moral law even is
no more "stablished for ever" than the mountains with
which it has been compared.   Nor is the case altered
one whit if I adopt the pragmatic contention that a
principle of unity is not to be found, that the world will
submit to no kind of comprehensive synthesis.   For
those who assert the principle of unity and for those
who deny it the position is the same.   The Pragmatist
is no less a world-builder than the Kantian.   His
philosophy is the offer of a new kind of world—the
world of adventure—a world as strongly characterised,
as sharply differentiated from others, as it would be if
informed by any attributes which a rigid rationalism
could confer.   If you want a non-creative philosophy,
you will not get it by exchanging Kant for James,
Hegel for Spencer.   When you have made the exchange you will find that you have not escaped from
the necessity of constituting your world, but merely
given up one way of constituting it in favour of another.
The passage from the one system to the other is a

stage in the evolution of the thought-process: it is one more illustration of the endless transformations to which the universe is subject under the alchemy of interpretation.

By no great thinker has this truth been missed, though often forgotten, and those who are not among the greatest can seldom overlook it for long. How else shall we explain the ardour, the eagerness, the moral tension, the sense of a burden almost too great to be borne, which, easily discernible between the lines of all earnest thinking, betray the thinker in the acknowledgment of a tremendous responsibility? Why so much in earnest, we may well ask, if all you are doing is to take a reproduction of the world which makes no difference to the thing reproduced? It is with the thing and not with your reproduction that life has to do. Cannot Reality be trusted to take care of itself? If systems of philosophy are to be treated as so many photographs of Reality, which, needing not their aid, effectually asserts its own principles and declares its own nature independently of them, then it must be confessed that, of all the strange exhibitions man has made of himself before high heaven, his attempts to interpret the universe or to prove it non-interpretable are the masterpiece.

At this point in the discussion we must compare the result of the present argument with that which was offered at the conclusion of the former essay. On the comparison of those results the possibility of further progress depends. Putting them side by side, they appear to be contradictions. In the first argument the conclusion was that interpretations of the All-of-Things

proceed from that Reality which they profess to interpret ; that to explain the world is, for anyone who
regards himself as organically one with the world, to
proclaim the ability of the world to explain itself,—thus
attributing to the All-of-Things precisely that kind and
degree of intelligence of which the interpreter's own work
is the manifestation.   On this view systems of philosophy are so many self-confessions of Ultimate Reality,
whether we call this God or by any other name.   In
the second argument just offered, we reach the opposite
conclusion.   Instead of the universe creating its own
interpretation, we now see the interpretation creating
the universe.   In the first case we were led to see that
the individual thinker, when he reflects on the part he
is playing, and catches himself in the very act of trying
to solve the riddle of the universe, finds himself compelled to surrender the torch, by the light of which he
is working, to that universe whose riddles he is trying
to solve.   So then it would appear that the individual
thinker is completely swallowed up in the universal,
and that no further proceedings are possible by which
the universal may be compelled to disgorge him.

But now all this has been reversed.   In flat contradiction, as it would seem, to what has been before advanced,
we have made the thinker responsible for the world,
instead of making the world responsible for him.   We
have given a charter for world-building to an indefinite
number of persons who may happen to be inclined to
construct systems of philosophy.   We have said that to
interpret experience is to control it, *i.e.* to determine
its conceptual form, to make it mean what it does
mean, and therefore to create a world of experience for
thought.   Here, then, the individual thinker recovers

his rights—recovers them with a vengeance, for he gets back more than he wants. And here again there is no logical possibility of escaping the conclusion we have reached. If you insist on reading your experience exclusively from that end of it at which the experient stands, you will find that the philosophy at which you finally arrive actually creates for you the world you are investigating, and in so doing charges that world with all the problems and all the answers your philosophy professes to handle. We stand, therefore, in the presence of a situation which has all the characteristics of a fierce antinomy. Either conclusion has only to be stated to evoke the resistance of the other. Yet both conclusions follow inevitably from certain assumptions; and the assumptions from which they follow are of such a kind that we cannot avoid making them in the ordinary process of thought.

Nothing can be further from the aim of the present writer than to disguise the intensity of this contradiction. Rather his aim is to bring the contradiction into the full light of day and to set it up, where it is seldom seen, by the main entrance to the City of Speculation. The statement of this antinomy is of course nothing new; but it is not usually recognised that the seat of the opposition is in the philosophic consciousness itself. We find it in knowledge, and we propound a theory of knowledge to solve it: but what we may easily overlook—for no less a thinker than Kant overlooked it—is that in the theory of knowledge so propounded the antinomy turns up again in a conflict of opposites yet more intense. Not until we pass from the sphere of νόησις and enter that of νόησις νοησέως do we encounter the antithesis in the

extremest form, and grasp the principle in which, if at
all, reconciliation may be found.   In other words, the
only hope for a solution of this problem lies with that
philosophy which begins at home.

It is plain that the world may be read in two ways.
I have sought to indicate both ways in these essays;
and we have seen that each reading contradicts the
other. But the active principle which so reads the
world must not be confused with what is read; and the
reader must not be forgotten in the reading. If we can
catch ourselves in the act of discovering the contradiction, we shall perceive that the conflicting elements
stand over against one another just because they are
so *held* by the mind. The contradiction in which we
are all but finally involved is within us. By means of
this deeper unity, and because mind is in possession
of it, we may be able to grasp the truth that the
two processes of thought we have considered, each
leading to an opposite conclusion to that of the other,
are not two but the same, differing only as it is read
from left to right or right to left. The contradiction
is born from the very logic which tries to deal with
the situation. As the two ends of a straight line are
extreme opposites because it is the *same* straight line
of which they are the opposing ends, so the negation
of our first position by the second, or our second by
the first, reveals to us that it is only a *line* that we
are dealing with. This revelation, as we have now
to show, is *the philosophic consciousness itself*, a true
meeting-ground of God and man, in which the whole
work of thought is suffused by the light of a higher
meaning indicated, but never fully expressed, bv the
language of religion.

The results of human speculation are not a mere aggregate of inconsistent systems. The history of philosophy is the exhibition of a single life continuous with itself through the ages. In tracing the process of this life backwards from the mystical synthesis by which the soul loses and finds itself in God to the most rudimentary forms of knowledge, we follow in an inverse order the steps of the process of evolution in the external world. And again, in connecting one system of philosophy with another we shall find ourselves dealing with an organic whole, the parts of which, like the parts of a living body, are so related to one another that the withdrawal of any one of them, far from leaving the others more intelligible by its absence, has the immediate effect of weakening the vital principle in virtue of which all the systems have their being. So closely knit is the organism of the world's thinking that the deletion of any one of its members would threaten the life of the whole. A universe which is tolerant of the spiritual interpretation cannot dispense with the sceptical; just as, in the absence of the spiritual, there is nothing for the sceptic to doubt. The very affirmation of God is an unthinkable contradiction in a world which provides no room for His denial; and the sceptical denial, when it comes, always turns out to be undertaken in the interests of a positive Better which presupposes a positive Best. This point attained—and I freely admit that it is not easy: but what deep truth is?—a heavy burden will fall from the shoulders of thought. The problem with which we set out, that of understanding diversity in the self-confessing of the Supreme, will pass out of sight. The universe stands no longer chargeable with self-stultification in the multiplicity of its utterances. These utterances are the self-revelations of one reality. In their diversity they are as the single words of a sentence, meaningless till we read into them the one meaning which the sentence conveys : they are as the scenes of a drama, which tell us nothing when torn from their context in the action of the play : they are as the organs of the body, which live and die, flourish and perish, in the unitary life of the system to which they belong. The total life which is rich enough to require the tiger as well as the good Samaritan for its full manifestation requires also Nietzsche as well as St John, the Pragmatist as well as the Kantian, and Thomas à Kempis as well as James Mill.[1]

The philosophic consciousness has received but scanty treatment in the British schools. From Plato to Plotinus its rights were recognised by the Greeks ; but by Plotinus its contents were refined away until it came to mean nothing but a vision of pure truth abstracted from all contents whatsoever. Such vision was supposed to be the prerogative of God and godlike minds. This remains the standard account which the philosophic consciousness gives of itself. But it is evident that no intelligent consciousness can be associated with these conditions. To be aware of truth in the abstract, i.e. to be aware of truth only as true, is to be aware of nothing. Intelligent consciousness is comparative and self-discriminating, and to suppose a higher form of consciousness to which this does not apply is to speak of a consciousness which is not conscious. A being limited to any single experience, whether of truth or anything else, obviously would not

[1] See Royce, *The Spirit of Modern Philosophy*, p. 14 *seq.*

rise even to the level of knowing that anything was the matter with him ; unless, indeed, we commit the atrocious fallacy which has been the bane of psychology by supposing that it means to the experient himself precisely what it means to us, the students of the situation. In the same way the common talk about beings who enjoy an unclouded vision of the truth is disguised as to its absurdity by the reservation that the visionaries in question, in addition to their vision, have been let into the secret of our philosophy, and know what they are after as well as we do. On this supposition, no doubt they will understand the blessedness of their condition and be able to join us in our hymns. But it is evident that in this way we have altered the supposed character of their experience. The simplicity of their contemplation must be utterly broken up before they can know, as we know, how simple their contemplation is. Until we thus break up the conditions of a pure experience of the truth, the consideration of such experience cannot be proceeded with : which is another form of saying that the whole undertaking is absurd. The attempt to set up a form of consciousness occupied in the sole contemplation of the truth does not carry us *upwards* to God, or to man at his highest, but *downwards* to the worm and the amœba.

This may serve as a warning against that over-refinement in the conception of God which springs from timidity and would keep him sacrosanct in the holiness of exclusion, lest he be stained by contact with the finite. The disposition to refine this conception is natural and strong : hence the danger lest we refine it away altogether. In the whole realm of thought there is no partition so thin as that which divides God from Nothing,

and such is the eagerness of the soul in its flight God-
wards that it constantly breaks through and plunges into
the abyss on the other side.   Certain forms of Buddhism,
and Plotinus among the mystics of the West, have done
this.   But when once philosophy has reached the point
of conceiving God as the only True, or the truly Real,
the moment has come for thought to return upon itself.
Not a step further can be taken, and the warning to
turn back is instant and peremptory.   If thought
neglects the warning, and tries to refine once more its
last refinement ; if thought ever seeks to rest in its goal
and refuses to continue the endless cycle of its allotted
movement, it passes the boundary between God and
nothing, and enters the realm where all distinctions
are lost.   More precisely, we are helped by the negative
result that the correlate of a unitary whole is not the
single experience of the Truth as true.   The unity of
the whole must not be taken as the mere equation that
the whole $= 1$, nor is the self-consciousness of such a whole
— " I am one " — exhausted in the consciousness that
$1 = 1$.   To be conscious of self at all I must be conscious
of myself in many forms, including that of not-self,
and conscious of my own variability among them.   It
is either with this meaning or no meaning that we
attribute self-consciousness to the whole.   If the whole
knows itself at all, it knows itself as many-wise interpreted and determined ; and it is this principle that
enables us to regard "the Monism of Spinoza, the
Dualism of Martineau, the Pluralism of James," as the
self-confessions of a Single Being.

Thus even within the single field of the attribute of
Thought we find that same diversity of self-expression
in the universe which appears when we approach it as

clothed with the infinite and eternal attributes of a Work of Art.

Every system of thought, as we have seen, has its being in relation to the systems from which it differs. If we tear any one of them from its place in the living whole, and regard it without reference to the body of which it is a member, we find ourselves in the presence of a perfectly empty conception. Let the reader who doubts this try to explain to some novice the meaning of Monism without employing the conception of Pluralism as a means for making his explanation intelligible. He will find himself making bricks without straw. Systems of thought other than *this* are to philosophy what facts other than *this* are to perception, what organs other than *this* are to the living body: and just as *this* concrete fact fades into an empty abstraction when the relations are broken which bind it to others, so a particular philosophy sheds all its contents the instant you regard it as self-contained. A philosophic consciousness which contains nothing but its own system of thought contains nothing at all. The absolute idealist, for instance, whether he be a god or a man, is one who offers a solution of problems which have arisen from systems other than Absolute Idealism. Remove these other systems from the contents of the philosophic consciousness, and no problems are left for him to answer — his occupation has gone, and himself, as absolute idealist, has gone with his occupation. Let us suppose that in course of time the whole race of man comes round to his way of thinking, and let the victory of Absolute Idealism be so complete as not only to refute all other systems, but to erase them from the world of thought and cause them to be utterly forgotten. It would be a Pyrrhic victory. In forgetting the others, Absolute Idealism would forget itself. It would drag itself along with its opponents into the pit of oblivion, and none would be left either to rejoice over its fall or to celebrate its triumph. A world possessed of a single type of philosophy is a world which has ceased to philosophise; and as there is no knowledge which is not knowing, so there is no philosophy which is not philosophising.

Once again, the pragmatic consciousness contains a manifold of elements which, while essential to its being, need careful distinction from Pragmatism itself. The significance of Pragmatism is bound up with its attempted rejection of Idealism, and one may well ask what would become of Pragmatism if there were no Idealism to reject. The conflicts of the philosophic consciousness are determined not otherwise than the conflicts of desire in the moral life. As in the conflict between hunger and honesty I must ideally present myself as satisfied in both ways before I can freely determine myself in either, so I must reproduce Idealism and become ideally an idealist before I can decide that Idealism is not for me. This is what is meant by a thinker's rejection of Idealism, viz. that he rejects it as a mode of the philosophic consciousness *through which he has passed and into which he can return,* but in which he has decided not to remain. Short of having thus reproduced Idealism and made it his own, he has no competence to reject it, whether pragmatically or otherwise. You must pay your adversary the compliment of understanding him before you prove him in the wrong. And understanding him means that for the time being you take up his consciousness into your own. Ere you can escape from the Kantian position, or persuade me to follow your line of escape, you must show that you are really there yourself; *i.e.* you must reproduce in yourself (and so must I) the Kantian consciousness. Then, and then only, are you and I in a position to discuss the question of getting away from that condition into a better. It is an interesting question how far the pragmatic method can be applied to the process, through which every pragmatist must pass, of understanding the systems which are not pragmatic; how, for instance, the comprehension of Kant by James, as the logical *prius* to his rejection, conforms to the principles in the name of which he is rejected. But that is beyond the limits of our subject.

The points I have desired to make clear by these illustrations are that the very conception of philosophy involves a variety of progressive but divergent forms, for the same reason that morality involves a variety of conflicting desires not on the same level; that philosophy is an organic whole, the logical *prius* of all the philosophies; that its history is the evolution of a continuously developing life; that this life in each and all of its diverse manifestations is the expression of one and the same ultimate principle; that the full expression of this principle is the goal of the whole process, never attained under finite conditions; that no system is unnecessary which another system can use as the point of departure for a fuller expression.

To guard such conclusions against all possible misapprehension is here out of the question. But it will help to reveal their true nature if I simply set down what in my judgment would be the extreme form of misunderstanding them. If it were said, "Your one philosophy, then, is just the sum total of all the systems, each of which stands in relations of equality to all the rest, externally coexistent in one collection, so that none is afore and none after, but every one as good as his neighbour,"—I should answer that such a position is not only unwarranted by the course of the argument, but is negated by it at every point. To say that philosophy is the mere sum-total of the systems is as absurd as to say that a fully developed organism is the sum-total of the stages of its evolution; while to treat all the varieties of human thought as equal manifestations of the truth is to make the acorn equivalent to the oak.

We are so absorbed in explaining what we in our philosophies think about God, that we seldom pause to inquire what God may be thinking about our philosophies. When so much is being said of the unity of God and man, it is at least not irreverent to ask what part or interest, if any, the Divine Being is taking in these manifold human speculations as to his own nature. Various alternatives suggest themselves.

1. We may suppose, if we will, that these speculations lie entirely outside the sphere of Divine knowledge. The Infinite, we may say, knows the secret of its relation to the finite, but we have no reason to suppose that this knowledge coincides, either in whole or in part, with the account of the matter given by any human intelligence; perhaps God may choose to ignore such accounts altogether. Knowing himself as he really is, God may know nothing of himself as proved by

Descartes, presupposed by Hegel, or postulated by James.

2. We may suppose that there is some one among these accounts with which the Divine self-consciousness is somehow identified. God may know himself as the postulate of James or as the Moral Ordainer of Martineau, and know nothing of himself as the *Ens entium* of the scholastics, or the One Substance of Spinoza. As a person recognises himself in his own photograph, so the Divine Being may recognise himself in *this* philosophy and reject all the others as false. I imagine that this is the way in which most persons who think about the matter at all tend to think about it at first. And with this a good, honest, mechanical theology may rest content. That a God who is one among the objects of the universe should identify himself with one among the many theories of his own nature seems consistent enough.

The doctrine of Divine Immanence, in the form which represents God as the Life of Thought, " the Master-light of all our seeing," is now so common, and endorsed by thinkers otherwise so sharply opposed, that we may take it as the clue to the final issue, which is now before us. Like much of the language of which religion makes frequent use, the description of God as the Life of Thought is apt to be adopted by persons who have the vaguest notions of what it means or involves. If it means anything at all, it cancels both the alternatives we have just discussed. For, as we have seen, human thinking, throughout the ages, is not a chaos of fragmentary and unrelated efforts, but a continuous organic process, each moment of which has a necessary function in the constitution of the whole.

It is only, therefore, as the Life of the whole process that the conception of God as the Life of Thought has any meaning whatsoever. To reserve this view of God for the moment when our favourite philosopher is thinking, and to refuse to apply it when the torch passes to his critics, is as much as to say that divine light is limited to that kind of thought which happens to commend itself to us. This, of course, renders the whole doctrine perfectly futile. We must either abandon the conception altogether, or be prepared to say that God is not less able than man to regard himself as either postulated, presupposed, proved or denied, and that, as the Life of the total organism of thought, he could not regard himself under any one of these forms did he not also regard himself under the rest, and no doubt in infinite other ways which human thought does not touch.

The final step is taken when the doctrine of Divine Immanence is extended to that very doctrine itself—when, that is, God is regarded as the life of that thought which thinks Him as immanent in all thinking. Here the philosophy which begins at home will end where it began. The doctrine of Divine Immanence must submit to its own yoke. Let the reader who believes that the life of reason is the manifestation of a divine principle be on his guard against reserving one moment in the life of reason in which the divine principle has no part, the moment, namely, when reason declares for the Immanence of God. The reservation of such a moment as outside the circle to which Divine Immanence applies is tantamount to saying that, whereas God is the life of all other thought, He is *not* the life of that thought which is turned upon himself. An admission more fatal to the conception of an immanent God it would be impossible to frame. If this, the last deliverance of the reflecting process, has to stand on one side as a human product; if, that is, while the science which is turned upon Nature and man is a reproduction of Divine thought, the science which has God himself for its object is an affair for which finite minds alone are responsible, we can only say that the doctrine of the Indwelling God is cleft and shattered into an incoherent and unthinkable proposition. This point reached, the further consequences must be faced. Having admitted that God is the life of thought concerning himself, we cannot limit this truth to our own mode of thinking. If God is in the thought that is about himself, He is in that thought *in all its organic diversity* as the living Principle progressively revealed in its growth. We have seen that to tie self-consciousness to any single form is to annihilate it altogether. If, therefore, any meaning whatsoever attaches to the idea of a self-conscious Absolute, there is involved in the Absolute a plurality of self-expressions so diverse as to comprise the extreme forms of difference, even as they are comprised in self-consciousness such as our own. Not only, therefore, is a plurality of self-expressions *compatible* with the unity and self-consciousness of the whole, but it is an inherent logical *necessity* if we are to speak of God in any of the terms that are applicable to Spirit.

VI.—INSULATED PHILOSOPHY

THOSE who dream of Happy Isles have been guided by a true instinct in their choice of locality ; and the more one considers the particular forms of bliss these lonely places are supposed to offer, the more clearly he sees how impossible it would be to cultivate such happiness on the mainland. The criticism of the fault-finders would be too severe ; the jealousy of the unhappy too aggressive ; the pressure of the past too insistent ; the interruptions of the present too irritating and incongruous. How hard a thing it is to control the present with all the forces of the past marching down upon us by the open roads of history ! How easy a thing to construct the future if only we could place an ocean of empty time between to-morrow and to-day !

Abstractions are indigenous to Islands, thriving best on those which are not, and never can be, inhabited by Man. The power of abstractions increases with the insularity of their position, and diminishes with every approach to the context of the mainland. On the mainland abstractions must be content to *serve* ; but on Islands, and especially on Desolate Islands, they are the monarchs of all they survey. Whosoever, therefore, would set up the Kingdom of the Abstract, let him choose for himself an Island—so remote that no ship can visit its shores, so small, if possible, that it cannot

be divided against itself.   Abstract Thought, like Pure
Happiness, hungers for isolation and, oddly enough,
breathes freely only in an atmosphere of Strict Limits.
Remoteness and minuteness are the foundations of its
throne.   No marauders from the realms of Old Habit
must be suffered to enter; no room must be given for
self-criticism in the Kingdom where Abstract Thought
is King.

" The Thought of mankind," said the Plain Man, " is
still in the militant stage of its evolution.   It lives, as
it were, in the hurly-burly of vast continents, and joins
in the strife of overcrowded populations.   The various
systems of Philosophy are now, as they have been all
along, engaged in a wasteful war of mutual destruction.
Their best energies, their finest genius, are required, if
one may so speak, for the business of knocking each
other on the head.   We hear a little from time to time
of the application of Philosophy to life; but when we
open the works of our great writers and search for these
applications, how meagre, how disappointing is the
result!   Life is the goal they all have in view, or
profess to have; but seldom indeed does any one of
them succeed in getting there.   Their business is to
accomplish the overthrow of rivals.   ' Criticism ' is the
name of it; and under that name we may behold a
desperate struggle for existence, a veritable Arma-
geddon, if you will, of contending intellectual hosts,
charging down upon one another with incredible fury,
hacking, thrusting, and skull-splitting, until the poor
Plain Man who is looking on and waiting for Truth to
arise from the confusion, flees in terror from the scene,
bolts the door behind him, and puts up a trembling

prayer to the gods that the tide of battle may not flow
his way, that his ox, his ass, and his little ones may be
spared, and that no fiery dart may light upon his cottage-
thatch.   Thus Philosophy remains at the militant stage ;
an outlet for the love of fighting or the spirit of con-
tentiousness ; a thing of armaments, of fortified posts,
of tactics, manœuvres, field-days, excursions, alarums,
the beating of sonorous drums and the detonation of
mighty cannon ; and a real battle now and then.   Of
how many systems of thought, ancient or modern, may
we not say that they live by the mistakes of their
opponents, and have little reason to show for their
existence save the need of proving some other system
to be wrong ?   Hence the application to life, which we
plain men have been promised since who knows when,
never comes off, or at least is ever postponed to some
indefinite future when Thought shall have passed its
militant period and entered on that of peaceful development from within.   And just as nations engaged in
fighting for existence are bound to linger on the confines of barbarism, their development being held in
abeyance, while the Arts of Life fail to emerge, or
having emerged, suffer arrest, so these systems of
Thought, kept back from their proper business by the
brute necessity of confuting each other, have never yet
had a chance of showing what they could do for the
world under the kindly fosterings of Peace."

In the presence of these oft-repeated accusations,
is it not strange (we are now summarising for the
Plain Man) that no one has yet devised a plan for
testing philosophies under conditions of artificial tran-
quillity ?   Our botanists, our zoologists, do this every
day with the wild creatures of the natural world which

it is their business to study and evaluate for the use
of man.   They isolate their investigations so as to
secure them from disturbance.   Might not the same
thing be done, with even more beneficent results, with
the various systems of thought which, if the Plain Man
is right, are at present trying to choke each other like
beasts in the jungle, or wild trees in the forests of the
Amazon?   What is to hinder, for example, some
enlightened government or private society, for the
matter of that, from purchasing or leasing a sufficient
number of Desolate Islands for the purpose of segregating selected adherents of various schools, and of
setting up on each an Experimental Farm for the
practical cultivation of the particular system assigned
to its solitudes?   Idealism, Realism (both New and
Old), Pragmatism, Hedonism, Rigorism, Determinism,
Free Will would thus be separated from each other
by vast expanses of sundering sea, freed from the
wasting claims of self-defence and aggression, and
exposed no more to the interminable jolt and jar of
their mutual differences.   Each system would get at
last the chance of showing the world what it can do.

In the Isles of Hedonism, for example, it would be
taken for granted that Happiness is the end of life,
and all the energy of mind and heart hitherto expended
on proving that Happiness ought to be promoted, and
on confuting the people who proposed some other end
—a large proportion, truly, of the total energy at the
command of the School—would now be devoted to
the actual work of promoting Happiness.   Thus the
Application to Life, so long delayed by what one may
term the foreign wars and international complications
of Hedonism, would receive an unrestricted oppor-

tunity; and persons like Mr Spencer, who prophesy what the world will be like when all men are Hedonists, would be able to check their predictions by experiments on a world *in petto*, a world artificially provided in advance with all the conditions that will obtain when mankind in general hold the opinions which Mr Spencer, or any other thinker, desires them to hold. Some allowance, no doubt, would have to be made for the knowledge, which we must imagine the inhabitants of each Island to possess, that the thing was only an experiment; but a scale for discounting this rather troublesome circumstance might be devised; and when that was done Philosophy would be in the position long enjoyed by all the other sciences, and laboratory work would begin.

And not only would a need long felt by philosophers be satisfied, but the public would derive even a greater benefit. For on each of the Farms or Laboratories a careful register of results might be kept; trained experts would watch and record the civilising influences of the various systems; and after a sufficient time had elapsed these records would be tabulated and compared. Thus the public, for the first time in the world's history, would be able to judge Philosophy by its fruits and justly estimate the relative merits of the different Schools.

In picturing the result of such an experiment, all kinds of possibilities suggest themselves, and the reader may instruct himself by imagining them of this kind or of that. For example, he may suppose himself reading a Report from the Isles of Hedonism, and learning therefrom that the devotees of Happiness were developing a profound melancholy and confessing themselves aweary of the world. Pursuing his inquiries he might read, in

the proper sections, how the Pragmatists were reverting
to savagery; how the Idealists were going mad; how
the Determinists were losing the use of their limbs;
how the Free-willers were engaged in mutual exter-
mination; how the Realists had forgotten their language
and were hooting at one another like owls. From such
Reports he would conclude that the philosophies under
review were severally productive of race-failure, and
neither he, nor anyone else, would trouble about them
any more. Or he may please himself by imagining
results of an opposite kind and then go on to construct a basis for further experiments. Reassured, for
example, by a good Report from the Isles of Free
Will, he might suggest the plan of introducing a few
Determinists into those Islands; so that by the cross-
breeding of minds and careful study of the hybrids thus
produced, and by comparison of these with the original
types, he would see at once the relative merits of the
pure strain and the cross. And so on in Permutations
and Combinations without end.

It is probable that the actual result of insulating
philosophies in the manner here suggested by the
Plain Man would be startling. It is a result I should
never have thought possible had it not been confirmed
by the experience of Devil's Island, and I shall trust to
the narrative, presently to be delivered, to make the
prediction good.

I believe, in short, that the result of segregating any
school of thinkers would be the conversion of that
school to the tenets of some opposing party. The
Hedonists would all become Stoics and the Stoics
Hedonists; the Free-willers would embrace Determinism
and the Determinists Free Will; the Pragmatists would

learn to swear by Hegel and the Hegelians by William
James; the Idealists would go back to Common Sense,
and Common Sense would go forward to Idealism.
There would be a general interchange of parts and
agreement in nothing save in the common determination
of all parties to get back to the mainland at the earliest
possible moment.

It may be said in passing, for the point is important,
that if the same experiment were tried with the sects
of Christendom a like result would almost certainly
follow. Let some Pontiff conceive it his duty to extirpate a particular sect, say the Muggletonians, or
what you will. How may he best succeed in effecting
his design? Not by issuing a Bull against Muggle-
tonianism; not by persecuting its adherents with the
stake or the sword. That, as we know, will merely
serve to give the movement a new lease of life. Let
him rather transport the offending Muggletonians to
one of our Islands and provide them with all the
necessaries of life and with ample funds to build
Muggletonian churches and endow Muggletonian
schools; let him arrange that no voice shall be raised
in protest against Muggletonian practice or in criticism
of Muggletonian theory; let him give them twenty
years of undisturbed enjoyment of each other's company,
and I warrant him that if he visits the Island at the
end of that time he will find not a single Muggletonian
in the place.

One cannot pretend, however, that all philosophical
difficulties would be brought to an immediate conclusion
by the adoption of the experimental method as suggested
by the Plain Man. It is probable, for example, that
interested parties on the mainland would have their

favourite Islands ; and we may be very sure that if an
unfavourable Report were issued concerning any Island
in which distinguished philosophers had a vested interest,
that Report would be severely criticised and its standard
of judgment condemned.   In short, this question of
the standard for judging results would be very troublesome—at least for a time.   Even in the extreme case
of all the Islands turning out to be utter failures, we
should still have to deal with the pessimist verdict,
namely, that this was the very best thing that could
happen in a world where nothing is worth while, and
that the alleged failure was therefore a triumphant
success.   Perhaps the matter would be ultimately
settled by some one adducing the doctrine of what I
may call the Absolute Insularity—the doctrine, I mean,
which teaches that the whole Universe is an Island of
Being fixed in an immeasurable ocean of Nothing ; that
whatever conserves Insularity must therefore be considered good ; so that in the last resort any Island whose
inhabitants had preserved their abode from contamination
by the influences of the mainland might be considered
as having satisfied the ultimate test.   But of course the
public would pay little heed to all that.   They would
judge by plainer tests and give the palm to that system
which produced the ruddiest cheeks, the brightest eyes,
the broadest foreheads, and the strongest arms.

It was my fortune to be cast away for many years
on an Island where a state of things existed which
provided most of the conditions required for such an
experiment.   I say most of them, for the Island was
too large and too near the mainland to provide them all.
Moreover, the inhabitants were not perfectly unani-
mous ; there was only enough unanimity to provide a

basis for induction. It was called Devil's Island, after the individual who discovered it and planted the first colony.

With the other Isles of which I am to speak I have no direct acquaintance; but I learnt a great deal about them from one of the Omniscients whom I encountered on Devil's Island—all of which I shall recount in its proper place. I have, indeed, seen the Isles of Omniscience many times, but only from a distance, with leagues of cold salt water between them and me; and all I can tell of their appearance is that, when viewed from afar, they seemed to be covered with eternal ice. A dense fog usually blotted the horizon in the direction where they lay; but now and then a hurricane blast blew out of the North, and, as the mists parted, those Islands would appear, hanging in air at the confines of vision as though they were aloof from the world.

VII.—DEVIL'S ISLAND AND THE ISLES OF OMNISCIENCE

AN ADVENTURE AMONG ABSTRACTIONS

"I asked Friday who made the sea, the ground we walked on, the hills and the woods. He told me 'it was one Benamuckee who lived beyond all'; he could describe nothing of this great person but that he was very old, 'much older,' he said, 'than the sea or the land, the moon or the stars.' I asked him then, if this old person had made all things, why did not all things worship him? He looked very grave, and with a perfect look of innocence, said, 'All things said "O" to him.' I asked him if the people who die in his country went away anywhere. He said 'Yes, they all went to Benamuckee.'

"He told me one day that . . . . Benamuckee could not hear till they went up into a great mountain to speak to him . . . . and that their old men went to say 'O' (so he called saying prayers) and then came back and told them what Benamuckee said. By this I perceived that there is priestcraft among the most blinded and ignorant pagans in the world. . . .

"I endeavoured to clear up this fraud to my man Friday and told him that the pretence of their old men going up into the mountains to say 'O' to Benamuckee was a cheat."—*Robinson Crusoe.*

I

DEVIL'S ISLAND is at no great distance, on the map, from the Isles of Omniscience. The Omniscients can see it in clear weather bearing a point or two north of west, and if the wind blows fair a well-found boat will make the passage in a few hours.

There is a legend that the ancestors of the Omniscients were a colony from Devil's Island, driven thence by an outburst of religious persecution, and though documentary evidence is lacking the story is impressively

confirmed by linguistic affinities. Not only have they
many words in common, but the syntax of both languages betrays an identical structure. The language
of Devil's Island has developed from the first on the
principle that affirmation is implied negation, the
peculiarity being that instead of implying the negation
as other races do, the Devil's Islanders make it explicit
in their common mode of speech. Instead of saying
"that thing is a cooking-pot" they say "that thing is
not what it would be if it weren't a cooking-pot." Or
if they want to indicate everything else in the world
except the pot they say simply "the not-pot." Thus
the universe is the not-pot, just as the pot is the not-
universe. The only difference between the two
languages is that the principle of negation has been
more thoroughly carried out in the language of the
Omniscients, whose practice when at home, as we shall
see, is to say nothing-at-all, because they have nothing-
to-say.

The principle which determines the grammar of the
Devil's Islanders pervades their whole life, and may
be illustrated either from their religion and their science,
or from their performance of the humblest task.

They are, of course, idolaters, but I was greatly
puzzled at first by my failure to discover any of their
idols. I observed that they were very devout after
their manner, that religious processions were constantly
taking place, and that the air was always laden with
the smell of incense or of sacrifice. But where they
kept their gods I could not, for a long time, discover.

I had noticed, however, that the ground of the island,
when struck by a stick or the heel of one's boot, frequently sounded hollow. This I attributed at first to

the burrowings of some strange animal, perhaps a
gigantic land crab.   More than once I felt the ground
giving way beneath me, and a horror of falling into the
claws of the crab would cause me to clutch for support
at any object on which I could lay my hand.   I came
to the conclusion that walking was thoroughly unsafe,
and I fell into a habit of looking around me for something to catch hold of in case I should feel the surface
sinking beneath my feet.   It was this habit which led
me to discover the idols.

One evening, when the light was failing, I came to a
dangerous piece of ground with a very thin surface,
honeycombed, as I could plainly see, by innumerable
burrowings.   I stood still and resolved to advance no
further until I was sure of my wonted supports.   There
was one of them just ahead of me, and it looked
like a statue beautifully framed in the foliage of a tree.
I now advanced, confident that in case of accident I
could easily save myself by throwing an arm round
the neck of this figure.   I had not gone many paces
when my foot began to sink, and perceiving that in
another instant I should be entombed, I flung an arm
round the statue, only to find, to my horror, that I had
clasped the empty air.   Instantly I was at the bottom
of a hole ten feet deep.   I clambered out as best I
could, coughed the dust out of my lungs, and, retreat-
ing by the way I had come, sat down to think.

While thus engaged I heard a great noise and saw
a crowd of angry people rushing towards me.   One of
them, who seemed the most infuriated of all, and was,
I suppose, a priest, accosting me with great trucu-
lence, and speaking his native tongue, said: " Are you
aware, sir, what you have done?"   " I know nothing,"

said I, "save that I am much shaken." "And you deserve to be," said the priest, "for you have broken the head of our highest god and committed a hideous sacrilege by falling into his belly." "But," said I, "the fellow had nothing inside him." "The contents," answered the priest, "are presupposed, and your failure to see this increases your crime tenfold." And then he proceeded to argue with me at great length; that, as I afterwards learnt, being the usual form of punishment on Devil's Island for all who have done wrong. On my side I contended that the thing into which I had fallen, seeing that it was hollow, couldn't be divine. He answered by proving, from the principle of negation, that the Hollow was the only Real. Beaten from this position I took refuge behind my former argument— the absence of content. To this he replied that I was quarrelling about terms; that the Absent was only another name for the Hollow, that if I would recur to what he had just said I should have to admit that the essence of an idol's belly was its Hollowness. Thus he continued to dress me down until the full penalty had been inflicted, leaving me in the end a beaten man.

From this the reader will understand the secret of the idols. They make the images of their gods in Devil's Island, not by the process of filling them in, but by the contrary process of hollowing them out. That is to say, having cut the form out of the matter, they throw the form away and worship the hole that is left by its removal. Sometimes the statue would be made by clothing, or encasing, the hollow form of the artist's ideal, after the manner of the Irishman's recipe for making a cannon. Sometimes a solid block of matter would be taken, and the artist would either cut the figure out of this in a single piece and, of course, throw it away; or he would gradually scrape the substance by an instrument designed for the purpose till the requisite form and degree of hollowness was attained.

This instrument, by the way, was a wonderful tool, and it was said that the mightiest brains of Devil's Island had spent three thousand years in bringing it to perfection. It was guaranteed to tear the inside out of anything whether living or dead, and, being made of all conceivable sizes and powers, was equally effectual for driving a shaft through mountains of granite or taking the core out of a grain of dust. When at work it made an ear-splitting, heart-rending noise. Its insistency was like that of the electric riveters as you may hear them at work on the steel frame of a New York sky-scraper. At the same time there was something in the sound which reminded one of an extremely harsh human voice saying "no" at the rate of twenty "noes" per second. To those unaccustomed to the sound it was an amazing experience to listen at night to these mighty engines roaring and screaming an infinity of "noes," like things in conversation with each other, as they tunnelled the everlasting hills and tore their way through the foundations of the Great Deep. More appalling still, I often thought, was the sound of the more delicate instruments, such as they used for the hollowing of small objects or the evisceration of minute living things. These when held close to the ear pelted out an endless stream of little "noes" like sparks from radium. The sound thus produced was comparable to nothing else I have ever heard. It was malign beyond expression, and when heard for the first time would often paralyse the brain and stop the beating of the heart.

Thus in course of time the whole island came to be hollowed out in a manner which not only rendered walking extremely dangerous but demanded excessive care in respect of everything one touched. The objects which stood above the ground had been treated in the same manner as those which lay beneath, so that you could never push aside the branch of a tree, or remove a pebble from the beach, without the risk of disturbing some artistic enclosure of empty space and thereby displacing the pediment of a temple or breaking the nose of a god. Though, as I have said, a casual observer would have thought the island utterly destitute of religious symbols, the truth was that it swarmed with idols, temples, and altars, both above ground and below. The whole place indeed was like one of those children's picture puzzles, where faces are indicated not by drawing them but by leaving them undrawn. Any arrangement of objects one came across was almost certain to be, as it were, a hollow mound which, if you could have filled it with molten metal or plaster of Paris, would have yielded you an arm, a leg, an elephant's proboscis, a fish's tail, or what not.

The distinction between virtue and vice on Devil's Island turned upon a man's power of walking among the hollows without falling in, and of moving among the stencils without disarranging their encasing forms. It was a very difficult matter to avoid these catastrophes, even for those born in the island ; and saintship being reckoned by the fewness of a man's falls, it came to pass that as the island grew hollower and hollower the number of saints diminished and saintship became

almost entirely a thing of the past. Great as was the
number of persons engaged in scraping the hollows,
there was an even greater number whose business was
to restore the shells which careless fingers had marred,
or mend the hollows after sinners had fallen in, as I did
when I fell into the belly of the god. All this, of course,
involved an immense expenditure of labour, which the
few Dissenters in the island hotly condemned as useless
waste. But anyone who ventured these opinions was
at once punished by argument, the logic of Devil's
Island being equal to any emergency, and able to make
the punishment most severe. It was conclusively
proved against the dissident that by his objection to
falling in he had already taken the first step towards
his fall. He was challenged to furnish an answer to
the question, *Why should I not fall in?* and, being unable
to do so, he was required to confess in public that the
hollows were their own justification. Such was the
mental constitution of the islanders that any person
condemned to this punishment winced under it as under
a lash.

Everything in Devil's Island was managed in the
same manner. Suppose, for example, that you wanted
to cut a chip. To accomplish this feat you must first
attend to the principle that a thing is always defined by
its opposite, for the islanders were fanatically devoted
to the rule *omnis determinatio est negatio.* Now it is
obvious that the opposite, or " true other," to the chip,
is the entire universe from which the chip has been
withdrawn. Thus, in Devil's Island practice (as well
as in its terminology) you were not allowed to cut the
chip off the universe; what you had to do was to cut
the universe off the chip; then by contemplating the

negated universe so cut off you got the corresponding
affirmation, which was of course the chip. Contrariwise,
if you wanted the universe minus the chip, you first cut
off the chip, and then by contemplating its negative you
got the universe.[1]

II

During my sojourn on Devil's Island I became a
fanatical convert to the cult of Hollowness. The
change through which I passed ought perhaps to be
called inversion rather than conversion; for I learnt to
see everything from the end opposite to that which I
had previously occupied. The principle on which my
thought came to rest was that the nature of Reality is
revealed by the manner in which it withdraws itself
from observation. That which I had hitherto regarded
as Appearance I now learned to interpret as Withdrawal. Thus when a light was turned on I would say
to myself, "The darkness, which is the true reality, has
withdrawn. The light is just a hole in the darkness, and
the inner surface of the hole is the form Reality has now
assumed." Again, when I was looking at the sunset I
would say, "These colours are the modes under which I
perceive what is *not* happening. What is happening is
undulation of the ether at various velocities, and Reality
has withdrawn these waves from observation by pushing
them out of sight behind yonder coloured veils." The
ether, in its turn, resolved, or (as we always said in Devil's
Island) "withdrew," itself behind a veil of electrons, and
these, when explained, bolted (or withdrew) into ions
or what not.

[1] *Cf.* the article on "A Pluralistic Mystic" by William James in *The
Hibbert Journal,* July 1910.

And here, perhaps, I may interpose that on Devil's Island we never spoke of explanation. The term by which we indicated that process was "dismissal." Instead of saying, for example, that a philosopher had explained virtue as the pursuit of happiness, we said he had *dismissed* virtue *into* the pursuit of happiness. Scientific men in like manner dismissed matter into vortices of atoms, dismissed atoms into electrons, electrons into ions, and so on *ad infinitum*. We congratulated one another on the advent of the age of enlightenment, in which, as we said, everything has either been triumphantly dismissed or has received notice to quit. A candidate for honours in philosophy would be asked, "What do you mean by the dismissal of a mystery?" and was expected to show in his answer that the mystery could be made to disappear only by dismissing the thing that was mysterious. Thus the colours on a bird's egg ceased to be mysterious as soon as you were in a position to say these colours are, for thought, not colours but protective devices; and the problem then awaiting science was, of course, to dismiss protective devices into examples of universal mechanism or something else. Emerson's saying, "Things are in the saddle and ride mankind," would have seemed nonsense to any intelligent Devil's Islander. He would have said, "Things have taken the bit in their teeth and are bolting." The progress of science was measured by the number of things that had thus bolted. I well remember an article in *The Times* of Devil's Island for 31st December of a certain year in which it was proudly claimed that during the past twelve months a large number of fresh holes had appeared in the substance of Reality owing to the splendid labours of

Professor So-and-So; and no higher honour was ever paid to a Devil's Islander than that contained in the simple epitaph which a few years later was engraved on this man's tomb:

" He drove his ploughshare into the Bowels of Being ;
   He tunnelled the Universe ;
   He found a Fact, and left a Vacuum."
Si monumentum quaeris, circumspice.

One day when I was thinking about myself and trying to pierce the mystery of my own consciousness, I suddenly made the discovery that my mind was just a hollow shell or mould, the walls of which were composed of certain mechanical or chemical changes proceeding in the blood or brain. I saw, just as Hume did when he tried to contemplate his own identity, that nothing was there. But, unlike Hume, I was greatly interested in the way in which Reality had withdrawn itself so as to leave behind a nothingness of that particular shape I called "my mind." I could not overlook the fact that though the mould was hollow, its hollowness had a perfectly determinate character. And I found myself continually feeling the interior surfaces, passing my hand, as it were, over the integument of my nothingness and marvelling at the way Reality had scooped itself out, or thrust itself back, so as to leave behind that particular configuration of nothing.

In fine, the whole universe of mind and matter became to me an infinite stencil. Every tree growing by the roadside, every little pig grunting in his stye, was interpreted as so much Reality put out of sight in such and such a way. The starry heavens presented themselves as a perforated darkness. Between the shining stars I saw a solid wall of good substantial not-being, which had, so to speak, negated itself, or perhaps run away, wherever a star appeared. If the reader will take an engraving and consider the artist's work as constituted not by the black lines but by the white interspaces left untouched, he will have a fair idea of my habitual Weltanschauung during the Devil's Island period of my history.

We were all Kantians on Devil's Island, or at least we thought we were—though I doubt if Kant would have acknowledged any one of us. We held that Kant's greatest achievement was the doctrine of the thing-in-itself. That the thing-in-itself was no possible object of knowledge seemed to us the foundation of philosophy. We contended that so long as things remained in themselves no knowledge of them could arise, the lodgings, so to speak, being occupied; but when they came *out of* themselves, there was an opportunity for knowledge to step in and fill the vacant room. We held that Kant had lost a golden opportunity by failing to set up the thing-out-of-itself as the proper antithesis to the thing-in-itself, and we proceeded to supply the defect. The thing-out-of-itself was our equivalent for the Kantian "phenomenon," and with that substitution we adopted the principle that only phenomena can be known. But here a distinction became necessary, by making which we departed from the letter, though not perhaps from the spirit, of Kant's philosophy. A thing "appears," we said, precisely through this act of coming out of itself, and it is this appearance that we know. But what is the "appearance"? Plainly it is not the thing standing outside-of-itself, for such a thing, properly considered, is only another thing-in-itself; the difference between it and the original out of which it had come being little else than the difference between a dog in his kennel and the same dog taken out for a walk, or, better, between a glove in its usual condition and the same glove turned inside out. The mere shifting of position from in to out, therefore, makes no difference to the possibility of knowledge; for " in " and " out " are relative terms, what is " in " in the first case being " out " in the second, and *vice versa*. What, then, once more, is the appearance that we know? Plainly it can be nothing other than the blank or hole left in the inner being of a thing when that thing goes out-of-itself into something else. Knowledge, we said (for we were fond of metaphors on Devil's Island), must always be content with the leavings, and the leavings are the empty spaces in being occupied by things prior to their dismissal by science into the circumambient Beyond. By another figure, which formed the starting-point of a great movement in the history of our thought, Knowledge was described as the Incoming Tenant, to provide for whose arrival everything in the universe was under Notice to Quit. The act of Quitting, we said, took place in Time, but the Notice to Quit was eternal.

Thus, we argued, the understanding is always one stage *behind* the fact. We understand, that is, not what a thing *is*, but what it *was* before thought dismissed it to find a resting-place elsewhere. To illustrate this process we referred to the manner in which our scientific men constructed their knowledge of bygone monsters, such as the Dinosaur or the Megatherium. All the scientific man has to go by is the mould of the creature's body or the print of his hoof left in the mud before he departed and was no more. And from such evidence, which, of course, is the evidence of holes, the scientific man will body forth the entire structure of the monster and describe his general walk and conversation in the primeval slime. Now, all our knowledge, we said, is constructed in that manner. Paradoxical as it may seem, a thing must pass out of sight in order that it may be seen, must go on a journey in order that it may be found at home, must be dismissed—explained, as other folk would say—in order that it may put in an appearance. " He who would capture the fortress of reality," said one of the more picturesque of our thinkers, " must lay his plans with care. He must wait patiently for the moment when the active principle which rules the citadel is not at home. The thing must first come out itself. Let the besieger therefore "—here I am afraid there was some mixture of metaphors — " test the walls with his battering-rams, and withhold his main attack, until the stones have responded with a hollow sound. Then let him open his batteries and storm in. The fortress will be his."

In short, the method of our philosophy on Devil's Island was the method of evacuation, and the process of thought consisted simply in sucking the meaning out of things, the things thus treated being then set up, like squeezed oranges, as the only real. The principle was not unlike that of the Vacuum Cleaner, carried, as one might say, to its logical conclusion. To every object of knowledge thought applied its mouthpiece, and sucked away until not only the superincumbent dust, but the stuff of the fabric, the floor on which it rested, nay, even the walls of the containing house, had disappeared into the belly of the monster that was hissing and pounding in the street below. The last act of Thought was to initiate the process of mystical absorption, for it must be noted that in spite of the prevailing idolatry, or perhaps in consequence of it, mysticism occasionally broke out on Devil's Island. This last act can only be described by saying that it consisted in turning the mouthpiece of the Cleaner on yourself and awaiting results in a state of wise passiveness, until your consciousness became absorbed in the eternal sputter of the machine. The end was, of course, that you yourself followed your carpets and furniture into the belly of your system. Arrived there, you mingled with the universal dust and lost all sense of your separateness from it, while from a spy-hole provided for the purpose you looked forth at intervals on the vacant space once occupied by yourself, and reflected, " Such was I."

Of all the islanders I have known there is none to compare with the Devil's in the matter of logical thoroughness. I could never detect any flaw in their logic, and although their philosophy was a philosophy of gaps, I could never find any gap in their philosophy. But I could not help observing that in all other respects they were a miserable set. They had big heads and stunted bodies; they were polite in manners, and eloquent in discourse, but abominably sneakish in behaviour. For solemnity of carriage I have never met their equals ; but there was not a man on the island whom I would have trusted with the loan of a pin. According to their system of morality nothing was right unless you could prove, by the principle of negation, that it was not-wrong ; the consequence was that sneakishness, which stood the test better almost than any other quality, was reckoned one of the highest virtues. The chief controversy among their moralists was as to the precise significance of the word "not," on which many great volumes were written; the majority holding that the word meant nothing, the minority that no other word meant anything; and this latter opinion led at one time to a very dangerous outbreak of honourable behaviour which the Sneaks, then in power, promptly suppressed.

Again, if you had been in one of their churches you would have thought them very religious; nowhere else in the world was to be found such eloquence, such pious attitudes, such grave demeanour. But it meant nothing, and what was more, they knew it; nay, their philosophers openly taught that only as meaning nothing was religion to be professed, practised, or desired. There was no end of grandiose talk about "ideals"; but the reality of an ideal, they would tell you, was precisely its hollowness. Did you ask, "What, then, was the good of it?" they would answer, "Why, to talk about, of course."

But I must return to the metaphysics of the island. In some respects we Devil's Islanders had advanced beyond Kant. Most of us had adopted the principle of Evolution, and our interpretation of this doctrine was, I think, consistent on the whole with the turn we had given to the Kantian philosophy. That things acquire their characteristics through the modifying influences of the environment was a commonplace of our thought, but we avoided the one-sided form in which this doctrine is held in other parts of the world. It was quite true, we admitted, that a midge, for example, might be fully explained, or as we said dis-

missed, by reference to the totality of its environing
conditions, this environment being co-extensive with
all the remaining universe after the subtraction of the
midge. Understand the environment and you have
all that is necessary to get a complete account of the
origin, structure, and behaviour of the midge. But
this, in which we followed the common doctrine, was
only one side of the matter. The distinctive feature of
our thought lay in the doctrine that what was true
of the midge was true also of the totalised remainder of
the universe from which the midge had been subtracted.
Here on one side was the midge—the organism ; there
on the other side was the remainder of the universe—
the environment. Look at the matter fairly and you
would see that organism and the environment, like in
and out, were merely relative terms; and while no
doubt the rest of the universe was environment to the
midge, yet from the other point of view the midge had
an equal claim to be considered the environment of the
rest of the universe. The midge and the rest of the
universe made up between them the totality of everything there was ; the rest of the universe, therefore, could
have no other environment than that which the midge
provided. Now, what was sauce for the goose was
sauce for the gander. There could be no doubt that
while on the one hand the midge owed its character
to the reaction upon it of the rest of the universe, on
the other hand the rest of the universe owed *its*
character to the reaction upon it of the midge. In
this way we sought to correct the one-sidedness of
the evolutionary hypothesis as propounded on the
mainland.

It must be confessed, however, that we developed

a difference of opinion when we applied this wider
hypothesis to the problem of the creation of the world.
Some held that the original datum of creative activity
was a midge or some such creature and that the
process of creation consisted in fitting on the rest of
the universe to the midge; others held the inverse
doctrine, namely, that the datum or given material
was all the rest of the universe and that creation
consequently was the process of fitting in the midge
to the totality of everything else. The adherents of
the first position were appropriately called the Fitters-
on; of the second, the Fitters-in. There was a great
deal of confusion, and I must admit that the thinking
of Devil's Island on this matter had not the clearness
characteristic of its general procedure. The first school
contended very justly that the process of fitting-on
could not proceed unless the midge, to which the
universe was adapting itself, retained a fixed form
throughout, any more than a tailor could make a suit
of clothes to fit a man with a fluctuating body. The
fitters-in, on the other hand, demanded a like fixity
in the universe for which the midge was being contrived; but both parties being evolutionists, no satisfactory reason could be given by either why midge
or universe should retain its form for two consecutive
seconds. Finally, a few metaphors were invented, one
of an evolving tailor who made evolving clothes to
fit evolving bodies; another, of a criminal assiduously
fitting himself to the punishment which at the same
time was being fitted to him; and, as you could always
settle a dispute on Devil's Island by a brilliant metaphor
and by the pooling of issues, the main difficulties were
ultimately got rid of. The distinction between organism

and environment was abandoned, and a doctrine of mutual inclusion which substituted " both " for " either " made everything grammatically clear.

III

And now the question may be asked how it came to pass that I ever found myself in this outlandish place? What brought me hither, what was the manner of my arrival, what reasons induced me to stay? Frankly, I know not. Often have I asked myself the same question, but in vain; the secret of my coming to the island remains to this day the deepest of all the mysteries that baffle me. Sometimes I have thought that I must have been drugged. Perhaps some drowsy syrup was administered, poppy or mandragora, and a passing vessel may have dropped me on the island; or perhaps I was shipwrecked and carried ashore in my sleep. Often, as I recall the incidents of my sojourn, the words of Dante recur to me:

> " I' non so ben ridir com' io v' entrai;
>   Tant' era pien di sonno in su quel punto,
>   Che la verace via abbandonai."

But though the circumstances of my arrival are utterly obscure, there is no mystery about my departure. I have a good recollection of every relevant detail in the causes which led to my leaving Devil's Island once and for all. Indeed, it happened not so long ago. How it came to pass I will now relate.

Not far from the place where I lived there stood an ancient crannied wall. The crannies were many and deep, and because of this the islanders let it stand, for, said they, the wall is fairly hollow, its hollowness increases, and if left alone it will become perfect, and tumble down in course of time.

In one of the crannies of this wall there grew a flower of a species especially dear to me. It was an antirrhinum, or snapdragon, and it had for me a moving interest, for it reminded me of thoughts too deep for tears. I don't ask the reader to concern himself in the tragedies of my life; no doubt he has his own, and they are enough. But for the purpose of this narrative I must tell him that in bygone years, long before I voyaged on the strange seas of thought, my life had been wrapped up, as we say, in the life of a little boy, to whom I had given a patch of garden ten feet square. This he sowed with antirrhinums, and stood all day beside it to watch them grow. They came red and yellow; the yellow ones, he said, were his Auntie Rinums, and his Uncle Rinums were the red; and he used to laugh immoderately at his little joke. Well, he died; and " oh, the difference to me."

I have sometimes thought that my departure from the mainland and my arrival at Devil's Island was not unconnected with his death. Longer and more disastrous voyages than mine, I reflected, have often resulted from such incidents; besides, the presence of this flourishing snapdragon in an island where flowers were almost extinct, always seemed to me a hint that the two things were in some way connected. But I must not interrupt my narrative with these sentimental excursions.

As I said, the flower grew in the crannied wall, renewing itself year by year, and changing its colours, sometimes red, sometimes yellow, sometimes a mixture of the two, as the manner of antirrhinums is. All this was very eloquent to me, and in the season of blooms not a day passed but I visited the spot and indulged in thoughts which are hard to reproduce and perhaps not worth reproducing. I admit they were unnatural thoughts for a Devil's Islander, even an adopted one like me, and they were strangely out of keeping with the place. But as I looked at the flower I thought of its human counterpart; I thought of the place on the mainland where this had once flourished; I thought that if ever I visited that place again I should look in vain for my flower, for the wind had passed over it and it was gone. These meditations, if they may be called such, were the sole luxury my mind enjoyed during its long incarceration in that island; and the luxury had to be enjoyed in secret, for I knew there was not a soul in the entire population of Devil's Islanders whom I could take into my confidence, for they were all incapable of understanding what such things meant.

One day while thus engaged my reverie was broken by the apparition of a stranger. He was regarding me with interest, and I got the impression that he had been standing in the same attitude for some considerable time. I saw that he was a foreigner, but a foreigner accustomed to travel, for though in strange parts he had the air of a man at his ease.

I was half attracted and half repelled by his appearance. I believe that he got himself up to look like Michael Angelo's picture of God in the frescoes at Rome. That, as the sequel proved, was the part he wanted to play, and on the whole I must confess it was a clever make-up. So far so good; but beyond this there was something about him I did not like. Like other people who fancy themselves gods he had thought

it due to the character that he should assume something
of the air of a bully, as though swagger were a mark of
the divine.   His figure and expression were imperial
enough until you came to the eyes ; but in them there
was a furtive, restless look which seemed to say that
the part of a god was one which he knew he couldn't
sustain, and that if opportunity were given he would
immediately lapse from his dignity and betray himself
a vulgar snob.   And yet as the man stood before me—
for he remained without speaking long enough for me
to study him and draw conclusions—my feeling was
that in the long-run he might turn out to be a likeable
fellow ; and that all these grand airs of his belonged to
a part which had been forced upon him by an unkindly
lot.   Also I noticed there were lines of sorrow on his
brow.

" You seem a stranger," I said.

" Yes," he replied.   " I come from the neighbouring
Isles of Omniscience.   I have just been released for my
annual holiday."

" I thought that your people needed no holidays," I
said.   " When you know everything it must be rather
difficult to find a change, either of air or scene or anything else.   And I can't imagine why a change should
be necessary."

" Oh," he said, " you're quite mistaken about all that.
Things are uncommonly quiet over there "—and he
pointed to the south-east, where I could see the Isles of
Omniscience shimmering on the distant edge of the
ocean-floor—" uncommonly quiet, I can assure you.
Except for our annual holidays I doubt if we could
stand it.   Some of us take a trip to the mainland ; but
for my part nothing does me so much good as a visit

to this island and a fortnight's romp with the jolly islanders."

" Jolly islanders ! " I cried. " Why, we are the dullest dogs under heaven."

" You wouldn't think so if you lived in *our* islands," said he. " Everything, you see, is relative to everything else. You can form no idea of the *tedium vitæ* we have to endure, nor of the relief it is to have a run in a place like this."

" But," I said, " it's a dangerous place to run wild in. The whole island is full of holes, and unless you keep a sharp look out you'll be down one of them in no time and perhaps break your neck. I've had many narrow escapes myself. The fact is, I'd clear out to-morrow if I could, for I don't half like it."

" Oh," he said, " you needn't be anxious about me. Trust an omniscient for knowing where the holes are, and for keeping himself out of trouble. Besides, it's part of our holiday fun to smash them in, and then get into argument with the islanders. Of course we can always beat them at that—they're just babes in our hands. How do they like it ? Well, they pretend not to like it, and they make us pay pretty smartly for the damage. But in their heart of hearts they enjoy the fun just as much as we do."

" I notice," I said, " that you speak of our islanders as ' they.' Please to remember that I'm one of them."

" Pooh ! " he replied. " You can't take me in. I know all about you. You're no native of this island, and you play the part of one pretty badly. No born Devil's Islander ever wore an expression on his face such as yours had when I first saw you staring at yonder wall. However, if you don't like the place why do you stay in it? Try *our* islands for a change. We'd soon find you a billet, and you'd get accustomed to our ways in a month."

"But," I exclaimed, "you said things were even duller there than here; and though I can't understand why, I take your word for it, and I assure you that the Isles of Omniscience wouldn't do for me. Why, the dulness of this place is already more than I can stand; anything duller would kill me outright."

"You're changing the ground of your argument," he said. "Your last point was that this island is unsafe, and I suggested the Isles of Omniscience as a place where danger cannot exist. You couldn't break your neck there, because, if it is to be broken at all, it must have been broken from all eternity."

"Well," I said, "I don't understand that. Give me ten days to think it over and perhaps I may be able to follow you. Meanwhile, tell me more about the dulness you complain of. I should have thought that it must be very interesting to know everything."

"My good fellow," he replied, "you've no imagination whatsoever. Can't you understand that knowing everything is precisely the same as knowing nothing at all? Just consider what it means! In our islands it's impossible to think of anything, because everything has been already thought of. It's impossible to do anything, because everything is for ever done. It's impossible to say anything, because everybody knows what you're going to say. It's impossible to find anything, because nothing can ever be lost. Why, if you write a book, the whole population takes it as read and you can't sell a single copy. I've often told these stupid folk on Devil's Island that they ought to

migrate in a body to our part of the Archipelago.
Why spend your lives on explaining things away when
the very next island to your own would provide you
with Nothing-to-explain? That's what I say to them.
But I suppose it's crossing the sea that frightens
them. They're poor sailors. However, you can't
imagine how dull it is."

"Is there no means," I asked, "of laying your
omniscience aside when you find it inconvenient? I
have heard of such things being done in another
island."[1]

"Well," he said, "some time ago a movement was
set on foot to improve matters. It was proposed that
the post of Omniscience should be reserved for one man,
who should be a kind of king, while all the rest of us
should reduce ourselves to a condition of partial knowledge. It looked promising, but when it came to
business nobody could be found to take the kingship;
everybody wanted it to be given to somebody else.
So it all came to nothing, and then, of course, it turned
out that, being omniscient, we had known that it would
come to nothing all along. Looks like a huge farce?
Not at all. You don't understand. There can be no
farce when you know how everything is going to turn
out. That's the trouble! Our people would give half
their kingdom for a farce. But they can't get one up.
Complications? Well, your stupidity is colossal. Of
course, our standard of intelligence is high, and perhaps

---

[1] "Mais il convient que ma prescience n'entreprenne pas sur leur
libre arbitre. Afin de ne point porter atteint à la liberté humaine
j'ignore ce que je sais, j'épaissis sur mes yeux les voiles que j'ai percés
et, dans mon aveugle clairvoyance, je me laisse surprendre par ce que
j'ai prévu."—L'Ile des Pingouins, p. 44.

11

I judge you unfairly, but your suggesting complications
in the Isles of Omniscience does strike me as discreditable
even in a being of partial knowledge like you.   Why, my
dear sir, if you will come over to our islands and introduce a few complications the people will worship you as
a god.   They'd give even more for a complication than
they would for a farce.   And if only the complication
were a complete mystery!   Ah me! there you touch
me on the tenderest spot.   Despair of mystery—despair,
I mean, of ever finding a mystery to tackle—that is
our settled mood, and it is the one interesting emotion
that is left us.   Were it not for this despair we should
all die!"

" No fear of that," I said, for I was now catching the
spirit of the argument.   " No fear of your dying.   Did
you not tell me that in your islands nobody could break
his neck, since to omniscience it must have been broken
from all eternity?   How, then, could an omniscient die?
You can't introduce anything new into the experience
of a being who knows everything.   If ever you die,
therefore, you must have known yourself as dead all
along.   In your experience what isn't happening always
can't happen at all."

I could see that I had given him a home-thrust and
that he was a little staggered.   Seeing him thus my
suspicions were aroused, for I reflected that a being
omniscient, as he pretended to be, ought not to be
taken by surprise or knocked off his perch by any
conceivable argument.   " The man," I said to myself,
" is an impostor after all."

"Come now," he said, after a little, " let us understand one another.   I know the kind of man you are.
You're one of those fellows who go about trying to

make logical trouble for other people. But you'd
better not try that with me, or you'll get the worst of
it. This accursed Devil's Island is full of people like
you; I suppose it's a habit you've picked up from the
rest of them. Take my advice and give it up, especially when you meet a man from our islands. You
can't make logical trouble for us, and don't you forget
it!"

I knew, of course, that all this was bluff, and I
resolved not to let myself be browbeaten even by an
omniscient; nor would I abandon the advantage I
had already won. So I said: "You spoke just now
as though a little logical trouble were precisely what
you wanted—I mean when you were speaking about
complications. That's why I offered my last remark.
I was in hopes you'd fall down and worship me as a
god. Instead of that you fly into a rage and threaten
me with I don't know what."

He laughed, and I saw a total change come over his
countenance. "Well," he said, "let us try to understand each other, as I proposed just now. I'll tell you
something in confidence. One of the chief pleasures
of my annual holiday in this island is the pleasure of
being frank. I'm going to be frank with *you*. I
don't deny that there is a touch of humbug over
there"— he pointed to the shimmering islands in
the south-east—"though it's mainly professional and
therefore innocent. The fact is, our claim to omniscience needs to be taken in a certain sense. It's true
that we know everything *in general*, but we don't
know each thing in particular. Or, as you would say,
we know the All *as such*, but not otherwise; and if you
ask for particulars we are apt to get into a muddle.

But to know the All, even *as such*, is no small achievement, I can assure you.   I was years in attaining it,
though I am not sure that I am much the gainer by
the attainment."

"The dulness you complain of," I interposed,
"suggests that you are not."

"No doubt there are disadvantages," he said, "though
it would be hard to explain them.   So long as you know
the All—as such—at intervals only, it's a very interesting experience; but when you can't help seeing the All
in everything you look at, you begin to lose heart, and
life becomes pretty blank.   I'm like that myself sometimes.   The All obsesses me, never leaves me, comes
between me and my business, and turns existence into
something of a nightmare.   When that state comes on
I know that I want a holiday, and I take the next boat
for Devil's Island."

At this moment one of the great boring-machines to
which I have previously alluded—the machines which
had cost the intellect of Devil's Island three thousand
years of labour to render perfect—began tearing the
ribs out of a mountain immediately to our right.   The
sound was deafening.   In a few minutes ten thousand
"noes," each as loud as a cannon shot, were exploded
into space.

"How would you like to have that kind of
thing going on under your windows night and day?"
I asked.

He replied with enthusiasm, " I should like nothing
better—at least for a time.   That sound is the principal
attraction that brings me to Devil's Island, and it does
me more good than I can tell you.   We've got a worse
machine than that in our islands.   It says 'yes, yes, yes,'

all day long, until the whole universe seems to hiss like a serpent. I tell you, my friend, it's an infinitely more trying lot to have to stand up to the bombardment of the everlasting yea than to endure an occasional visit from the Vacuum Cleaner. Why, it's a positive relief to hear a few negations. Ha! It's beginning again!"

"Can you relate any instances," I asked, when the noise had subsided, "to illustrate all this? As yet I don't quite understand why the All should make your existence such a burden."

"I could give you many," he said, "but the subject is a painful one, and just now I wish to forget it. Remember I am on my holiday, and am trying to escape from this very thing. Tell me rather what you yourself are after. Why were you looking so sad when I saw you first?"

"That also," I replied, "is a painful subject; but, unlike yours, it becomes less painful when talked of, though I don't often get the chance. In this God-forsaken place they don't care for such things. But you are different, and, if you like, I'll tell you the story."

I stumbled through it as best I could, and when I had done I looked up to see what impression it had made on the Man from the Isles of Omniscience. To my great embarrassment I saw that he was staring at the flower in the crannied wall with a vacant and most melancholy expression in his eyes. But I thought it best to go on. "It's not much to look at," I said. "It's only a snapdragon, and not a very good one neither; but from what I've said you'll understand why it means so much to me."

"Snapdragon?" he said, in a tone of irritation that

distressed and surprised me. " What fool is talking of snapdragons ? There are no snapdragons here."

" But what's that you're looking at ? " I cried, pointing to the flower in the crannied wall.

" God-and-man," he groaned ; " God-and-man ! Will the awful thing never depart ? "

" Great heavens ! " I thought. " What's to be done ? "

At that moment he turned his eyes upon me, and the utter vacancy of their look made me shudder. Then in a flash the secret of his trouble was revealed to me. " He's at the universal standpoint," I thought, " and sees nothing. It's the blankness of omniscience. The Oneness of the One has got hold of him."

" Come," I said after a little, " take a walk ; the air of Devil's Island will do you good." And linking my arm in his I led him, still groaning inarticulately about God-and-man, to the summit of a promontory from which one looked at a vast expanse of sea and sky.

"This," I said, "is my favourite point of view. Yonder is the sun, sinking beneath the ocean floor. The clouds are edged with crimson fire ; the breeze awakens, and the eagle in the upper air, like the tireless messenger of heaven, wings his steady flight for Chimborazo."

" Metaphysics ! " cried the man, now in the very crisis of the omniscient fit, " metaphysics, and bad metaphysics at that ! Throw your metaphysical eagles to your metaphysical dogs ! A pin for your ' favourite point of view '! Stick to the plain fact of the All, and prate no more of ' points,' either of ' view ' or anything else. Flowers in crannied walls, Chimborazos, clouds edged with crimson fire—have done with your mystical flummery ! Vain abstractions ! Metaphors masquerading as facts ! Impotent strivings to escape from the One! Airy nothings dressed out in pompous words! Oh, my young friend, if only you would spend one short week among the honest, plain-dealing people of our islands! Try on them your high-flown nonsense about seas and sunsets, and they will have you down from your metaphysical perch in a twinkling. No, sir, it wouldn't *work* with men who know things root and all and all in all."

" What!" I said. " Do you mean to tell me that the people on your islands can't recognise the Flower when they see it ?"

"Oh," he cried, "we've been through that on the Isles of Omniscience. We had our metaphysical period like the rest of you ; and for ages too long to measure our philosophers laboured in vain to prove the existence of the Flower in the Crannied Wall. There were even mystics among us who said they had seen the Flower and smelt its fragrance. Ah, how they used to prate of their vision ! But when plain men, who knew the All, challenged them to show the Flower, how helpless they were! 'I have never seen it,' cried one of our plain men ; 'I have swept the All with my telescope and found the All everywhere, full and perfect in a hair as heart, but no vestige of a flower or a crannied wall did I ever see. I have also heard your arguments for its existence, both *a priori* and *a posteriori*, and have tested them by experience, and found no tittle of confirmation anywhere.' And all these mystics could answer was, 'Trust the experience of those who have seen the Flower and sat on the Crannied Wall.'"

" That great man of yours who swept the All with his telescope," I said, " must have been a muddle-headed fellow to give himself away in the language you quote.

What did he mean by saying that he found the All full and perfect 'in a hair as heart'? If he found the All full and perfect in each of them he would see no difference between the two. What, then, made him call the one 'a hair' and the other 'a heart'?"

"A mere concession to the deficiencies of language," he replied. "Language was made before people had learnt to think; it belongs to the period when the mind was plunged in the metaphysical darkness of the flower and the crannied wall. The consequence is that we are compelled to use metaphysical metaphors such as 'a hair' or 'a heart' for expressing even the simplest apprehensions of the All."

"But," I said, "I don't see what you want with two of them. And since you pass both 'hair' and 'heart' I can't understand why you won't allow 'the flower' and 'the crannied wall' as well, and so have four metaphors, or any number for the matter of that."

"And so we should," he replied, "if those rascals on the mainland would treat them all alike. But they will pick and choose. They get hold of some metaphor that sounds prettier than the others, like that of the flower, and because of its prettiness they forget it's a metaphor and set it up for something real. Now nobody would lose his head in this way about 'a hair' or 'heart,' and that's why our great man was justified in using such terms."

"You've not removed my difficulty," I said. "However, tell me this. Is there any difference in your islands between a hairdresser and a cardiac specialist?"

"Only as distinctions of thought," he answered. "There is no difference in being."

I could think of no reply to this argument. So,

remembering the old men who went up the mountain
to worship Benamuckee, I turned to my omniscient
visitor and said simply, " O ! "

" Who more than I has reason to speak of these
things," he went on, " for have I not been through it
all ? Am not I the man at whom they pointed and
said, ' There goes one intoxicated with the Flower-
Consciousness ' ? Indeed, I have had my visions and
spoken in tongues. The strange gibberish comes
back to me even now. ' A simple primrose by the
river's brim ' I would babble. ' Trees are green, pigs
grunt, aloes are bitter, it's hard work pulling the cart
up-hill,' and so on in endless maundering, till the honest
folk of our islands deemed me mad."

I must confess that up to this point I had never
doubted that I should ultimately succeed in putting
my omniscient visitor to confusion and forcing him to
admit that he was a fraud. He had seemed in a state
of metaphysical intoxication, and therefore deprived
of right reason ; and I had waited to deliver the final
blow until he should return to his senses and converse
like a rational being. But these last remarks of his,
assuming, as they did, that it was I who was intoxicated
and himself who was sober, reduced me to a state of
helplessness such as I had never before experienced in
any argument. How was I to prove my sobriety or
his intoxication ? I saw the thing was impossible. I
had always thought that a man who took a primrose
by the river's brim for a simple primrose and nothing
more, whatever else might be the matter with him,
could not be accused of being metaphysically drunk ;
while another person who saw in the primrose not the

primrose but God-and-man, whatever good qualities *he* might possess, could not rightly claim, *pro tanto*, to be a plain man.   Yet this was the way in which my visitor insisted on arranging the situation.   And now it occurred to me that he had just as good a reason to arrange it thus as I had to arrange it in the contrary manner.   May it not be, I thought, that taking a primrose for a primrose is nothing but the last stage of metaphysical madness, whereas the taking it for God-and-man, the vision of the Whole of Things displacing and replacing the flower, is just the plain, normal, business-like, sensible way of dealing with the matter? May it not be that there is more metaphysic in Hodge's notion of a pig than in the νόησις νοησέως of Aristotle? Why not?

Enough has been said to show that this was, at all events, the normal way of regarding the matter in the Isles of Omniscience, and what right had I to treat the mere accident that I lived in Devil's Island, and adopted its ways of thought, as a conclusive reason for taking the opposite point of view?   Both points of view seemed to me equally tenable for island philosophies; I mean, that whichever of the two you take, you only need an island sufficiently far from the islands where the other is taken to have all the grounds you want for ascribing plain sense to your own islanders and mysticism to the rest of the Archipelago.   I reflected, however, that while both of them might be tenable on islands, neither of them could be adopted on the mainland; at least not without great inconvenience and perhaps disaster, because the controversy as to who was drunk and who was sober would be perpetual, would precede and overshadow all other discussions, and would doubtless lead, in course of time, to bloody quarrels between individuals and to wars of mutual destruction between communities.

While these reflections were passing in my mind, a change came over my companion. I noticed that the air of strain and distress which had accompanied his expositions of omniscience gave way, and he seemed once more to assume the mien of cheerfulness, even of jollity, with which he had originally greeted me.

" Let's go back," he said, "to your crannied wall and take another look at the bonny flower. I still retain some of the old mystical habits, and I don't mind indulging them a little during my holiday—if only for the purpose of understanding the confusion of the mystical consciousness in persons like yourself. Now that the light has faded it may be that the flower will look less like God-and-man than it did, and it may even have some colour and perhaps a little scent. Besides which, I should like to hear more about that boy you mentioned."

" Pardon me," I said. " I would rather keep that matter out of the discussion; for though I recognise that you are no longer in a professional mood, yet the fact that you are capable of such moods, and may therefore fall into one of them again, makes me most unwilling to mention the boy."

" Ah ! " said he, " I understand. You are afraid lest I should treat the boy as I treated the flower. You don't want to hear that the boy, like the flower, is a figment of your metaphysics, a mystical illusion diverting your attention from the All and from—— "

" That will do," I said. " Don't go on. If you were to convince me of that it would kill me. Or perhaps

I should kill you. I can stand it with the flower but
not with the—— "

" Yes," he said, " there is nothing so strange as the
ineptitude of philosophers in the choice of illustrations "
—ignorant, apparently, that it was a poet who had
chosen this one.

Never shall I forget the night of horror which followed
this strange interview. For many hours I lay awake,
full of troubled thoughts, and when sleep overpowered
me at last, these thoughts became a nightmare of
monstrous and appalling imagery. I was in the Isles
of Omniscience, and there was one by my side who
would not depart. " Art thou in Heaven or in Hell ? "
he kept repeating ; " there shall be no rest for thee till
thou knowest." Evermore a weight oppressed me,
and the weight was the question which I could not
answer—" Art thou in Heaven or in Hell ? " Wherever
I turned I found the All confronting me. Now it
would present itself as a black and solid sphere which
grew bigger and bigger till it filled space and time ;
and again it would shrink to the dimensions of the
tiniest seed. As it grew, it would crush me with an
intolerable pressure ; as it shrank, it forced me to shrink
with it, and the rigour of the contraction was like to
crack and comminute my bones. Whether it grew or
whether it shrank, the sphere seemed in some way to
identify itself with the question that tortured my soul—
Art thou in Heaven or in Hell? And now the immensity
of this question would appal me, and now its littleness
would fill me with loathing or contempt. I tried to do
things, and then the black sphere would rend itself
asunder and show me the thing already done. I tried

to move my limbs, and could not, for I saw they were
already moved; I tried to speak but could utter no
sound, because everything was said. Great processions
came marching out of eternity; among them was one
dressed out in scarlet, which I recognised as my own
sins. As they approached they became fused into
a river of blood; the black sphere bulged out towards
them, becoming horribly lopsided, and then, having
lapped up the scarlet stream to the last drop, suddenly
recovered its spherical shape and began expanding to
its largest and contracting to its smallest with incredible
rapidity, as though it had eaten food and were refreshed.

Blank misgivings, nameless fears, horrors of nothing,
storms of panic, swept over me in an endless flood.
Presently I would see what I was afraid of. The firma-
ment was falling down on my head; the deeps were
rising to swallow me up. And then I would burst
out of it all into scenes acted on a stage. Two men
were fighting a duel, and I was one of the seconds.
I was loading a pistol for my man, when the other
second stepped up to me and said, "These fellows know
how the affair will end." "Then," I answered, "there
can be no fair fight." Whereupon the two principals
laughed and cried, "Precisely; we knew it would come
to this." And the problem was, "Ought I, or ought I
not, to have foreseen the turn events would take?"
Then a dirty fellow from the pit of the theatre called
out "Try a Many and One," and threw a halfpenny
cigarette on to the stage.

I was walking in a procession of old men who were
climbing a steep mountain. When we reached the top
all of us said "O" to Benamuckee, and then Benamuckee
said "O" to us. I asked one of the old men what was

the good of this? He answered, "O, all is O and O is all."

I was in a merchant's office, with an enormous book before me full of figures, which I was trying to add by the rule that the totals were in each of the items and each item in the totals. Panic seized me, and I rushed away crying, "Is there no balm in Gilead?" I came to my doorstep and a thing named the All opened the door, threw its arms around my neck, and kissed me. A friend dropped in. What news? None; for the All is neither new nor old. "Then why that knocking at the door?" I asked.

It was the man from the Isles of Omniscience. "You've had a bad night," he said; "your groans have been terrible. I suppose you've been dreaming about that flower. In my opinion you're haunted by metaphysical monsters. If so, be warned in time. You ought to try a change of air. Come with me for a spell to the Isles of Omniscience."

"Thank you," I said, "but I'm not coming. I've done with islands. I'm going back to the mainland."

VIII.—SELF-DEFEATING THEORIES

I

THERE never was a philosophy without an end in view. The philosophical knight-errantry which goes out in quest of Truth, sublimely indifferent to the form that Truth may assume, and equally content whether she turn out to be a flame-spitting dragon or a beautiful lady, is a thing that exists only in dreams. Every philosopher knows what he is looking for. We give him credit for all the impartiality the circumstances admit of, but we cannot close our eyes to the fact that his selective attention is at work all the time. If by an impartial philosopher is meant a person whose attention to the field of thought works without selective purpose, then we do not hesitate to say there never has been, and never can be, an impartial philosopher. And there never was a great thinker who pretended to be impartial in that sense.

The student of philosophy should use this as a test, and he should apply it with especial rigour to any thinker who may protest that he is indifferent to the form of his results. In every case the student will find that the philosopher has an object—he *wants* something, perhaps a certain kind of world; he is looking for something, perhaps a rule of safe-conduct through life; he is after something, perhaps a particular kind of intellectual satisfaction, or even a particular set of emotions. Well, does his system give him what he wants, enable him to find what he is looking for; or does it end in giving him something that he doesn't want, in his not finding what he undertook to find but something else ? This is a fair test.

The test will never fail to yield important results, for, as we have said, there is no philosophy without an end in view. No matter how the thing is evaded, or wrapped up, philosophy shares with life the inability to advance one step without selecting its path, though often at a great risk. The "ends" of the thinker are many, as are also the ends of life. To say this is not to impugn philosophy; on the contrary, we thereby claim philosophy as a genuine vital experience. As we cannot live without bias, so neither can we think without selection.

Testing thought by its own results, one cannot but be struck by the existence of many self-defeating theories. By a self-defeating theory is meant a theory which, when accepted, thwarts the purpose or destroys the interest it was originally put forth to serve. Admitting that the thinker's purpose, implied or avowed, is always the enrichment of experience, we must not too hastily pass on to the statement that the process of reflection does *de facto* enrich the experience of every person who reflects. There seems to be some confusion between the two statements. Enrichment may be the purpose, but impoverishment may be the actual result, of the thinker's work. If the process of reflection leads us to an honest belief that the Good is the pleasant, that the Beautiful is the useful, that the world is a fortuitous concourse of atoms, that human life is "ruled by chance," it is by no means self-evident that our experience as a whole is "enriched" by these results. Persons who have come to more "enriching" conclusions will no doubt be tempted to treat our impoverishment as due to the arrested development of our thought; they will accuse us of having stopped too soon; they will say we have not reflected *enough*. But this, of course, will merely lead to our addressing a *tu quoque* to our accusers. To assert that a "reflected" experience is always richer than its opposite, that we are always better off, therefore, when reflection is complete, may be true; but it will be found, as we shall endeavour to show in the sequel, to involve a very big assumption as to the ultimate character of an experience. For the present we shall do well to confine ourselves to the matter of fact by asking how far certain theorists, who avowedly seek "enrichment" on particular lines, do actually succeed in getting what they seek. We shall find that they frequently fail. Thus there are theories of religion which kill religion; there are theories of happiness which would, if received, make the recipient profoundly unhappy; there are theories of conduct which prompt men to rebellion against the principles of morality; there are theories of freedom which would cause us all to regret that we were free; and again there are predictions—about the future course of evolution and such like—the bare mention of which sets us scheming with all our might to prevent them from coming true. These theories are intended to make us more interested in Religion, Morality, Happiness, Freedom; they end by making us less interested. Therefore they are self-defeating.

Again, there are Cosmologies which set out to explain

12

the Universe and end by explaining something which, whatever else it may be, is certainly not the Universe. And, once more, there are theologies which raise our hopes by undertaking to prove the existence of God and do indeed succeed in proving the existence of something. But this something whose existence is proved turns out again on examination to be very different not only from what the reader means by God but from what the theologian himself meant when he first undertook his task. When the theologian *began* he meant by God what we all mean when we spell that name with a capital letter and pronounce it with reverence; by the time the proof *ends*, however, the meaning of the term may have become so changed—changed, indeed, by the very process of proof—that there is no longer any need to spell it with a capital, or pronounce it with any reverence whatsoever. The God about whom our hopes were raised was God; the thing whose existence is proved *may be* a phrase, a concept, an idol of the mind; or, more simply, an idol. It is futile to pretend that we are satisfying the seeker after *God*, that we are giving him what he *wants* to find, if all we can give him is some hypothesis that accounts for the Universe. Nobody can say his prayers to a hypothesis, even though it accounts for the Universe; nobody can shed tears of repentance in its presence or call upon it in time of trouble. These, too, are self-defeating theories.

After prolonged study of many such, one gets a strange impression. The impression is that the Universe is full of secrets which fulfil a very useful office so long as they are *kept* secrets, but which cease to do their appointed task the instant they are found out. The resultant feeling is one of regret that the philosopher

as been so candid as to communicate his discovery.
t is as though a very dangerous cat had been let out of
he bag. "Would it not have been better," we say to
urselves, "to keep this useful secret dark?"

1. Among many instances that might be given we
vill first consider Hedonism. With Hedonism as a
moral theory we have here nothing to do; let us only
glance at its results. Suppose, then, with the Hedonist
hat happiness is the true end of life and that the
promotion of happiness is the whole duty of man.
Not many Hedonists have thought it worth while to
nquire whether they themselves are promoting happiness by letting this particular secret out of the bag.
May it not be that the happiest man is precisely that
man who doesn't know that he is pursuing happiness;
and may not this piece of knowledge, rashly communi-
cated by the Hedonist, be the means of putting the man
at odds with himself in a most distressing manner?
Most Hedonists admit that the less a man thinks about
happiness the brighter are his prospects of success.
Why, then, should they take such elaborate pains to
make him think about it? If the Hedonist would
cease his argument, this not-thinking about happiness,
which is so essential for its attainment, would be easier
for all of us. Psychologically, therefore, the disclosure
appears to be a mistake.

And there are other reasons for regretting it, of which
we will mention only one. The doctrine that happiness
is the end is not the cheerful thing it seems. Accepting
it, one can't resist a most depressing conviction that
human life has been a lamentable failure. Nor is it
likely to be anything else. For, if we were all to
urn Hedonists to-morrow, and set to work promoting

happiness with all our might, it is extremely doubtful whether the amount of happiness so produced would in the long-run be sufficient to make any of us very happy. Can we doubt, indeed, Life being what it is and Death being ever on the watch to stalk its prey, that any race of beings which should deliberately devote itself to the pursuit of its own happiness would end in the misery of disillusion, disappointment, and defeat ? Supposing the happiness-doctrine to be true, can we respond to it otherwise than by a somewhat melancholy sigh ?

If it be true that the best results in the way of happiness are obtained by those persons who think they are aiming at virtue, or beauty of character, or obedience to God, then on Hedonist principles it must be highly undesirable to make them think that they are aiming at anything else. A Hedonist who publishes his theory is like a conjurer who betrays his profession by explaining to the public how the thing is done. On his own showing he ought to drown his book ; for surely a doctrine which is only practicable when forgotten is a doctrine that ought never to be divulged. In this connection it may not be out of place to quote from a letter written years ago by a person who had made a close study of the literature of Hedonism. " The very name of Happiness," he said, " now gives me a feeling of nausea. And of one thing I am firmly resolved. Come what may "—the reader will recognise the attitude—" come what may, I will *not* work for the Greatest Happiness of the Greatest Number ; and if any friend of mine has the bad taste to work for my happiness I will cut him on the spot. Of this, I say, I am resolved ; and if I must go to Hell for so resolving, then to Hell I will go. I owe this resolution to—you know whom." It needs perhaps to be pointed out that the author of these remarks was neither a murderer nor an incendiary, but a most estimable citizen of no mean city.

2. With the "Paradox of Hedonism" we may compare the less noticed "Paradox of Prediction," to which allusion has been made in another essay.[1] The "Paradox of Prediction" may be expressed by the rule—"If you want your predictions to come true, keep them to yourself." Prediction of what is going to happen in human affairs differs from prediction about the course of inanimate Nature in the highly important fact that the former kind frequently provokes a successful conspiracy against its fulfilment among the persons whose interests are affected. When this happens the prediction is self-defeating. Thus it is a highly dangerous thing to forecast what social evolution is going to bring about unless you are sure that the social beings interested in the result have no power to break the evolutionary entail whose secrets you are disclosing. In presence of such a power these predictions should not be dignified with the name of prophecy; for they are nothing better than ill-considered blabbing. Indeed, all prophecy of this sort that would be successful should be carried on in an unknown tongue; and this, we believe, has been the invariable practice of experts.

3. A third instance of a self-defeating theory is provided, if I rightly understand it, by a famous passage of the late William James[2]—a philosophical genius to whom in general the present writer can only profess

[1] See the essay, "Is there a Science of Man?"
[2] *The Will to Believe,* p. 180 *seq.*

his veneration and indebtedness.   In this passage,
James, with his usual incisiveness, suggests a mode of
reconciling Free-will with the idea of an overruling
Providence.   We are asked to contemplate a game of
chess in which the players are a Moral Providence on
one side and a free humanity on the other ; Providence
being a consummate player and humanity a novice.
The consummate player knows all the possible moves
his antagonist may take, but which particular moves
he will take at any given turn in the game has been
left a matter of chance.   Here is the opening for Free-
will ; which, however, does not endanger the final
result.   For Providence, knowing all the possibilities,
has so arranged them, and is so sure of its own ability
to play the winning game, that come what may, it is
going to win and bring all right at last.   Thus man
enjoys a measure of freedom on the one hand ; and, on
the other, the ends of Providence are secured.

This is highly ingenious [1] ; but on examination it
turns out to be another instance of letting in daylight
on a matter which ought to be kept profoundly dark.
For if this figure correctly describes the working
arrangements of a moral world, it is essential that
those arrangements should be known by only *one of
the parties engaged in the game*, namely, by the consummate player.   The moment the novice is let into
the secret the game is up.   So long as the novice is
ignorant that his consummate antagonist is sure to win,
and thinks he has a chance of winning himself, he plays
for all he is worth, and the game goes on briskly

---

[1] Dr Hastings Rashdall says : " This is perhaps the best attempt that
has ever been made to deal with the difficulty."   *The Theory of Good
and Evil*, vol. ii. p. 343.

enough.   But when the philosopher comes along and whispers in his ear the true state of the case, namely, that play as he will the issue is pre-determined in favour of the other side, the interest of the novice instantly vanishes; he perceives that he is being mocked by a bogus game; he refuses to make another move, and rises from the table, not, perhaps, without addressing a few uncomplimentary remarks to the consummate antagonist who has inveigled an innocent beginner like himself into a fool's business of this sort.   It is obvious that philosophy here plays the part of the serpent in the Garden of Eden by inducing the human subject to eat of the Tree of Knowledge, of which in a world so arranged it is evidently intended that he should not eat.

4. The last example is from Professor A. E. Taylor's *Elements of Metaphysics* (p. 399) :—

" My own conclusion, then, which I offer to the reader simply as my own, is that anything less than the Absolute is an inadequate object of religious devotion, and that the Absolute itself has the structure which such an object requires.   If it should be further suggested that at any rate, when we come to actual experience, we find that we cannot represent the object of our worship to ourselves in an individual form of sufficient concreteness to stir effectual emotion and prompt to genuine action without clothing it in imagination with anthropomorphic qualities which meta-physical criticism proves inapplicable to the infinite individual, I should be inclined to reply that I admit the fact.   And I do not think we need shrink from the conclusion that practical religion involves a certain element of intellectual contradiction.   Thus, though God is not truly God until we deny the existence of any independent ' evil ' by which His nature is limited, it seems probable that the thought of ourselves as ' fellow-workers with God ' would hardly lead to practical good works unless we also inconsistently allowed ourselves to imagine God as struggling against a hostile power and standing in need of our assistance. But this only shows that the practical value of religion in guiding action is not necessarily dependent on its scientific truth."

If this is the scientific truth about Religion, the conclusion we feel inclined to draw is, not with Professor Taylor that the practical value of religion doesn't depend on its scientific truth, but that the two things cannot be made to live in the same house or within sight of each other; for where the one comes it is obvious that the other must go. The presence of an element of make-believe is certainly no barrier to worship so long as the worshipper is unaware of his own feigning. So long as the make-believe is unknown for what it is the worship may go on. But the situation is entirely changed when the worshipper, thanks to Professor Taylor's book, is informed of what he is doing and learns the nature of the trick he is playing on his own mind. To worship a figment is one thing; to worship a figment found out is quite another, representing, unless we are mistaken, neither more nor less than a psychological impossibility. For our own part we can only say that if we accepted Professor Taylor's view we should not go to church. The wonder is to find anyone supposing that information of this kind will persuade other people to go. Perhaps we are wrong in supposing that this passage is written in the interests of practical religion. If it is, we can only say that it affords one more instance of a self-defeating theory.

II

" In all the wide world of things that challenge reflection," says the Plain Man, " there is nothing so wonderful, and nothing which ultimately becomes so illuminating, as our faith in the beneficence of progressive thought. Is it not an amazing thing that men should select the thinker as the one person upon whom no restraints are to be imposed ? Admitting to the full all that can be claimed for him as a Builder, who will deny that his power as Destroyer is equally great ? In both respects his work may be beneficent, but in the second he is terrible as the winds of God. Where will you find so dangerous a person as he ? He is, and he has been, the Prince of the Disturbers of Peace. It is he who allows humanity no rest. He is the chief wrecker of the works of man. He troubles all waters ; renders ancient rivers undrinkable, and drops his philtres into every well. A social order which has been a thousand years in the building he can shatter, as Heine says Kant did, by a few strokes of his pen. 'Beware,' says Emerson, ' when the great God lets loose a thinker on this planet. Then all things are at risk. It is as when a conflagration has broken out in a great city, and no man knows what is safe, or where it will end.' Who can tell what the thinker will be after next ? Who can tell on whose roof-tree his lightnings will fall, or on what deepest interest his tempests will be let loose?

"Yet he is the one who claims liberty in widest measure, and gets what he claims. He is the one to whom humanity gives a blank cheque on its moral and religious capital. He is the one to whose mercies we all submit. On the face of it there is no vocation of man which stands so sorely in need of justification as does that of this same thinker. But challenge him on the subject, and you will find nine times out of ten that he is dumb. There is no devourer of widows'

houses, there is no robber of shrines, who has less to
say for himself than he. 'Justify my calling to the
world?' he cries, at length. 'Who ever heard of such
an insolent demand? Was not a charter to go where
I will given to me at the foundation of the world?
Who ever doubted the beneficence of Truth?' So he
is apt to think himself exempt from all human restraint.
And so perhaps he is : but upon what ground?

" Amid much disagreement as to the nature of truth,
there is one thing about which we all seem to agree—
viz. that the more we have of it the better. That
nothing but good can result from the deepening of our
insight and the extension of our knowledge seems to be
implied by everyone who takes the trouble either to
support his own opinions or to confute those of other
people. Even the pessimist who holds that everything
is as bad as it can be, makes an exception in favour of
his own book. The world would be a little worse than
it is, he thinks, if his book were not published. By
publishing these pessimistic opinions of his he makes
one small oasis in the desert, and thus does a little good
—the only good, in fact, there is.

" Among the powers which influence human life, truth
stands alone as the object of an unqualified trust. To
no other of the so-called 'powers' of the Universe
do we extend the same warm welcome, the same
ungrudging hospitality, the same undiscriminating and
enthusiastic acceptance. Towards most of the others
our attitude is essentially one of distrust, even of fear.
They come in the form of earthquake, famine, pestilence,
conflagration, sudden death, and they seem to play us
the vilest tricks. They are ineluctable and highly
dangerous. On no account are they to be let loose

at any time and in any form.   No one in his senses would throw away the end of a lighted cigar and be equally confident that whether it fell into a water-butt or a powder magazine the resulting developments would do him good.   But the thinker is encouraged to fling his brands about in every direction.

" There is a story about a professor of physics who had discovered a hitherto unknown force of Nature, whereby he was enabled, on pressing a button, to destroy a city or even a continent.[1]   He lived in some wicked Babylon and had come to the conclusion that, for moral reasons, it would be a good thing to wipe this city off the face of the earth.   So he was just about to press the button when the heroine rushed into his laboratory and smashed his machine.   Most persons would commend the deed for saving the city from the destruction threatened upon it by the free-will of an individual professor of physics.   But if some similar Amazon were to invade the studies of our Newtons or of our Kants at the moment when they were about to let loose some intellectual earthquake on mankind and burn the MSS. of the *Principia* or the *Critiques* and knock the authors on the head, should we not all agree that the deed was ill done ?

"Apparently, then, our Universe is so constituted that while in its physical aspect it cannot be trusted for an instant, and is known to contain a reservoir of imprisoned mischief, in its intellectual aspect it is not only safe but friendly,—nay, even bursting with the

[1] That such a discovery is not beyond the bounds of possibility is suggested by the statement of Sir Joseph Thompson about the forces contained in the atom. See his Presidential Address to the British Association, 1909. Verily, knowledge is power !

will to bless.   To be afraid of truth at the present day
is almost tantamount to being profane.   If the suggestion were offered that a philosopher who had discovered
the origin of evil, or the nature of truth, would be well
advised in keeping the discovery to himself, the author
of the suggestion would run a serious risk of being
considered no better than he ought to be.   In China,
perhaps, such a man would be esteemed, and would
be admitted to great honours; but in the more enlightened West he would be condemned.   Here people
are hunger-bitten with desire to have the truth let loose
upon them in every form, and without respect of time
or place; and a class of professional thinkers is maintained for the express purpose of so letting it loose.
Every gate that is barred must be unlocked, in the
sure and certain faith that when the cage is opened
a fat and succulent sheep will come forth and walk
straight into the butcher's shop.   It would be profanity to suggest that the animal inside may turn out
a hungry wolf or a hissing serpent.   Varying the figure,
may we not say that the professional thinker is one
whom a thoughtless public encourages and even per-
secutes into turning on every tap from which a single
drop of that high explosive called truth can be made
to flow ? "

The story is told of a certain evangelist who once
prayed in public as follows: " O Lord, save us from
the perils of modern thought "—and then, after a
pause — "yea, O Lord, deliver us from all thought
whatsoever."

" Well," asks the Plain Man, "why not ? When
one thinks of the desolations that have been wrought
in the earth by the launching of new ideas, is it not

prima facie as reasonable to pray for protection against the unknown powers of truth as for deliverance from shipwreck, thunderbolt, or sudden death? Does any of us know enough about the Whole to make him dogmatically certain that the continual liberation of its secrets, by thinking, will conduce to the best interests of that extremely insignificant part of the Whole represented by human life? Have we any means of knowing in advance that the nature of experience is such that its value will be increased by the revelation of what it is?"

There are some things in the life of thought which are their own justification. You can criticise them only by appealing to the very principle you are criticising. If you question their truth, your question already assumes they are true. Thinking cannot go behind its own principles. If you ask, Why should we think as we do? your question is only another specimen of thinking, and begs the answer before it can be given. All inquiries into the nature of the Universe are based on the assumption that the Universe is worth inquiring about. We ask the question because we believe the answer will pay. We reflect because we believe that in the upshot good will come of it. Short of this assumption there is no reason why one should think, inquire, doubt, or question anything. This, then, is one of the things in the life of thought which can never be proved; but if any one denied it, we may point out to him that his denial involves the very principle denied.

That the ultimate truth of things is good and worth knowing is a presupposition which lies concealed

behind all the thinking of all the world. We make it
unconsciously before we begin to think. The public
make it when they encourage us to go on thinking.
Faith in the ultimate soundness of the constitution of
things is implied equally by the unquestioning com-
placency of the philosopher in the pursuit of his task,
and by the encouragement to go on, no matter what
the results may be, which he receives from the public.
The philosopher and his audience share the same conviction—that all will turn out well at the last.   No fear
of poking one's stick into a hornet's nest, nor of opening
the lid of some Pandora's box, restrains the thinker
from pursuing his inquiries or the public from standing
by to hear what will come of it.

It is good sometimes to get away from the question
of what particular thinkers have taught, and to take
stock of thought as one continuous movement going on
from age to age.   Let us ask ourselves, not what are
the teachings of this philosophy or of that, but what is
implied by the fact that the process of reflection on
ultimates goes on deepening and broadening as the ages
pass; and not only so, but goes on with the sanction
and support of every reasonable being, no man fearing
it, no one doubting but that this Universe is so constituted that the deeper you mine into its secrets the
richer you will find its gold.   The very existence of
this stream of thought, and the encouragement it receives, betokens a fundamental confidence in the last
issue of things.   It illustrates on a scale which is world-
wide and age-long the great saying of Paschal, "that
God is a being whom we could not seek had we not
already found."

But if that is so, philosophy is at once face to face

with a paradox.   The existence of philosophy in any or
all of its varieties rests on the assurance that the deepest
truth of the Universe is good.   But if this assumption
is made in advance, what is there left to philosophise
about?   Is not the very question at issue that of
the ultimate goodness or badness of things?   What,
pray, is a philosopher?   Is he not a man appointed
to solve the question whether this world is God's
or the devil's or nobody's?   Does not his business
spring from doubt as to the answer?   How, then, is it
possible without self-stultification to treat the question
as answered in advance?

By asking these questions in the full earnestness of
our souls we bring ourselves into the presence of the
ne plus ultra of thought.   *We discover that the very
process of seeking an ultimate world-formula involves that
which cannot be explained by us, but must be left, like
Spinoza's Substance, to explain itself.*   Every theory
which fails to recognise this is self-defeating.

Pessimism is such a theory.   The opinion may indeed
be hazarded that there has never lived a man who
regarded the ultimate badness of the world as a conceivable truth.   No world can be ultimately bad so
long as it contains a single being who is capable of
knowing how bad it is.   The presence of one mind in
the Universe which is capable of condemning it, of one
being who is able to say " This is not good," or " It
might have been better," relieves that Universe from
all risk of being ultimately consigned to the black-lists
of thought.   For a thing can only be condemned as
bad when measured by some standard of good.   And
where, except in the Universe itself, do you find that

standard of good which authorises you to condemn the Universe as bad ?

One consolation there is which may be received forthwith. If the world is thoroughly bad, it will be impossible for any of us to find it out. No world could keep up its reputation for badness in face of the fact that it has produced out of its own loins beings who know of something better than itself. Pessimists seem to have a very feeble idea of what kind of a thing the worst of all possible worlds would be. Surely a bad world would understand its own business better than to suffer the pessimists to publish its secrets and arm mankind against itself! Or, if we assume with Mr Huxley that Nature is engaged in an offensive warfare against the moral ideals, must we not conclude that Nature blundered most egregiously and showed herself incompetent to conduct war either against moral ideals or anything else when she produced Mr Huxley, armed him with a knowledge of her plans, and provided him with the means of spreading them broadcast over the world ? A thoroughly bad world would assuredly have the sense to keep its own secret. A pickpocket or a burglar who himself sends for a policeman to witness his crime is not a very dangerous sort of person. This is precisely what Nature did when she sent Mr Huxley to give the Romanes lecture; what the Universe does when the pessimist finds it out. The pessimist is the policeman whom the guilty Universe has produced out of its own loins for the express purpose of witnessing its own crimes, apprehending the criminal, and saving the public from his depredations.

It would be admitted that if you want to be thoroughly and successfully bad you must put intelligence into the business. Above all things, you must not let people know how bad you are. You must deceive them. If you go the length of advertising your own badness, as Nature does through the voice of the pessimist, the inference is that you are not really bad, but only playful. To be seriously bad, to play the game with success, is on these terms impossible. When once you have labelled yourself a villain you can do no more villainy, except the people on whom you practise are more incredibly stupid than you are yourself. We can attach no importance to the badness of a world which allows its secrets to leak out. As to its being the worst of all possible worlds, the thing is ridiculous. A bad world which had the sense to keep its own counsel would be infinitely worse than this one.

Let us assume that the opposite of Huxley's doctrine is true, namely, that Nature takes a friendly interest in the moral ideals of man and is anxious to help him in fulfilling them. How would she set about it? What would she do by way of helping him? Well, she would be perfectly candid about herself and her own failings. She would show him all the weak spots in her own arrangements. She would make him see how badly things would turn out were the human contribution withheld. She would confess that her brute forces and her laws of evolution and her struggles for existence are incompetent to improve the world—nay, are certain to disimprove it if left to themselves. By thus making a clean breast of it she would, in fact, tell the story which every pessimist tells on her behalf. But does this prove her bad? On the contrary, it proves that she is taking the only course she can take in order

13

to help the beings who have to set things straight. What if the story as she tells it is full of horror? The more Nature dwells on her own horror and ugliness, the more pessimists she produces to underline her failures and waste and cruelty, the more certain she is to provoke those reactions of the will that turn her failures into success and her ugliness into a garment of praise. By thus helping us to *know* the worst she is helping us to *do* the best. In responding to our demand for information about her character—and science is nothing but such a response—Nature seems to be acting on a principle which is the reverse of that which the pessimists have assigned her. Instead of making war on our ideal, she is providing us with the means we need for applying those ideals to facts. If her intention were to thwart us, what worse thing could she do for herself than she does when she answers our inquiries into her policy? All human inquiry assumes that the Universe is willing to tell. That is what no bad Universe would ever do.

I repeat, then, that our expectation of an answer to inquiries implies an ultimate but quite unprovable confidence in the nature of that concerning which we inquire. We should not ask the question unless we were pretty sure that the answer would pay. Pessimism is thus a crowning instance of a theory that defeats itself. Pessimists and optimists alike, when once they have chosen to treat the Universe as a Problem-to-be-solved, must play the game up to the last move.

IX.—IS THERE A SCIENCE OF MAN?

"Le dernier mot de la verité restera toujours à dire."—M. Loisy

If there is a Science of Man its terminology must be fluid. Unlike the other sciences to which fixity of meaning is essential,[1] the Science of Man must provide for an endless transformation in the meaning of its terms. They must be like water which takes the form of any cup into which it is poured. And the form of the cup must be undefined. We may go further and say that the laws of this science must be, not merely laws of life, but living laws. They must be formulæ which retain their identity while changing their form. If, for example, we lay down the Love of one's Neighbour as a law of life, it must be with the reservation that the beings to whom it refers are not tied to any fixed meaning either of "Neighbour" or of "Love." The question, "Who is my neighbour?" is continually answered and yet remains open; so does the question, "What is love?" There are perhaps no two individuals in the world, there are certainly no two epochs in history, for whom the meaning of these terms either are, or ought to be, the same. We may say

[1] Scientific terms are "fixed" by the purpose of science which abstracts them from their context. Restored to their full context they become as "fluid" as any others. See the essay on "The Usurpations of Language."

of all such principles that they gather meaning in their application.   Their meaning cannot be defined in advance of the performance to which they refer; we must wait upon events to say what they mean.

Whether or no a Science of Man, constructed in fluid or in living terms, is possible, it is certain that we cannot make the same use of it that we make of the other sciences.   We cannot use it to predict or control the behaviour of men, as we use the others to predict or control the behaviour of the bodies or forces to which they refer.   To those who believe that the value of science lies in its uses this difference is very important. Indeed, its importance is so great that confusion and disaster seem likely to result from giving the name of Science to something which differs so fundamentally from those other bodies of doctrine to which the name is generally applied.   Since the other sciences carry the fixity of their terms into all their applications, and are indeed useless on any other assumption, it is certain that men in general will assume a like fixity in the proffered Science of Man; the fluidity of its meanings will be overlooked; expectations will arise which can never be fulfilled, and efforts will be made which are bound to come to grief.   Misled by the term Science, men will try to make the same use of this doctrine as they make of the others to which it is commonly applied, and in so doing they will wrong both their neighbours and themselves, and they will encounter a great disillusion.   From the confusion that follows this double usage it seems to us that great harm accrues, especially to Morality and Religion.

Such, in brief, is the contention of the two following essays.

It is perhaps a truism that Theistic religion can exist only among men who are conscious of a vital *need* for God. "I cannot live without Him" are words which express with essential accuracy the attitude of the believer's mind. If men should come to feel that they can live, that they can "get on," as we say, as well without God as with Him—if, that is, God should ever seem to be irrelevant to the essential issues of life, a superfluity, a luxury, or even a bare hypothesis —Theism would certainly die. God is either a vital necessity or no-*God*.

To feel God as a vital necessity is to feel that God does something for His creatures which it is essential should be done, and which, if undone, leaves one's life maimed, incomplete, and unsatisfying. Theism gains nothing, or very little, by a conception of God which completes and satisfies our speculative *thought*, unless we can show that in so doing He completes and satisfies our life as a whole. To show this, one would have to exhibit some kind of equation between thought and life; and it must be confessed that important tendencies of modern philosophy are averse to this. One of the most significant movements of contemporary thought is a protest against the attempt to make the conception of God do duty for God himself. The protest is that God, even if secured as a logical necessity, would fall far short of being that *vital* necessity which Religion ever finds Him to be. The word "necessity," like the word "reason," is multi-dimensional and points in all directions towards satisfactions which no conception and no system of such can ever yield. There is, indeed, no room in the world for God, until He is seen to answer the human need in all the fulness of its implications, and not alone in that restricted form which is adequately met by a logical system.

When Laplace described God as a needless hypothesis, he meant, of course, that He is needless for the purpose of human logic—that the business of science can be carried out without requiring at any point a reference to the conception of God. This may or may not be true ; but even if true it is not necessarily fatal to Theism. If it can be shown that man has vital needs, other than the needs of logic, to which God and God alone is the answer, then we should always be able to plead that Humanity cannot *live* without God ; and Theism would be safe. But if this cannot be shown, if we can point to no vital needs to which God is the only answer, or if such vital needs as man has are adequately met by something which is not God, then indeed the disappearance of God from the list of our *logical* requirements, the statement that He is a needless *hypothesis*, would be the removal of the last straw to which our drowning faith could cling.

At this point we encounter the full force of the antitheistic tendencies of our time. Their force lies not, of course, in any demonstrated disproof of God's existence, but in the claim that the vital needs of man are better met and more fully satisfied by something else. This something else is the Science of Man. If all that is hoped and all that is claimed for the Science of Man, as commonly understood, should ever be made good, we should be forced to admit that there is nothing that God can do for man which man cannot do as well, or better, for himself. God would now become needless, not merely in the sense that logic no longer requires Him, but in the far more serious sense that we can

live, and get all the good that life has to offer, by
attending to the teachings of science. All that has
been expected of God could now be provided for by
the Science of Man. We have only to suppose that
men are fully possessed of the strategy of Nature and
the fixed laws which govern their own lives, and it is
obvious that their destinies would be in their own
hands, assuming, of course, that they still retain the
power of independent action. In such a world, God,
even if we suppose Him to exist, would have no function: His occupation, so far as this consists in exercising
beneficent influence over human life, would be gone.

We have only to ask further *what precisely* God could
do for a being who was thoroughly master of the science
of his own life, to satisfy ourselves that He could do
nothing. Could He, for example, make us happier or
better than we should be without His assistance? To
say that He could is to say that there is some outstanding area of our life which we do not understand, and
which, therefore, must be left to the management of
Him who does understand it. The existence of such
an area, however, beyond our knowledge and our power
of choice, is incompatible with our possession of a
science of life. Were such a science ours, there would
be none of these outstanding areas, none of these deeper
interests, stretching beyond and beneath the limits of
our knowledge and therefore of our will. Just as a
person perfectly acquainted with the science of bodily
health would never need to commit his health to the
care of a doctor, except, perhaps, as a matter of etiquette or convention, so a being or race of beings
which had mastered the law of its own interests and
been equipped by science with a complete set of clues

to the path of its betterment, both moral and material, would obviously be able to attain every one of its desired ends without any appeal to the assistance of God.

If, for example, Ethical Science should really succeed in teaching us the whole secret of becoming better men, what need would any of us feel to ask God to help him in the process? To suppose the assistance of God necessary is to suppose our ethical science incomplete and fragmentary, and every step we take towards making it complete brings us nearer to the point at which, if I may so say, we shall be able to dispense with the appeal to God. So long as we are asking Him to give us clean hearts, or to show us the path of life, we are confessing that the Science of Man doesn't yet exist; for if it did we should know how to cleanse our own hearts, and the path of life would be sufficiently shown by text-books appropriate to the subject. With the full-blown Science of Man at our elbow, we should know how to master all the passions which menace our interests, we should know how to avoid the ways of destruction and death, we should know exactly what steps to take in order that our best possibilities may be realised and our happiness fulfilled. To admit that there is any one essential good which our science can never teach us to procure, and for the attainment of which we must look to the help of God, is to strike the ground from under the claims of the Science of Man. Even to hope for such a science is to hope for a time when the human race will be able to do without God. He will then become, in a far more serious sense than Laplace intended, a needless hypothesis. For he will cease to be the Helper of men.

The result is, of course, precisely the same, if the

formulæ of the Science of Man are held to cover the
action of the human will.   Everything, our own action
as well as God's, is now provided for by the fixed plan
of the universe; nothing further, or other, can be done
either by God or man, and there is nothing for it but
to wait upon events in a wise passiveness.   By extend-
ing the realm of necessity so as to include within it the
action of the conscious will, we pass by a single step
from a state of mastery over life into a state of helplessness.   And it is well to remember that in a universe
whose ultimate structure must be always "taken as
read," God—if we can now attach any meaning to that
term—would be as helpless as we are.   We could only
think of Him as the cosmic steersman, paralysed at the
wheel of the universe, and therefore, so far as we are
concerned, a wholly negligible entity.   How close
together, in the human mind, are the two thoughts of
mastery and helplessness, how rapidly each passes into
the other, may be seen in the writings of Mr Herbert
Spencer, who alternately raises our hopes by pictures
of what Science will enable us to do, and then dashes
them to the ground by exhibiting some world-formula
in the grip of which we are powerless to do anything.
More will be said of this hereafter.   For the present
we have merely to note that God is equally superfluous
on either supposition.

Nor is all this a picture of what might conceivably
happen under conditions that are never likely to be
realised.   There is at least one great system of thought
which illustrates how men who think themselves
possessed of the innermost laws of conscious life are
immediately led to dispense with God.   The initiate
of a certain form of Buddhism claims to possess

under the Law of Karma a complete Science of Man.
You have only to acquire the knowledge of Karma
and your destiny at once passes into your own hands.
Nothing can be done for you better than that which
you can now do for yourself. And all you can do
for yourself is to attain the Gnosis of what *is being
done* under the unalterable laws of the universe.
Whether the salvation thus obtained deserves its
name may be a matter of dispute; but the science
or Gnosis of which you are now master entitles
you to say it is the best attainable. Naturally and
logically the appeal to God is superfluous; accordingly,
for this kind of Buddhism, God does not exist. And
any kind of mystical initiation which equips the
believer with the knowledge he requires for the
complete management of his own life, whether by
way of action or submission, involves the same result.
It was characteristic of some of the ancient Mysteries,
for example, that those who had passed through them
were wont thenceforth to treat the gods as con-
ventions. And though it may seem a far cry from
these Mysteries to modern science, yet a little reflection will serve to show a striking resemblance
between the two, in that both claim to equip man
with the kind of knowledge which enables him not
only to dispense with the gods, but even to defy
them, should any gods happen to exist. We are only
prevented from seeing this by our habit of holding
apart two thoughts whose significance depends on our
taking them together. The first is the thought of the
universe as having a fixed strategy in regard to man;
the second is the thought of science as informing man
of the strategy he has to face. Hold these apart and

their significance escapes you. Put them together—
think, that is, of man as fully acquainted with the
strategy of the universe in regard to himself—and it is
immediately apparent that God is no more master of
the situation than man is. Man, therefore, can dispense
with God.

For these reasons it is a matter of supreme importance to inquire whether the Science of Man is possible.
We must, of course, take the terms in their strict
meaning. And we shall not be doing this if we allow
any body of knowledge which has even a remote
bearing on human interests to masquerade as the
Science of Man. We must think of man throughout
as a self-conscious being, as a living will, and ask
whether the interests of such a being are amenable to
scientific definition, and whether the activities of his will
in the pursuit of those interests can be brought under
formulated laws. Nothing short of this is entitled to
rank as the Science of *Man*.

That the intellectual temper of our time encourages
the belief in the possibility of a Science of Man and the
hope of its realisation in the future admits of little
doubt. A state of the world when the system of
natural laws shall be thoroughly understood and when
all human action shall be in accordance with this
knowledge is the far-off divine event to which vast
numbers of persons are vaguely looking forward.

This millennium of science has been often described.
Physiology and its cognates will enable us to control
our bodies; we shall eat by science, dress, warm and
house ourselves by science. Psychology will have
given us command of our minds; we shall know

how our intellects, our emotions, our wills, act under given conditions, and we shall prepare them for acting accordingly; education will be thoroughly scientific; we shall teach nothing but what the laws of the mind allow the young to assimilate, and to assimilate in the most favourable manner. Society, too, will be sociologically enlightened; statesmen will know the laws under which communities develop, flourish, and decay; and legislation thus informed will avoid mistakes. This is the kind of prophecy in which our age likes to indulge, and it seems to rest upon a general assumption that there is some final body of knowledge concerning man, some fixed system of laws as yet partially known but destined hereafter to be thoroughly known, and that the end will have been attained when this system in all its fulness is discovered, accepted, and obeyed.

In many of its details this dream will probably come true. But were it to come true in all it would cover but a fragment of the future of the race. The vital interests of humanity lie outside the scope of the picture; what it tells is small compared with what is left untold. In thinking otherwise we are the victims of a false analogy which has its source in the one-sidedness of our scientific enthusiasms. Physical science rightly assumes that if we can discover the rule under which things are behaving themselves and have behaved themselves up to date, we have in that rule a statement of their behaviour under like conditions for all time to come. The law of gravitation is not going to change. Knowing that bodies attract each other in such and such a way, we may confidently base our dealings with those bodies on the assumption that they will always so behave. We can *manage* them on that assumption, and there is no risk that our management will ever miscarry through the body taking upon itself to modify the law of its own action.   And no one needs to be told of the vast extent to which our power of management has already grown, and of the incredible profit we have won thereby.

But if we have gained so much by the management of mere physical masses, what should we not gain if, in like manner, we could learn to manage ourselves and our fellow-men ?   Imagine a statesman legislating for an empire under the guidance of a formula which defined with mathematical exactitude the relation between national wealth and national well-being.   What immeasurable powers for good that statesman would possess !   Imagine a wise man in any station of life adjusting his relations to other men by scientific rules whose results were as certain as the results of burning so much fuel under the boiler of a steamship or applying so much force to the end of a lever.   Surely it only needs that we should learn to handle men as we handle the forces of Nature, and we should become masters of our human destiny to a degree which would lift us to the level of gods.   And what is to prevent us from learning this ?   Are we not agreed that the reign of law is universal ; that what happens to our bodies, that what goes on in our minds, is as surely law-abiding as the union of two elements or the fall of a stone ?   And what save present ignorance deprives us of the enormous power we should possess if we knew the laws of human life as we know the laws of elements and of stones ?

This is the analogy which misleads our imagination. When we say, for example, that teachers in elementary

schools must be trained in psychology, the assumption
too often is that psychology has something to say which
will enable these teachers to control the minds of the
taught in the same sense that a knowledge of physics
enables an engineer to control the speed of his engines
or the resisting power of his bridge.   When we say that
politicians ought to be sociologists, do we not mean
that there are fixed laws in human nature and in history
with which the legislation of the State must be made to
harmonise?   Nay, when we say of ourselves, or of life
in general, that right conduct is obedience to discover-
able principles, are we not conceiving of these principles
as existing things, laid down and unalterably formulated
in the very constitution of the world?   Behind all this,
is there not the notion that life is an object to be
handled by rule just as you would handle a spade or a
gun; that man is a being to be managed by the book
just as you manage electricity or fire?   Are we not
thinking of masses to be moved, of bodies which yield
to pressure and follow the direction of the strongest
force; of materials to be arranged in certain patterns
and to remain in the positions that have been assigned
to them?   Do we not, I say, introduce into our
proposals for dealing with life that notion of an equation between cause and effect which governs our
management of things and powers in the physical
world?   You want your engine to do more work: you
put more steam into the boiler.   You want the community to be more honest: you put so much energy
into the teaching of honesty in elementary schools.
You want the drawing-room to be more commodious;
you rearrange the furniture.   Well—you want Society
to stand on a more equitable basis, and you readjust

the relations between man and man.   For is there not
a pattern of the perfect State?

In all these things we are apt to be ruled by one
set of ideas, to be guided by one set of principles.   But
may it not be that we are here classing together things
so fundamentally different that the rules which give
us success in the one case may ensure our failure in
the other?   We would reform society, but what if
society, unlike our drawing-rooms, is precisely of such
a nature as to be impatient of any form we may impose
upon it?   We would construct a formula for the
government of life, but what if the essential principle
of life is insusceptible of formulation?   We would
manage men, but what if man is by nature a rebel
against all external management?   We would handle
him as we handle matter; but what if matter, by
growing into man, grew out of the form in which it
could be handled at all?   What if, as M. Bergson says,
the intellect, so adroit in dealing with what is inert,
is the clumsiest of instruments for dealing with what is
alive?

It is one of the most singular and yet most familiar
facts of life, that when you inform a man of the law of
his action, you make it possible and indeed probable
that he will henceforth act on a different law from that
which you have laid down.   You tell me, for example,
that the law of my character is so-and-so; that my
past behaviour reveals a principle at work in virtue of
which I fail to keep my promise three times out of a
hundred.   Confronted by this piece of information
I am clearly in a position different from that which I
occupied prior to your discovery.   So long as I knew
nothing of the law that was at work within me, I con-

tinued to break my engagement three times out of a hundred, thereby yielding confirmation of your accuracy. But now that I *know*, the situation is completely altered. I do not like this law; and because I do not like it I mean to break it. Henceforth I keep the three engagements I used to miss; and what now becomes of the law? I shall cause no trouble to science so long as you are content with the abstract statement that my action, or my character, is law-abiding. But make your statement concrete, give me the precise formula of my character, tell me the specific law of my action, and I will at once put science to confusion by adopting another formula and by acting under another law. So, then, if you desire to maintain the scientific accuracy of your account of my character, if you would point to my actions as confirming the specific laws under which you say it goes on, one thing is essential—you must rigorously conceal all this from my knowledge. In my ignorance I shall continue to play the part of an example illustrating the conclusions of your science. But once reveal these conclusions to me, and I shall at once assert my right to upset them all. The very knowledge that I am acting under such and such a principle is precisely what enables me to act under another principle, perhaps undreamed of in your philosophy.

To bring out this point more clearly, let us suppose that these inert masses whose behaviour is so amenable to intelligence were in the same condition as ourselves— let us suppose, I mean, that they were endowed with reasonable souls, that like ourselves they could hear when science speaks, could understand the laws of their own behaviour when science announces them, and were

able to respond to these announcements, to criticise
them, to pass judgment upon them, and while remaining
like ourselves essentially law-governed things, were yet
capable as we are of choosing the law under which they
would act, of changing the principle of their past conduct if they did not like it, and substituting another
principle at will. Is it not obvious that science would
immediately come to a standstill, and that prediction
would be impossible? If we imagine the planets listen-
ing to Kepler as he announces the law of their elliptical
orbits, and forthwith calling a meeting to consider the
situation and passing a resolution to the effect that
ellipses were highly inconvenient or inartistic figures,
that the rate of revolution was far too high for safety,
that the position of Jupiter was too near the sun for
economical efficiency, that there was gross inequality
in the distributions of solar heat, that Saturn's endow-
ment with rings was a flagrant example of the unearned
increment—that, in short, all these things must be
reformed—if, I say, we imagine such resolutions taken
and that power existed to give them effect, is it not
obvious that no science of planetary behaviour would be
even conceivable? Yet is not this the situation which
science has to face in human affairs? Let science, for
example, formulate the law of the distribution of wealth.
Would not the mere announcement of this law jeopardise
its continuance as the working principle of industrial
society? "It is true," Society would say, "that this is
how wealth has got itself distributed up to date; but
knowing this we are in a position to set on foot a new
method of distribution. No doubt industrial civilisation
as it has so far developed is well explained by the
principle announced, but anyone who assumes that the

14

next phase will be explained in the same manner is reckoning without his host. It is irrelevant to say that things always follow in a certain order; that a state of society like the present has existed in past ages and has always been followed by such and such another state, and that therefore this other state will recur as soon as the present has passed away. It is irrelevant, because the fixed order of which you speak was maintained in times when men were not only ignorant that it was fixed, but didn't dream that there was any order at all. Thus nobody interfered; the cycle went on repeating itself; the human lives affected being like so many inert masses following the path of their destiny as the planets follow their orbits. But now that these human lives have become through your discoveries aware of the true state of the case, they are going to stand it no longer. That B has followed A in human affairs a thousand times may be a fact; but it has only to be stated and made known to those who previously knew it not, and at once the resolution is taken that it shall never occur again without consent."

Thus it is that the discovery of tendencies in human society, no matter how long they have been in existence; the announcement of sequences in history, no matter how often repeated; the formulation of evolutionary principles, no matter how comprehensive their sweep,—all this fixes nothing, renders nothing inevitable, affords no certain clue to what is coming next, imposes no destiny on man, but leaves his future uncharted and free. Knowledge of the past, when offered to a self-conscious being, is indeed a challenge to construct the future on *different* lines; it can never yield the formula which the future is bound to fulfil. It is a vain thing, therefore, to base predictions of what is coming on the knowledge of what has come. Nay, the prophet who makes the attempt imperils his result by announcing it. Who, for instance, can study the social prophecies of Mr Herbert Spencer without perceiving that the one condition on which everything depends is precisely the condition which lies outside the formula of social evolution ? What if the picture he offers of the future interplay of Altruism and Egoism prove so little attractive that men begin to conspire and say to one another, " Go to, now, let us put a spoke in this evolutionary wheel and prevent the grinding out of these melancholy results " ?

Perhaps we shall be told that this is beyond our powers ; that we cannot help ourselves ; that the fixed strategy of Nature must have its way with us, conspire against it as we will. But this surely is not to give us that control of our destiny which science has promised. The promise was, that as science applied to Nature has enabled us to bind inanimate forces to our will, to leash the lightning and to harness the storm, so science applied to Man shall make us masters of the currents of history and teach us to build at pleasure the future of mankind. But now, in the last resort, you turn upon us with some formula of evolution and tell us that the future rests with this ; this, you say, is the process of your life, this is the wheel on which humanity is hung, and if you resist its turning it will grind you to powder. Towed through Time in the wake óf evolution, held fast in the grip of some final formula which he can neither guide nor alter nor suspend, man is no more master of his life than if he lay at the mercy of any brute force you please. The process from undifferentiated homogeneity to differentiated heterogeneity, for instance, has no blessedness in it save what it owes to the length of the words; and I cannot see that a race whose ultimate destinies are dependent on such a process is any better off than if it lay at the mercy of wild forces or wild beasts with less portentous names. Think of the human race as a unitary being carried on the back of the evolutionary process as described by Spencer or any other of its devotees; then think of a man clinging to a log in the current of a mighty river which is sweeping him onwards towards the sea, and ask what, in principle, is the difference between the lot of that race and the lot of that man. Is it not just as idle to talk of control in the one case as in the other? No doubt the man on the log enjoys a certain liberty. He can paddle his feet in the water and find out by observation and experiment which side of the log is most convenient for the purpose. He can wriggle his body into various attitudes, of which some are more comfortable than others. He can cry his woes to the silent stars or he can hold his peace. And to what, save to judicious wrigglings such as these, does the scientific control of life amount, when you set mankind drifting on the current of the world process? Nay, if the logic is thorough, you will have to admit that the very wrigglings fall over into the fixed order of your evolutionary formula, and that the victim can only wriggle as he must.

What, then, becomes of the promised power over his fate which the growth of scientific knowledge was to lodge in the hands of man? Surely when Science comes before us with these vast and comprehensive formulæ she must do one of two things: she must

either exhibit those formulæ as sealing the doom and
confirming the ultimate helplessness of humanity, and
thereby wreck for ever that dream of control with
which she started on her quest; or else she must
concede to man some power of successful conspiracy
against any strategy of Nature which she is able to
define.

All philosophies are equally depressing which end
by representing Man as tied to a system which he
must perforce accept. In this respect I can recognise
no difference among the various systems that are
offered. A world whose final secret was discovered
and formulated, whether in the language of British
science or German metaphysics, would be a world
robbed of living interest for the human will ; conscious
life, subject in the last resort to a rule from which there
was no escape, would be covered by the categories which
govern the falling of stones and the drifting of logs.
What difference does it make whether the system drifts
us into heaven or into hell ? If to heaven, let the
system do its own business and get us there in its own
time. We shall arrive no sooner by making a fuss.
If to hell, again let the system take its own time ;
we can't postpone the inevitable. In neither case is
any higher wisdom than that of sitting still and letting
ourselves drift. Nor is it the doom under a bad system
rather than under a good one that is terrible ; it is
the being doomed at all. To have heaven *forced* on
us would, from the human point of view, be indis-
tinguishable from a sentence of universal perdition.

The question of an ultimate Science of Man is identical
in principle with a problem which each of us has con-

stantly to solve in his daily life. In principle there is no difference between the position of an individual man considering what he is going to do next in the light of what he did last, and a whole race of men fashioning their future upon scientific knowledge of their past. Suppose, then, that walking yesterday on dangerous ground I fell unawares into a pit. Having to take the same walk to-day, I now ask myself, Shall I fall into the pit again? What we have first to note is, that if I do fall the second time, that second fall will be no mere repetition of the first. It will not be the same thing over again. To fall into a pit of whose existence you never dreamed is one thing; to fall into a pit whose position you know and into which you remember falling yesterday, is another and perhaps a much more serious affair. One couldn't do it again even if he tried. For if to-day you fell into the pit by trying to fall, you would by no means repeat what you did when yesterday you fell into it unawares. It would be an altogether different experience. Knowing that you have fallen once, no ingenuity on your part will avail to make the second fall an exact reproduction of the first. The nearest approach would be to forget what had already happened, according to the principle that the only history which can be repeated is the history that is forgotten. But even so you would only approach duplication; you would not attain it. The mere circumstance that the first fall occurred on Monday and the next on Tuesday will make all the difference between the two, to say nothing of the fact that the second set of bruises comes on the top of the first.

A being who remembers his past can never repeat the same action twice over; and what is humanity confronted with History except a being who remembers his past ? This consideration alone suffices to break down the analogy between the Science of Nature and the proffered Science of Man ; and at the same time stamps as unpractical the entire view of human life, and the entire method of dealing with human life, which have been founded on that analogy.

We have heard it proclaimed as a law of history, for example, that periods of democratic upheaval are invariably followed by periods of tyrannous autocracy ; we have been reminded of the Greek States and the Roman Empire, and of the rise of Napoleon after the French Revolution. Instructed by these instances there are people to-day who tell us, with some shaking of the head, that tyranny is the certain sequel to the democratic movement in the modern world. And there is no denying that if the modern world forgets this history, then history may repeat itself after a fashion ; but only after a fashion, for the tyrant who rules the modern world will have to be a different kind of person from the tyrant of old, or even from Napoleon. But is the world going to forget its history ? And if not, can we treat the situation as exactly what it was when there was no history to remember ?

The same reflections should serve as a warning to all those hardy spirits, and they are not a few, who think they can foresee what is going to happen to religion. Religion affords the most signal proof of the rule that history never repeats itself ; and yet religion is the theme which tempts more prediction than almost anything else. Thus we have recently had from the distinguished ex-President of an American University a singularly striking picture of the Religion

of the Future; and the religious journals of the day
provide their readers with much startling information
on the same subject.

But when the temptation comes over us to announce
that a particular type of religion is on the way, ought
we not to remember that while we and our friends may
regard the coming of this type as good and desirable,
there are other persons, perhaps more powerful than
we, to whom it will appear undesirable and bad ?   And
is it irrelevant to point out that these others, if they
take our prediction seriously (as the Pope and his
followers often appear to do), will accept it as a timely
warning and stir up their energies to the uttermost to
thwart the expected arrival ?   No doubt the prophets
will tell us that the predicted religion will come whether
or no ; that it has Power behind it greater than that of
the Pope ; and that if he or anybody else try to arrest
its arrival he will fail and run upon his own destruction
into the bargain.   But is not this a two-edged argument ?   Might not the Pope reply that a coming religion
which is immune from the hindrance of the one party
cannot be dependent on the help of the other ; and that
conversely, if it needs the support of the Liberals it may
be destroyed by the hostility of the Conservatives ?
The only alternative to this is for both parties to
regard the Religion of the Future as being forced on
the world *ab extra* and bound to come all the same
whatever the Pope may do to hinder or the Liberals to
help.   But then it is gravely open to doubt if a religion
thus forced on by the course of evolution, or by super-
natural agency, and bound to come whether or no,
would be one which anybody could regard as a good
religion.   A good religion is one which man attains, at

great peril and against mighty odds, by the travail of
his spirit and the faithfulness of his will; not one which
insists on coming whatever man may do or forbear.
The only safe assumption seems to be that unless all
parties, Conservatives as well as Liberals, exert themselves to the uttermost, the future may have no religion
at all. But *what* the religion of the future will be when
it comes is precisely what no man knoweth nor can
know.

Are we to conclude, then, that the intelligence is an
utterly useless faculty when applied to human affairs,
and that, no Science of Man being possible, ignorance
is as good as knowledge, the barbarian as wise as the
philosopher, and the Dark Ages as well off as any
other?

To this we reply that whether the intelligence is
useless or not depends on the purpose for which it is
used. It is useless if you ask it to reveal to you the
coming developments of the world or the future course
of your own life. It is useless if you ask it to do for
human affairs, or for your own life, what it does in
regard to Halley's comet, viz. provide you with a
chart of your own behaviour and tell you where you
or the world will be at a given date. It is useless
if you want a fixed pattern of the world's evolution, or a fixed code of human conduct, or a fixed
form which your own life is bound to assume. In
short, the intelligence is useless if you ask it to do in
the field of human life what it does with success in
the field of inanimate Nature. Whatever the intelligence fixes in this way, even though it be a scheme of
world-evolution like that proposed by Spencer, or the

form of the coming religion as foreseen by the American thinker, is liable to be instantly made fluid and undone when it comes into contact with the human will. There is no historical method of living; for life is not the repetition of a past but the endless creation of a future. The intelligence, therefore, is always too late for self-conscious life; for all it can do is to record and systematise what has been up to date, in order to provide the will with a point of departure, a *terminus a quo* from which to embark on some fresh venture of the spirit.

But what a service that is, if only we would take it aright! Historical science is the knowledge of how the world spent yesterday,—a yesterday which may have lasted a thousand years. And it is just that knowledge which puts humanity in position to spend to-day *otherwise*. The knowledge of his past is the raw material which man, the artist, weaves into fresh patterns hour by hour. Keep him ignorant and he has no material to work on and cannot live. Did he fall into the pit yesterday? Let the fact be recorded and to-day he may do something else, but *what* else no science can tell. Let the fact be forgotten, and he will fall into the pit again; he will not *live* as a self-conscious being at all, but simply roll and tumble about and go on repeating what the law of his rollings and tumblings requires, like any helpless stone. The future is always the free reconstruction of the past, not the imitation or there petition of it; and without knowledge of the past man has nothing to reconstruct, and the work of the spirit cannot go on. Such is the inestimable service of the historical method—the method of the intelligence. Where that method has overreached itself has been in supposing that the study of the past can teach us any one fixed and final principle, according to which man, whether he likes it or not, must submit the free creative genius of his spirit in its endless work of transforming and re-fashioning the raw material of his life. Even though it take the comprehensive form of Hegelian Dialectics, such a fixed and final principle instantly turns fluid when brought into contact with the living will ; the will rejects it in the final form and insists on re-creating it after a new fashion of its own. For this reason it is certain that the suffrages of humanity will always be given in the long-run to the cause of freedom ; not because necessity is illogical, but because it has no application to *Life*. The mistake made by many of the advocates of freedom is that they reduce it to a fixed formula : for example, the formula of choice between two alternatives. The free spirit overflows that formula, just as it overflows every other. A formulated freedom is nothing but necessity under a new name.

A teacher who would unify all knowledge into a hard and fast system of truth, a philosopher who invents a system into which all our experience *must* go, a moralist who constructs a mould for the human will—any one, in fact, be he scientific man or metaphysician—who shackles conscious life with formulæ, is a dogmatist, and is merely trying to do on other fields what the Pope of Rome does in his more restricted department. To escape from the bondage imposed by the formulæ of creeds and to accept in place the formulæ of Evolution or Psychology, Ethics or Metaphysics, is to exchange whips for scorpions. Indeed no form of spiritual tyranny is quite so obnoxious, so completely deadening and deadly, as that proposed by

a cut-and-dried Science of Man. It has not even the
merit of being picturesque. The tyrant whom we now
serve is no longer a being of flesh and blood, but a
spectral abstraction, cold and pale as a sheeted ghost.
It cannot produce so much as a mythology. And
that alone puts it under suspicion. For though
mythologies are not " true," yet nothing that is " true "
ever fails to produce a mythology.

What, now, is the bearing of all this on Religion?
Does the view that Life overflows all formulæ, breaks
through all theory, goes beyond all knowledge, render
the task of the religious teacher more hopeful or the
reverse?

Let us ask ourselves a parallel question. How would
the prospects of Art be affected if someone were to discover a fixed formula of Art, by the application of which
anyone could produce works of Art at will? What
would the artist say if some prophet were to promise
that in a future state of the world this formula would
be as familiar to every man as A, B, C; that in those
halcyon days there will be no more inartistic people,
no more incompetent artists, no more bad pictures in
the Academy? What if some æsthetic counterpart of
Mr Herbert Spencer should show the world, by means
of a synthetic principle, a picture of the millennium of
Art when all difficulties will have been overcome and
the pressure of a button will produce an Elgin Theseus
or a Sistine Madonna?

Would not every artist turn away from this folly,
and tell us that what we are describing is not the
millennium of Art but the total disappearance of Art
from the world; that whatever is produced by obedience

to rules imposed from without lacks everything that Art demands ; that Art lives in a free creativeness, which ever makes new rules for itself, and rejects every formula which defines its business, or shackles its free movement towards a freely chosen end ? Is not all this a commonplace ?

How much more ought it to be a commonplace in regard to religion ! It is as impossible to graft religion on to any cut-and-dried theory of life as it would be to produce Art from any cut-and-dried theory of painting and sculpture. Indeed one may go further and say—what every artist knows in his own sphere— that if any cut-and-dried theory of life were possible, religion would be impossible.

The greatest dangers to religion have arisen from blindness to this view of the case. Religious men have been too ready to take over one or other world-formula and attempt to give it a religious character by grafting on to it the idea of Personality. God, under these conditions, is neither more nor less than the Impersonation of the world-formula, the eternal Embodiment of the abstract Law of Life. This is probably the least attractive form in which religion has been presented to the mind of man. The personation of the world-formula is a mere piece of bad mythology, which the formula itself does not require and will not sustain. The statement so often made in works of religious metaphysics that God is eternally what He means to be and eternally means to be what He is, is not only infinitely perplexing on the face of it, but when understood is precisely the sort of thing one would wish were not true. Candidly regarded, it is merely an effort to disguise the unpleasant fact that the person here called God is nothing but the abstract world-formula endowed with a proper name. But the christening makes no difference.

When the science of life puts forth these claims we must remember that in everything that comes before us we have an interest which goes far beyond our interest in it as a mere object of knowledge. Everything loved, admired, valued by man is both a known and an unknown, and the value of the thing to him is never exhausted by what he knows about its nature, its origin, or the laws of its behaviour. We know something about the sunset; but what we know about it is not what we most admire, not what makes us glad that the sunset is there. Are we to ignore its beauty on the ground that we cannot translate this into terms of knowledge? We know something about the people we love; we could write chapters of their physiology; we could draw their portraits perhaps; but neither the physiology, nor the portrait, nor any number of such things gives the reason why we love them. Shall we limit our interest in these people to what we know about them? If we did we should surely cease to love them. Is it not true that the life that lures us on is a life whose issues we cannot forecast; and if we could forecast them would it lure us any more? The world whose presence we welcome, the universe in which we rejoice, is it the world as defined in *any* formula or reproduced in *any* system? Nay, rather, the Nature we love is the Nature that runs wild, and the life that we seek is one on which the shackles of no system have ever fallen. To bid us live exclusively on the basis of formulated knowledge is to ask a self-contradictory thing, for life, and love too, is just an out-going beyond the formulated into the ever-open hinterland of the spirit. There at all events there is room for religion. "La science a trait aux choses sans lesquelles l'homme ne peut pas vivre ; la religion à celles sans lesquelles il ne veut pas vivre." [1]

[1] M. Emile Boutroux—Introduction to the English translation of *Science et Religion.*

X.—THE MANIPULATION OF MAN

I

To the question, "Is a Science of Man possible?" we have offered a negative answer. In so answering we have had in view throughout the essential feature of human life, viz. the conscious will. Self-consciousness, which is another name for the conscious will, escapes from all formulæ, and overflows all definitions. Hence it is that science, which bridles facts with formulæ and circumscribes them with definitions, can never capture the essential fact of life; and a science of life on those terms is impossible. If we were at liberty to omit from our notion of Man this essential truth of his conscious will, no doubt we could construct human science of many varieties. And "human science" of that kind does exist; and not only exists, but grows apace and does its work. Individuals considered as objects in time and space provide the subject matter of Physiology and its cognates. Communities considered as organisms that grow upon the surface of the planet, or as masses that execute mechanical movements and impinge one upon another, give rise in their turn to the science of History and to Sociology. Then there is Psychology, both individual and social; a science of which we may say that the weight of its claims bears an inverse proportion to the solidity of

its foundations. For Psychology claims to be, pre-
eminently, the Science of Man — undeterred by the
existence of a grave doubt as to whether it is a science
at all.

Leaving self-consciousness, or the conscious will, out
of account, we may then construct an indefinite number of such "human" sciences, and we may combine
them all under the general name of Anthropology.
But when the conscious will is reintroduced it will be
seen that there is one human fact which our Anthropology does not cover, namely, the Anthropos himself.
Whatever belongs to our Anthropos as an object moved
by external forces will fall within the scope of the
science and be explained by its methods; but all that
belongs to him as a law and end unto himself, as a self-
conscious personality, will fall outside; and, what is far
more important, will take up a critical and, if hard
pressed, a defiant attitude towards that part which
falls inside the area of proof. Whenever a Science of
Man is propounded we see this strange spectacle: Man
standing opposite that scheme of his life which science
has drawn, stroking his chin, as it were, in an attitude
of contemplation, and deliberating with himself as to
whether he will or will not allow the picture to be
realised henceforth as a concrete fact. There is
nothing like this in the natural sciences. The inert
masses of Nature may be considered as submitting
without protest to whatever the human intellect pro-
pounds as holding true of them; they have, of course,
no power to protest or even to criticise. But no sooner
does "human" science issue its pronouncements than
Man, who is the subject-matter of its formulæ, raises
the question, " Shall we suffer these pronouncements to

15

continue in force ?   Shall we suffer the facts, the laws, the percentages to remain as they are ; or shall we take measures for introducing another set of facts, another set of laws, another set of percentages ? "   Thus a complete Anthropology, if we may imagine such a thing, would do no more than provide Man with a fresh point of departure.   Published to-day it would require re-writing to-morrow.

No doubt we shall be told that in all this we are confusing what philosophers have been pleased to distinguish as the *that* and the *what*.   It will be said that while the particular truths of Anthropology are always subject to the criticism of Reason, yet the *principles* of this criticism are eternal.   But those who use this argument ought in all fairness to make it good by telling us explicitly what the " eternal principles " are.   To say merely that there are eternal principles either evades the issue or begs the question.   What are they ?   That " duty must be done " ; that " the interests of the part are subject to the interests of the whole " ; that " there is an infinite difference between right and wrong."   These are all true beyond cavil ; they are indeed deliberately constructed in such a form that no reasonable being could deny them ; but what do they all amount to beyond a restatement of the fact that Man is a self-conscious being ?   " To be self-conscious " is only another way of saying that we have a duty to do ; that our life has meaning as " a whole " ; that the difference between the interests of life as a whole and the interest of any single moment is " infinite."   Unless Philosophy can get further than this and tell us precisely *what* our duty is, the mere proclamation of an abstract duty announces nothing that any self-conscious being could possibly overlook. As to the confusion of the *that* and the *what* we gladly admit the charge. But we do so on this ground—that self-conscious life is itself the confusing, or rather—for the change of term is important—the *fusing* of the *that* and the *what*. Any scheme of thought which separates the two becomes by that separation inapplicable to Man.

Of all the sciences it is perhaps Psychology which is most apt to provoke the critical attitude, with its attendant readjustment of the situation. Take, for example, the Psychology of Desire. Turning to an accredited authority, I find the law laid down that " all men desire happiness." Now, let us consider the result of accepting this proposition as true. Plainly, the discovery creates a new situation. Prior to its announcement we knew not what we were doing; from generation to generation the desire for happiness held us in its grip ; and the times of that ignorance God winked at. But no sooner has Psychology enlightened us than reflection and criticism begin. Admitting that we have always desired happiness up to date, and even now desire nothing else, we begin to ask ourselves whether this universal desire for happiness is not, after all, a foolish desire, and one we should do well to discard, or to vary, as soon as possible. For our part, we think we should, and we mean to try. Assuming that we succeed in this attempt (and only dogmatism can assume that we shall fail), the law that " all men desire happiness " will no longer hold good.

The same result may be evoked by the more ambitious statements of Social Psychology. " Crowds " are said to be actuated by such and such impulses ; and the statesman is informed that he may count on the uniform recurrence of this or that impulse under given conditions.   What is here overlooked is that the " crowd " as well as the statesman can read and think and make use of the information concerning its own behaviour thus provided by the Social Psychologist. Indeed, as things are in the world of to-day, it is probable that the " crowd " will be the first to profit by the Psychologist's discussion, thanks to which it may learn to discard the impulses under which it is said to " act," and replace them with others ; so that when it comes to business we may see—and indeed we often do see—the curious spectacle of the " crowd " handling the statesman instead of the statesman handling the " crowd."

For these reasons, which might be multiplied indefinitely, we conclude that a rigid Science of Man is possible only on condition that we artificially abstract from our conception of Man the circumstance that he is a self-conscious being, or the possessor of a conscious will.   But when this feature is abstracted we cannot persuade ourselves that what remains is worthy of the designation " Man," nor that the science which treats of such an eviscerated being can properly receive the qualification of " human."

We cannot conceal from ourselves, however, that in putting forward this negative answer we shall have to encounter a most formidable prejudice ; a prejudice deeply rooted in the soil of our intellectual history and nourished by the whole atmosphere of modern life. It may even appear to some persons that by denying human science we degrade the conception of Man. For it is almost an axiom of the modern world that things of which no science exists are things that are not worth considering; whence it would follow that in representing Man as insusceptible of scientific handling we make him contemptible, or, at all events, of no account.

And it must be confessed that from a certain point of view this objection is serious. We admit its fatality to an entire class of ambitious designs. It is certain that if we want to turn electricity to the best account we must have a science of electricity as the basis of our operations; that to make poultry pay we must handle them scientifically; that to get the best results out of an acre of wheat, or a stud of horses, or a herd of shorthorn bullocks, we must rely on science and call science to our aid at every turn. It is certain that the Germans will oust us out of the market if their commerce is scientific and ours is not; it is certain that our ships will sink if we build them on the assumption that there is no science of naval construction. Deny science in any one of these or such-like situations, and the result is that we shall neither make money nor win victories, nor attain any purpose we may have in hand. And the same holds good in regard to Man. If there is no Science of Man it is certain that we can make no use of him, or at all events very little. In plain words, we can't make him pay. A Science of Man we must have before we can bend him or compel him to serve any purpose of our own. Nor does the nature of that purpose make any difference. You cannot say, "Science comes in when Man is exploited for his harm, but not when exploited for his good." Without science you cannot exploit him at all. It makes no difference whether your object be to

harness him in chains to your waggons, or to transform him into a seraph. Nay, for transforming him into
a seraph science is even more necessary than it is for
harnessing him to a waggon. Suppose, for example, that
our purpose be to compel all men to develop as rapidly
as possible into the sort of being with whom Mr Spencer
peoples his millennium. Without a Science of Man we
cannot take even the first steps towards the accomplishment of that benevolent design. Or suppose we lay
our plans for guiding the race into Mr Bellamy's Utopia.
The Science of Man must be our starting-point. Once
take the position that men are to be put to uses of
our designing or desiring; that their destinies are to
be controlled by a purpose which emanates from our
avarice or from our benevolence; that we, and not
themselves, are the arbitrators of what is good for them;
that the end they exist to serve is of our assigning and
not their choosing—assume any of these things, and all
our well-meant schemes fall like card-houses before the
announcement, "There is no Science of Man."

The case may be presented in another form. Let us
imagine the human race divided by a hard-and-fast
line into two classes in any of the following ways:—
(1) Men and Employers-of-men; (2) Crowds and
Managers-of-crowds; (3) People-to-whom-good-is-done
and People-who-do-them-good; (4) Brothers and
Brothers'-keepers; (5) Governors and Governed; (6)
We and They.

It will be observed that the division is between
those who take the part of active agents and those
who submit to the arrangements which those agents
ordain—in a word, between those who operate and
those who are operated upon. Now, it is implied in

such a classification that the operators are equipped for their business by an appropriate Science of Man. In each case the position is that the active party are engaged in moulding a certain raw material, namely, the passive party, into a shape which rests with the moulders, and not with the moulded, to determine. And to attempt this without scientific knowledge of the raw material to be handled would be to invite failure, or, at all events, imperfect success. To *employ* men for a purpose which is yours and not theirs is as impossible under those conditions as it would be to employ steam, electricity, or petrol-gas in a like ignorance. To manage " crowds " or " masses " implies that the managers understand their material and can predict its response to various modes of treatment, in the same sense that the manager of a powder factory understands the behaviour of high explosives when struck with a hammer or brought into contact with a lighted match, or ignited by percussion in the barrel of a rifle or a great gun. To " keep " one's brother, again, involves a power of expert control greater than would be required to " keep " horses or poultry or bees or tame leopards or a whole menagerie of wild beasts ; so that it becomes impossible even to imagine how the enterprise of " keeping " men could go on for a single hour in the absence of a firm scientific foundation.

Now, it is a fact that we do draw the above hard-and-fast definitions, that we do habitually class mankind in some one, or perhaps in all, of these ways ; and there is not a doubt that the whole body of mental habits and instincts which prompts that classification, and the vast array of interests involved in maintaining it, will rise up with one consent to protest against the announcement that there is no Science of Man. The managers-of-crowds, the manipulators of the "masses," the section who do good, the professional keepers of their brethren, the employers-of-men, the governors of the governed,— all, in fact, who take the active part in the business of Man-handling, will feel that their interests, their occupations, nay, their whole view of life, are really bound up with that Science of Man whose existence is here denied.

How the other, the passive, party will greet the denial need not concern us. It need not concern us, because for all practical purposes the passive party does not exist. I mean that if a census were taken of the human race, the number of persons who would enrol themselves as belonging to the purely passive side of the division would be so small, and the number who would enrol themselves on the active side would be so overwhelmingly large, that the question of what the former may think of our problem would not even arise. Indeed, were a census of this kind to be taken we should be confronted with a far more serious difficulty than that of ascertaining what the "crowd," or any other passive party, thinks about the Science of Man. Our difficulty would be *to find the "crowd."* No doubt from our own point of view the "crowd" is easily found; for it consists of everybody save ourselves. But that is not the way the crowd has of regarding the matter. Were we to adopt the fairer plan of consulting everybody else, the "crowd" would melt away before our eyes more rapidly than if charged by a regiment of armed dragoons, and we should be left in the unfortunate position of having no "crowd" to study and no raw material to which the teachings of crowd-

science might be applied.   In the long-run, therefore,
we should find that the whole of mankind, saving only
a remnant of the lame, the halt, and the blind, would
enrol themselves on the side whose interests are menaced
by our denial of the Science of Man, and present an
overwhelming confederacy of opposition before which
our humble plea would scarcely have a chance of making
itself heard.

But there are still to be found in Israel some who
have not bowed their knees to the Baal of the abstract They.   To them it seems that any individual,
or group of individuals, who treats his fellow men as
raw material to be forced into the mould of his own
ideals, who tries to harness them to the yoke of his
own purpose, who would impose his will on them, as
though they had no wills of their own, who would
use them or "make them pay" in the interest of any
scheme which his greed or his benevolence has fathered,
is not only undertaking an inherently impossible task,
but is committing the unforgivable sin against the
Holy Ghost.   The spirit of Machiavelli or Lord Chester-
field reincarnated in the Professor of some "Human"
Science, has not changed its essential nature, and pre-
sents no greater attraction under the new form than
under the old.   And the Pontiffs of Evolution, who
pretend acquaintance with the fixed Strategy of the
Universe, and command mankind to serve this Strategy
or die, are not one whit more terrible, nor more likely
to be obeyed, than any Pope who threatens us with
destruction for refusing to believe in the Virgin Birth.
Against such attempts to put men, considered as a
mere "they," under bondage to what "we" think good
or true, there rises up an inexpugnable opposition from

the very principle of self-conscious life; and it is to this that we look for support in our denial that there is a Science of Man. We are confident that its disappearance will leave no sense of loss in any thoughtful mind which has learnt the lesson taught long ago, that Man is an end unto himself.

That Man is an instrument to be employed by Man; that he is a thing to be made use of, exploited, turned to account, reformed, developed, compelled to serve a purpose, by beings who call themselves "we"; that "we" can raise him as though he were a bullock; that "we" can improve him as though he were a cart-horse; that "we" can breed him on Mendelian or other principles as though he were a Cochin-China fowl; that "we" can dictate his habits as though he were a hedge to be trimmed or a torrent to be confined—this, we repeat, is our deep-seated illusion. Remembering the conscious will in ourselves and forgetting it in our neighbour, we forthwith provide for his needs on the assumption that what "we" think good for him is what he will think good for himself, that when "we" have proved his interest to be so-and-so, he will forthwith accept our demonstration and act accordingly. And we defend this attitude by saying that inasmuch as the demonstration is "scientific" our neighbour *must* agree with us or forfeit his claim to be a rational being. But all this begs the question by assuming that the "must-be's" of science which are incontestable when applied to inanimate forces are equally valid when offered to human wills. Our neighbour is not bound to accept our standards of rationality in judging of what is best for himself. Were "we" the possessors of some despotic power, which left him with no will

of his own, we might perhaps (if sure of ourselves)
enforce our science at every point, just as we should
if we were dealing with a flock of sheep. But short
of this we can make sure of nothing; and since "making sure" is the very business of science, it would
seem desirable to drop the term, which, when used in
this connection, is bound to raise delusive hopes. By
using this term we disguise from ourselves the contingent character of our knowledge, clothe it with
attributes of universal validity which it does not
possess, ascribe to it a wholly fictitious value as a
guide for practice, and end by discovering that we
have built our house on the sand of an abstraction.

The power of these unwarranted expectations is at
the present moment very great, and is answerable for
plentiful mischief. To the scientific obsession we may
attribute in large measure the enormously exaggerated
estimate of the value of Law as a means of securing
the well-being of Society, so characteristic of Western
civilisation. Instructive theories have been put forward
for "reconciling" the Individual and the Social Will;
but these should not be allowed to blind us to the
growing tendency to rely on Social Science for the
construction of a legal mechanism which shall do for
us what it is perfectly certain we can only do for
ourselves. This tendency is sapping the will-power of
men. Under the same influence a vast amount of bad
treatment is being meted out to humanity, in many
parts of the world, by the people who call themselves
"we." The scientific obsession is largely responsible
for the mishandling of the young, whether by artificial
systems of "moral" or other education; for gross
wrongs done to subject races; for the disrespect of

alien religions; for arrogance and narrowmindedness of many sorts; and above all, for an interminable process of social doctorings and dosings and meddlings which, in spite of some professional pomposity, is but half-informed, and therefore greatly to be feared. There is one thing more dangerous than total ignorance: it is the pretence of complete knowledge. That, we venture to think, is a standing peril of our time, and the justification of our present plea. We are constantly embarking upon enterprises of education, of reform, of international policy, in which we take account only of what is done, of what is given, of what is taught, and give no thought to the reaction of other wills on the action of our own, thereby disregarding the most important factor in the production of the final result. To spread knowledge on a given subject is one thing, and a good one; to assume that other men will make the same use of this knowledge that *we* make is another and a highly dangerous thing. *What* use they will make of it we have no science to predict and no power to enforce.

We may, for example, be of the opinion that the process of "falling in love" which now determines the mating of mankind, and thereby seals the fate of the next generation, is a kind of chartered madness — a thing which has won a licence from poets to mock at sound knowledge and play havoc with the stock-breeding of humanity. We may point out that the human race will have no control over its own future until men have found some more rational method of choosing their mates than that of falling in love with the first attractive face or elegant figure that may swim into their ken. We may even plead, with a recent writer, that the custom of " proposing marriage " should be abolished and that " parenthood " should be proposed instead ; and we may imagine the blessed results to posterity if young people were to arrange their love-making exclusively on this basis and marry only after a careful study of the type of children likely to issue from their union.

Here is a picture of a young man in love, unconsciously taking the first steps in a process whose ultimate issue, for all he knows, will be anæmic, tubercular, or criminal offspring—one more contribution to the degeneracy of the race:—

> " Und herrlich, in der Jugend Prangen,
> Wie ein Gebild aus Himmelshöhn,
> Mit züchtigen, verschämten Wangen
> Sieht er die Jungfrau vor sich stehn.
> Da fasst ein namenloses Sehnen
> Des Jünglings Herz, er irrt allein,
> Aus seinen Augen brechen Thränen,
> Er flieht der Brüder wilden Reihn.
> Erröthend folgt er ihren Spuren
> Und ist von ihrem Gruss beglückt,
> Das Schönste sucht er auf den Fluren,
> Womit er seine Liebe schmückt.
> O zarte Sehnsucht, süsses Hoffen !
> Der ersten Liebe goldne Zeit !
> Das Auge sieht den Himmel offen,
> Es schwelgt das Herz in Seligkeit ;
> O dass sie ewig grüne bliebe,
> Die Schöne Zeit der jungen Liebe ! " [1]

From the point of view of the Science of Man, can anything be more absurd or pitiful than this ? Suppose a Chancellor of the Exchequer approaching his annual Budget in the utterly disorganised condition of mind

[1] Schiller : *Das Lied von der Glocke.*

and body ascribed to this well-drawn type of the amorous youth, bursting into sentimental tears before the complications of the income tax, trembling in every vein at the apparition of his surplus, wildly rushing from the Cabinet and hiding himself in the cellar at the bare mention of an old age pension or a brewer's licence. What would become of the Finance of the Nation if psychological phenomena such as these were the normal accompaniment of each attempt to adjust taxation or control expenditure? And what are we to say in presence of the fact that these phenomena *are* the normal conditions in which an enterprise of infinitely greater moment than Finance is most frequently begun — I refer, of course, to the breeding of the race? What cruel trick is this that Nature has played us—that she seems to suspend our reason at the very moment when everything depends on rational thought; that just when we ought to be calmly considering the interests of human stock-breeding, she either blots the whole question out of our minds or makes us look upon it as a loathsome, abominable, unholy thing—establishing an unutterable repugnance between all such calculations and that " Gebild aus Himmelshöhn " before which we stand amazed and trembling, our veins on fire, our brain half paralysed, our eyes blinded with tears, our foolish tongues unable to stammer one poor word ?

In so arranging matters, Nature, we must conclude, is either the most cruel of stepmothers, or else she has some deep design which the Science of Man has not yet penetrated and with which it would be well-advised not to rashly interfere. Leaving that aside, however, I think we may accept it as obvious that in this one

matter alone we are dealing with a human situation so
vast, so many-sided, so complex, that no scientific solution, no group of scientific principles, is quite far-
reaching enough to cover it.   Such bits or aspects of
it as we may abstract from the whole and consider
apart, are a mere inconsiderable fragment of the total
issue, of which the roots are in Tophet and the branches
among the stars.   Nor can we tell what will happen,
what new and unsuspected reaction of the conscious
will may take place, when, having solved to our satisfaction some fragmentary aspect of the total problem,
we throw that solution back, as a bit of new leaven,
into the boiling ferment of mysterious forces that are
here at work.   A pleasing fancy, too long indulged,
bids us hope that the ebullition will cease the instant
that science is cast on the flood.   But experience
teaches that science, thus introduced, joins the turmoil
instead of calming it, or gives new vigour to the gods
who trouble the waters and raise the wind.   Certainly
it will be a long time before we can induce the
amorous youth of Schiller's poem, who is here the
type of a portentous human fact, to restrain his
tears and his blushes, to act like a rational being,
and calmly study Eugenics with his beloved.   Whether
by so doing our youth would or would not make a
greater mess of the business he has on hand than
he now makes—whether, I mean, the stock-breeding interests of humanity have much to gain by the
introduction of the scientific temper into their pre-
liminary stages—is a question on which nobody has
the right to dogmatise in advance.   It is, at all
events, a permissible hypothesis that Nature, whose
arrangements at this particular point are so eminently

unscientific, is not the blind and blundering fool of our
first impressions. Were we fully informed of all that
is here involved, we might be forced to admit, in face
of all our scientific prepossessions, that the interests of
the family, of the race, of the future, are far safer in
the hands of Schiller's love-stricken, emotion-blinded
youth than they would be if his place were taken by
some prize-stallion of a man carefully chosen, *ad hoc*,
by a committee of experts. Be that as it may, we may
easily assure ourselves that the situation before us will
not reduce itself to the dimensions of any scientific
problem whatsoever.

II

That the life of Man can be brought within the four
corners of formulated science is, however, but a local
variety of a much more comprehensive assumption.
This assumption in its general form is the notion, to
which frequent allusion has already been made, that
the Universe itself is essentially a problem-to-be-solved,
and that, *per contra*, the one supreme concern of man
is to discover the secret which gives the solution. Than
this notion I know of nothing more deeply rooted in
the soil of modern thought, more strongly intrenched
in current habits of mind, more widely characteristic of
different schools (even of those most opposed to each
other in other respects), more insistent, more baneful,
or more difficult to combat.

The most general classification one can make of
modern thinkers divides them into those who teach
that the problem of the Universe can be solved, and
those who teach that it cannot. Both are agreed in
the implication, at all events, that the Universe is

essentially enigmatical; that it addresses the human mind primarily and fundamentally in the form of an *interrogation*.   Both are agreed that our ultimate business with Reality is to *know* what it is or what it means, to answer its challenge by showing that we have found it out.   The same implication runs through the whole literature of doubt and scepticism on the one hand, and on the other it forms the basis of many religious books and of much preaching. Religion is supposed to stand or fall with our ability to produce a triumphant answer to the Riddle of the Universe.   Hence it is that those who maintain that the riddle cannot be solved will, as a rule, have little to do with religion, while those who support religion claim that the riddle is not only soluble but solved— whether by natural reason or revelation matters not. Remove those underlying assumptions, and the greater part both of Gnostic and Agnostic literature would be meaningless; affirm that Man has more important business with the world than the bare discovery of its secret, and the ground vanishes on which we are conducting the larger half of our disputes.   If the appeal which Reality makes to *knowledge* is one element only in its total appeal to the whole man; if interrogation as to its own nature is only one of an infinite number of forms in which the divine Logos speaks to the soul, then the whole controversy between Gnosticism and Agnosticism, between faith and doubt, as now carried on, will sink into a position of minor significance, and the way will perhaps be opened into new realms of " spiritual " life.   We should then say to the Agnostics: " Granted that the question as to the ultimate nature of things cannot be answered, that the door of knowledge is for ever closed

16

against us on that side, there yet remain open a multitude of other doors through which familiar intercourse
may be carried on. The most you have done is to
convince us that Reality does not talk and cannot be
made to talk to us in the plain prose of the scientific
intellect. But this makes less difference than you
think, and is far from cancelling the terms of intimacy
between ourselves and a Reality which, though dumb
in prose, is eloquent in poetry and in infinite other
forms of expression that are not susceptible of verbal
reproduction." And to the Gnostics our speech would
be equally plain. "We are indebted to you," we
should say, "for revealing to us the secret of the
Universe. But even if you had failed to do so, we
shouldn't have lost heart. For just as a lover requires
no 'solution' of his mistress, and loves her perhaps
the more because she abides his question as a mystery
he cannot fathom, riding through thick and thin to win
her, all enigmatical as she is, for his very own, so we, in
accepting your solution, are conscious that on the whole
we could have got on without it, and are not quite
certain that you have done us great good. Nay, we
will be bold to remind you that if your own interests
in Reality are limited by what you can scientifically
formulate as to its ultimate nature, you are in peril of
encountering the fate of Lot's wife."

It were to be wished that more attention were given
to the part played in modern thought by the Will-to-
have-problems. It is certain that some of our most
distressing intellectual difficulties have no other justification for their existence than a love of problems
for their own sake and an obstinate determination on
our part that they shall exist. A consciousness without

problems seems to be a contradiction in terms.   Problem-
solving is treated as the air, and food, and raiment of
spirit, nay, as the spirit's very life.   The word " Problem " is indeed the name of our Grand Fetish ; it is the
Mumbo Jumbo of scientific ritual and intellectual
sorcery ; it is the Benamuckee whom our old men salute
on the mountain tops with long-drawn O's and to whom,
like the people in Friday's island, we shall, presumably,
all go when we die.[1]

Whence comes this strange obsession ?   Not from the
Hebrew, we may be sure.   Shall we lay it, then, to the
account of the Greek ?   Hardly.   Is it not rather a
Gothic inheritance, the spirit which in ancient days
looked upon the world as a thing to conquer, and which
now, revived in us with unabated ardour, treats the whole
universe as a defenceless country, sails up its navigable
rivers with invading fleets of thought, falls upon facts as
upon fat cities waiting to be spoiled, scatters knowledge
like a consuming fire, and wields the pen as though it
were a sword ?

" To overcome the world."   Are there not some
among us who take that expression as a literal statement of the business of human life ?   Is not the over-
coming of the world sometimes presented to us as a kind
of military, or, at least, a commercial project ?   Here are
we, yonder is the world ; and the question addressed to
us is, " What do you *make* of it ?   How do you propose
to get it into your power, to master it, to make it serve
your purpose and not its own ?   Is not the world in arms
against you ?   Are you not in jeopardy every hour ?
Does not the world threaten you and carry out its
threats ?   Does it not strike at your happiness through

[1] See Robinson Crusoe's conversation with Friday, quoted on p. 138.

your body and through your mind ; does it not persecute
you with its tempests and make you afraid with its
storms, and finally engulph you in an all-devouring
death ?   Does it not lay gins and snares for your steps
at every turn, and cunningly persuade you to your own
ruin, to become conformed unto itself ?[1]   On the other
hand, is not the world a mine of riches to him who can
turn its undeveloped resources to good account ?   Can
you not divert these destructive forces into useful
channels and turn the world's hostility into an alliance ?
Armed with a knowledge of its final strategy, possessed
of its ' secret,' can you not outflank and beat it, not in
mere isolated skirmishes but in one decisive action,
force it to capitulate all along the line, hoist your
flag on its innermost citadel and compel the beaten foe
to swear allegiance to your own cause ?   What, then,
do you *make* of the world ? "

To those who ask these questions, and to those who
think that the one thing needful is to answer them, the
world will necessarily present itself as a problem-to-be-
solved, and until the solution is obtained their life will
be baffled and their hearts unsatisfied.   Armed with no
comprehensive formula of life, and having only fragmentary knowledge of the enemy's tactics here and
there, they will feel themselves outmatched and doomed
to be beaten by that final strategy of the Universe whose
mysterious secret they cannot penetrate.   They will be
able to " make " nothing of the world ; for how can one
" make " anything of that whose final nature you do

---

[1] This seems to be implied in Huxley's famous comparison of life to
a game of chess.   The idea of *outwitting* Nature at her own game is
extremely popular and thoroughly characteristic of the temper of an
industrial age.

not understand? Can you "make" anything out of
electricity without understanding it? So then, instead
of being able to exploit the Universe, these people will
suspect that the Universe is exploiting them. They
will have to endure a complete reversal of what they
regard as the only satisfactory arrangement. They
will see no good in a world which they cannot handle,
manage, and control, as they could do and would do if
only they could master its "secret." They will despise
it, because they can "make nothing" of it. "It is not
a rational universe," they will say. "For a rational
universe is a universe which capitulates to man; which,
after due mining, breaching, bombarding, and general
besieging, renders up its 'key' to the intelligent
besiegers and bids them enter in and take possession
of itself. But here is a fool of a universe which refuses
to give in; which declines to be discovered; which
offers an impenetrable barrier-reef to the warships of
philosophy; which suffers no human formula to possess
its towers; which guards its fat cities from devouring
thought, and is uncut by the pens which we have
sharpened with swords. Therefore there is no God."
Conclusions of this kind are certainly inevitable if
you grant the assumptions on which they ultimately
rest. What are these? Well, unless we are grossly
mistaken, they may be summed up in a general assumption that Reality, or the Universe, is a kind of lock, and
that the supreme business of mankind on this planet
is to find the key. This metaphor, violent as it is,
does no injustice to the facts. There are few works
of modern philosophy which do not contain an avowal,
more or less explicit, that experience is problematical
—problematical in no incidental fashion, but essentially,

fundamentally, and through and through. The *problem*
that lurks in experience is its characteristic feature; this
stands out before all the rest of its elements, and however these may come and go, the "problem" is always
there. To take experience without its problem would
be to leave Hamlet out of the play. Experience *must*
present itself in the form interrogative "What am I";
presented in the form positive "I am so and so" it is
a contradiction in terms. Experience, therefore, is a
language which conveys no *direct* meaning, and has
to be translated into some other form of speech. Unfortunately, however, this new language turns out on
examination to be a kind of experience, too, which in
its turn requires translation into yet another, and so on
ad infinitum. Thus the only meaning we can discern
in experience is that of providing employment to an
endless succession of translators, and this, so far from
clearing the matter up and convincing us that we have
got to the bottom of things, ends by leaving the thing
to be explained more inexplicable than ever.

By reading the metaphor in different ways we may
distinguish the subdivisions of this lock-philosophy.
Sometimes it is "we" who have to find the key, this
having somehow got detached from the lock and become
lost or hidden. Sometimes the lock itself does the
business; it is in a state of timeless evolution, evolving
into its own key and yet remaining a lock all the same.

Now all this has no other result than to leave us in
the presence of a universe *pour rire.* "Rational" such
a universe may be; but if so, it is either ridiculously
rational or rationally ridiculous. That, of course, is
not a sufficient reason for rejecting these conclusions.
We must take things as they are and put up with them

as best we may; and if the Universe is ridiculous then
Philosophy does its appointed work in revealing the
fact. We have no more right to assume from the outset
that the world is a serious and not an amusing proposition than we have to assume that the world was made
in six days. We may justly express surprise at anyone
who does not perceive that there is *de facto* a grim
humour in these conclusions; but no reason, save an
unphilosophical one, can justify the attitude of a man
who should say to the philosophers, " I will accept your
teachings if they make me serious or force me to my
knees; but I will not accept them if they turn experience into a farce."

Our own reason for rejecting these doctrines is
different. We reject them because the assumptions on
which they rest appear to us to be gratuitous. We are
aware that there is contradiction in experience; but we
entirely deny that experience is *essentially* contradictory.
The contradictions that appear in experience seem to
us to arise only in so far as we treat the Universe exclusively from the point of view of those interests and
ends of ours which require us to understand it. But
outside this small and artificially limited area of our life
there are regions of experience in which contradiction
fails to appear, and others into which the bare notion
of contradiction cannot be so much as introduced.
Over against the relatively few moments of life when
things say to us " What are we ? " and we, trying to
answer, get involved in contradictions, there are an
infinity of moments when things say " I am what I
am," and when, no questions being asked, the contradiction that comes from trying to answer is entirely absent
from the situation. Thus, for example, if I insist on

treating Space as something to be understood, something which has no other function than to gratify my curiosity regarding its nature, immediately the well-known antinomies make their appearance. But why should I treat Space in that way, and in that way only? What duty do I owe to the Grand Fetish which forbids me to treat Space otherwise than a thing about whose *ultimate nature* questions are to be answered and problems solved? Surely Space enters into my experience in a thousand forms which have nothing whatever to do with the problem of finding out what Space is. I can master the whole science of Geometry without solving that question. I can measure Space and move about in Space without encountering even the faintest suggestion of a contradiction. In short, the contradiction does not appear until for a purpose of my own, a narrowly intellectual purpose, I force myself into its presence. And so with everything else that enters into experience—yes, even with that Tragedy of Good and Evil which is the hardest of all to "understand."[1] The contradiction appears only when we regard the object as having no story to tell *save that* which can be told in the language of our conceptional logic. But what right have we to regard it exclusively in that way?

We are inclined to think, therefore, that the demand for a Science of Man, for a key or bunch of keys to human life, is a special form or local variety of a much more comprehensive determination—that which

---

[1] Lest this should seem to be too lightly passed over, it may be added that the Tragedy of Good and Evil, *as a thing to be discussed,* can never be "solved." Nothing less than the *acting of the drama* can express the meaning.

insists on treating the whole Universe as essentially a lock. Now we who regard that determination as gratuitous or (in our suspicious moments) as a mere professional prejudice,—we, I say, are not in the least dismayed by our inability to produce a key either to the Universe in general or to human life in particular. Any shock of surprise we may have felt at first in realising that the key was not in our own pockets, and that keys in other people's pockets wouldn't act, was entirely swallowed up in the joy of discovering that the Universe keeps innumerable doors unlocked, that its alleged "secret" is *open*, and therefore no secret at all. There was a time, it must be confessed, when the Agnostic's proof that reality is without a "key" appeared to us not only convincing, but disconcerting. It still appears to us convincing, but it disconcerts us no longer. We now see that the reason Reality has no "key" is the simple one—that there is no lock on the door. Finding, then, that the notion of locks and keys is inapplicable to experience as a whole, we are willing enough to concede to the Agnostic that the key cannot be found. Only we are bound to add that the statement, so far as we are concerned, is entirely without meaning. If any one thinks it worth while to prove that there is no key to Art or Beauty, it is not for us to interfere with him ; we can only point out that his proof in no way affects our appreciation of the sunset, the ninth Symphony, or the face of the Sistine Madonna—which is the thing we mainly care about. In like manner, the proof that the ultimate nature of the Universe is unknowable leaves us un-moved, because we can still find business with the Universe which is, as we think, far more interesting and far more important than that of understanding its ultimate nature. Of course there is nothing to prevent a man who has a hobby for formulæ from turning his back on everything that cannot be formulated and from despising the world on that account; just as there is nothing to prevent a man with a hobby for chess from being insufferably bored by everything else. Such a person, however, appears to us perversely self-limited, and we are sorry for him. We are sorry because the most interesting phases of experience will not reduce themselves to the dimensions of his hobby, nor can we see that anything would be gained even if they would. Among the many self-denying ordinances which man can impose upon himself, none appears to us so supererogatory as this Positivist device of restricting one's concerns to the things he can understand. For our own part, were we under compulsion to confine our interest to any one type of experience, the type that we can thoroughly understand would be among the last on which our choice would fall. To have this type of experience along with others may be a good thing; to have no other but this is quite a different proposition, and it does not attract us.

XI.—MORALITY BY THE CARD

Καὶ εὑρέθη μοι ἡ ἐντολὴ ἡ εἰς ζωήν, αὕτη εἰς θάνατον

IT has often been remarked that the more a man talks about certain virtues the less likely he is to have them. The same suspicion, more widely generalised, was expressed by the cynic who said, " Whenever a man mentions his moral principles you may be sure he is going to play you a dirty trick."

These sayings are valuable, not for their scientific accuracy, but as indicating that men in general are awake to an important but elementary truth, namely, that deeds rather than words are the proper medium for the expression of morality. Just as movement cannot be represented by the stiff masses of architecture, so the Good, which involves a creative principle, is impatient of the rigidities of formal speech. Used as a vehicle for the conveyance of the moral fact, speech is inadequate to the burden. A stronger and a more elastic medium must be found before just expression can be attained. By common consent nothing less than action, life, personality, will do justice to the moral fact.

The tendency to make *talk* do the business, to substitute words for things and formulæ for facts—a tendency which, as we have seen reason to believe, has damaged whole systems of philosophy—is recognised by all men as one of the standing dangers of morality. The ques-

251

tion—"Why call ye me Lord, Lord, and do not the things that I say?" contains a point which none of us is likely to miss.

Deplorable as are the results which flow from this habit, we may, at all events, console ourselves by remembering the ease with which its presence is detected. In other spheres—for example, in the Theory of Knowledge—the substitution of formula for fact, of symbols for realities, can often be effected unperceived, even by the author of the substitution, and a generation or a century may elapse before men discover the trick they have played on their own minds. In morals, however, the distinction between the thing and the theory of the thing lies upon the surface, and he who runs may read. We can watch the process of substitution going on under our eyes, and have to wait only a moment, as it were, to see the disaster that results. We do indeed confuse ourselves at times by the use of such phrases as "moral precepts," "moral science," "moral education," and need to give our minds a sharp reminder that the adjective is here misapplied as entirely as it would be if we were to speak of a moral colour, a moral landscape, a moral drug. Yet we all know, though we sometimes forget, that the predicate "moral" attaches, not to the precepts, but to the man who makes use of them; not to the science or the education, but to the actual lives which result from either or both. "Moral" precepts might be as plentiful as blackberries and as excellent as the stars in heaven; "moral" science might have its text-books in every shop-window; the elementary schools might be humming and roaring with "moral" education from one end of the land to the other; but all this, morally considered, would of course, if taken by itself, amount to little or nothing. So widely recognised is the distinction between the moral fact and the non-moral formula, which often seems to do duty for the fact, that we might with advantage begin our investigations into the nature of all experience at this point. By thus beginning we should have a clue from the outset to an error whose serpent-trail can be followed over the entire field of Logic, Psychology, and Metaphysics.

Familiar as this distinction is, however, it can be, and is, forgotten with wonderful facility, and we have still to contend not only against fatuous metaphysics but against fatuous morals.

Morality, it may be said, shares with Religion in the proud claim of having survived millenniums of talk. Were Religion and Morality other than immortal they would have perished long ago—drowned out, disintegrated and swept away by a never-ending rain of words poured down upon them from the unkindly heavens. Watery skies have been the portion of both of them, with such occasional relief of sunshine as might come when it pleased God to send forth a prophet or a man of action on the earth. For the last hundred years, in particular, these two have had to bear up against a rainy season which, though broken by welcome gleams, has damped many fires and chilled many hearts. It is as though some god or demon were hurling water-spouts of verbiage at the things men value most, with Religion and Morality as his favourite targets. The obsessions of language are now indeed at the zenith of their power ; the boastings of the tongue, always shameless, have grown to a universal menace ; and morality, which has less to do with words than any other essential interest of life, is in danger of becoming with many of us a mere verbal experience. Encouraged by a pseudo-science the vain hope has gone abroad that by the gradual refinement of our formulæ we shall come to apprehend the Moral Fact—which, of course, can be apprehended only in the doing of a moral deed.

This is fatuous morality : it begins in confusion of mind and it ends in disaster. All of us are its victims —more or less.

For example. We are apt to believe that great good will be done by inculcating the precept " Imitate the Good Samaritan." That some good will be done by the mere repetition of this precept at appropriate times and by duly qualified persons need not be doubted ; at the same time it is equally certain that much harm will be done by exaggerating the good which this precept can do. Nothing, in fact, could better illustrate the limitations of fatuous morality and the dangers of forgetting them. For *how* are we to imitate the Good Samaritan, and what would imitation of him really involve ? The splendid thing about the Good Samaritan was that he refused to imitate any-body. Had his morality been of the imitative order he would have done after the manner of the Priest and the Levite, who were actually following approved exemplars of their time and place. So long, indeed, as our deeds of charity are mere imitations of somebody else, no matter of whom, the principle of our conduct is far nearer to that of the Priest and the Levite than to that of the Good Samaritan. When he showed mercy on the wounded man he was not imitating another Good Samaritan who had done the same thing on a previous occasion ; nor was he remembering some precept which

had been drilled into him by the masters of his youth
or the pastors of his manhood.   He was the first.   His
action, far from giving effect to any fixed rule that might
have been taught him by contemporary moralists, was
a flat violation of the respectable moral opinion of that
time and place.   A person who assists a wounded
man to-day and thinks he is thereby imitating the
Good Samaritan is therefore making a mistake, which,
though it may flatter his self-conceit, vitiates his moral
judgment.   To do this act for the first time, in defiance
of the accepted traditions of your race, is one thing ; to
do it for the ten thousandth time with the felt approval
of the world at your back, is another thing.   In no
relevant sense is the second an imitation of the first.
All the " subjective " factors of the two situations are
different.   Our pleasant consciousness that this kind of
conduct has been sanctioned by the highest authority,
ratified by the moral judgment of ages, celebrated in
art, proved sound in principle by science, and commended by the most illustrious philosophers—need it
be said that of all this there was no faintest glimmer
in the mind of the Good Samaritan ?   In place of it
there was, I suspect, an uncomfortable feeling that if
his best friends saw what he was after they would cut
him for ever.

How, then, can we imitate the Good Samaritan ?
We imitate him, not by reproducing his act, but by
being just as original, just as creative, just as indifferent towards fatuous morality as he was.   Without
the power of carving out for ourselves some expression
of the goodwill which no existing rules either cover
or contemplate, there will never be the faintest flavour
of the Good Samaritan about anything we do or

attempt.   Should we ever succeed in imitating him, one sure remark of our success will be *that we shall get into trouble*, even as the Author of the parable got into greater trouble for a similar cause.   True it is that not every one who does an unheard-of and surprising thing can set up as an imitator of the Good Samaritan. On the other hand, the Good Samaritan always does an unheard-of and surprising thing.   He shocks somebody. He " goes better " than his teachers, and there are few things that our teachers are apt to resent more bitterly, and punish more severely.

It comes, then, to this.   If rules for imitating the Good Samaritan are to be framed and " taught " by way of moral education either to children or adults, these rules must take the form of telling us how to be morally original.   And this, it will be admitted, is impossible.

The point is sufficiently important to deserve a second illustration from the same source.   Were one asked to describe the most odious form of hypocrisy conceivable, we should surely point to the man who deliberately reproduces the part of the Publican in the parable and deliberately abjures that of the Pharisee—the man who says inwardly, " I thank thee, O God, that I am not as yonder Pharisee.   I don't fast twice a week ; I don't give tithes of all I possess, but duly, and at the proper time, I smite upon my breast and cry, ' God be merciful to me, a sinner.' "   The splendid thing about the Publican —and here he resembles the Good Samaritan—was that he smote upon his breast *before any authority had laid it down that this was the correct thing for a man in his position to do.*   Surely we are well advised in not imitating the Publican ; even fatuous morality would shrink from such advice, though what other advice it *can* give is hard to say.   I remember reading a story— of Gallic *provenance*, I think—about a very respectable member of the middle class who confessed himself a sinner so often and so earnestly that the idea of himself in this character ultimately got hold of his will and began to express itself in sinful acts of the most incredibly repulsive types.   Psychologically the thing is not impossible, and in milder forms it is the actual result, too little noted, of exaggerating and overstraining the functions of book-learnt morality.

Among the various orders of fact which can be classified, moral fact is the promptest in declaring its impatience of bookish reproduction.   Significant evidence of this may be found, *inter alia*, in the reluctance of all healthy-minded persons to submit their characters to the verbal photographer.   Nobody, of course, wishes to hear himself described as " bad," but, on the other hand, who enjoys hearing himself being described as " good "?   An illustrious example seems to suggest that the loftiest natures are the least inclined to submit to this epithet; they wince under it as if stung by a lash.   It is from no fear lest a damning likeness may result that a man of high temper refuses to stand up before the descriptive artist.   The sting of the thing lies in the supposition that he desires to be provided with a verbal *alter ego*, to see himself " put into words " of any kind whatsoever.   Whatever else can be " put into " words, it is certain that personality will always escape them and always feel itself wronged when the attempt is made to capture it by a formula or an epithet. The only word in which character can be uttered is, of course, a word made flesh.   Not to be confined by the

17

limitations of speech, it is yet susceptible of luminous expression by other human media—by the grouping of personalities, by the ordered life of a single man, or by one of his actions, or even by the impression of his face left on a passer-by.

This may help us to understand why moral science, as written in certain books, differs from other sciences in being so strangely inapplicable to the moral fact—in a word, so useless. For morality if not concrete is nothing; it refuses, therefore, to provide the abstractions which make science, in the ordinary sense, possible. The other sciences reach their results, as everybody knows, by abstracting particular aspects of the object under consideration, leaving the results obtained in one department to be adjusted in practice to those which have been obtained in the rest. When each of the sciences—including the historical, the social, the economic—has had its say, the problem of the final adjustment of all results is precisely what is left over to morality. The word morality may thus be said to indicate that moment in life when the process of abstracting is over and done with and something else must now begin, viz. the selective and creative action of the will. The dinner, so to speak, has been cooked; the various dishes have been examined by experts and labelled wholesome or poisonous as the case may be; and the problem now is, " What, and how much, are you going to eat ? " If at this point a moralist appears on the scene and proposes to start the process of abstraction over again, nothing will come of it save a fresh cooking of the dinner and a fresh examination of the viands; the moral " problem " proper, which is always " What shall we eat ? " will remain at the end of the second cooking and the second examination exactly where it was at the end of the first. Reflection may change the content of the moral situation; it may enrich the data which the will has to handle, though it may also impoverish them; it may give the problem a form more favourable for action, though it may also do the contrary; but at the end, as at the beginning, the issue remains to be determined otherwise than by reflection. This process may be prolonged to infinity without getting one hairsbreadth nearer to the essential moral fact—the action of the will; this being always found just outside the boundary which abstract moral science has reached. Thus the problem which the other sciences handed on to morality is in turn handed back by "moral" science, and the solution of the problem is no nearer at the end than it was at the beginning— often, indeed, it is much further off.

Were these fresh abstractions undertaken by moral science called by another name—Social Physiology, for example—no exception could be taken; but by calling them "moral science" hopes are raised that definite formulæ for the action of the will will now be forthcoming analogous to those provided by physics and chemistry in their respective departments — in other words, that moral science will solve the moral problem; instead of which, however, the moralist merely joins his brother scientists in putting off the moral problem to another occasion. Thus moral science might be not unfairly described as the science which evades the moral fact. Hence those painful chapters found at the beginning of certain text-books in which the writer may be seen uneasily adjusting himself to his subject; hence the laboured defence of his scientific character;

hence the caveat that all *particular* moral problems must be relegated to a hypothetical department called "practical ethics," which the writer himself is careful not to touch, leaving it to those who are willing to imperil their souls by practising the black art of casuistry. Hence also the subsequent discovery by the student that the caveat so delivered covers the essential moral fact. Just as Kant, to quote our former example, setting out to explain the object, caused the object to vanish in the explanation and had to admit in effect that the only real object was the one he couldn't explain, so our moralists often leave us with the conclusion that whatever else they may be talking about it is not morality. Morality is "the thing-in-itself" which remains over when the last chapter has been written. For may we not say that a problem is moral precisely when, and because, it cannot be solved by any existing scientific rule, but compels us to make a rule for ourselves and to make it at our peril? Had men all along restricted themselves to the performance of those actions for which the warrant of moral science was then and there available, many crimes perhaps would not have been committed; but it is doubtful if the world would contain the record of a single noble deed.

We cannot remind ourselves too often that the most complete scientific knowledge of what has been done up to date will never enable us to answer the question, "What ought to be done next?" The thing that has-to-be-done next is never a mere copy of anything that-has-been-done; to some extent it is always a new creation; the "newness" amounting in some instances to reversal of what has gone before. This demand for something new, this attack upon the unknown, this advance into the uncharted Hinterlands of life, is precisely what gives its peculiar character to the moral situation.   Hence it is that even if a complete map were before us of all human actions up to date, the latitudes and longitudes correctly marked and the direction of every current and the date of every wind given on the margin, the information thus afforded would always stop short at the very point where the moral problem begins.   The subject-matter of science and the subject-matter of morality are entirely different and in a certain sense opposed : the first is the deed-as-done, the second the doing of a deed-to-be.   Between these two things the difference is so great that to consult astronomy about the treatment of an aneurism would be no whit more absurd than to expect abstract science of any kind to *solve* the moral problem.

Indeed it is only in a metaphorical sense that the term problem can be applied to the moral situation at all.   The problems of the will, concerned as they are with what-is-to-be, differ so entirely from the problems of science concerning what is and has been, that the direst confusion results from using the same word for the two things.   By calling the moral situation a "problem" we raise once more the vain hope that as other problems are severally settled by the sciences to which they are addressed, so there is some science which can solve in the same demonstrative manner the problem "What am I to do next?" But between this latter question and the questions addressed to the sciences there is little in common beyond the bare fact that both are put in the interrogative form.   We have only to note the differences

which go along with this mere formal resemblance and
we realise at once that nothing can be more quixotic than
the attempt to bring human conduct under the rule of
scientific formulæ.   If the moral situation is to be named
a problem at all, let us remember that it is a problem
unamenable by its very nature to scientific methods.
Persisting, as so many of us do persist, in the opposite
course ; treating the moral problem in the same class
and by the same methods as the others, we are bound
to end by the discovery that so treated our question is
absolutely insoluble.   Guided by conceptual logic alone
we are inevitably landed in moral nescience, and our
only answer to the question " What am I to do next ? "
is " We do not know; therefore do nothing."   It is no
unfair thing to say that of the many roads that lead
to ethical Pyrrhonism ethical " science " provides the
shortest cut.

Here a passing word may be said about the function
of books as instruments of teaching.   It is the fashion
of this age to assume that the teacher of any subject
must either write a book or make use of a book that
has been written by somebody else.   If you have anything to teach you "put it in " a book.   If, on the
other hand, you cannot "put it in " a book, what
more proof is required that you have nothing to
teach ?   Have you a message to your fellow-men ?
Produce your book.   Have you a mission to your age ?
Produce your book.   Or are you repeating the message
of others and helping to carry on *their* mission ?   What
books do you use — Goethe's, Carlyle's, Browning's,
Kant's, Comte's, Spencer's ?   No book, no message.

In making this requirement the fashion of our age
draws inadequate distinctions.   In all cases alike it tends

to look upon the bookless teacher as a kind of contradiction in terms. It does not, of course, go the length
of asserting that every man who writes a book is a
prophet, but it does tend to the belief that no teacher
of what is new ever fails to write a book. The non-
production of the book is therefore evidence of the
non-existence of the teaching. Nor does the weight of
this evidence vary very much in different departments.
It is generally conclusive. Whether you happen to be
a teacher of physical science or of ethics, few people
will believe in your originality till you have written
your book. Religion remains, perhaps, a doubtful
exception: here the bookless prophet is still tolerated
within limits. But claim for your friend that he has
made an important contribution to ethics and confess
yourself unable to name any book in which the contribution is *contained*, and who will believe you? Who
will even attach a meaning to your words?

Book-ridden as we all are, it is extremely difficult for
any of us to get away from the atmosphere of these
ideas, extremely difficult to realise that all this is
nothing more than a passing state of the spiritual
weather. The result of liberating oneself, even in
imagination, from the tyranny of books is so startling,
and so damaging to many of our vested interests, that
we can hardly trust ourselves to say what we then
think and feel. But making an effort just for once,
we can easily satisfy ourselves that without embarking
on any foolish tirade against books in general we can
yet draw an important distinction among their values
as instruments of teaching in the various departments
of life.

Of science proper we may say that books are its

fitting receptacles, and the necessary organs of its expression. The essential features of science may be "put into" books without diminution or excess. Books do no injustice to the abstractions of science, to its statements of general law. Science is a system of organised memoranda which are recorded and multiplied by books in a manner which leaves nothing to be desired. Considered as organs of expression for the purpose in view, they may be described as almost perfect—at all events, the best we have.

When, however, we turn to ethics the case is different. What is primary in the moral fact can never be contained in nor expressed by books, but only what is secondary. Here one is immediately struck by the inadequacy of the organ of expression to the thing which has to be expressed. Between the adequacy of the book when used for science and its inadequacy for ethics—which we contend is no science—there is a startling difference. Everything that is characteristic of science goes submissively into the book; everything that is characteristic of the Moral Fact—its vitality, its creativeness, its splendour—flatly refuses to enter in. The most the book can do is to touch, nay, to indicate, the Moral Fact as it flies, as one might point to an eagle in the clouds. That which expresses ethical truth must be *alive*; and lo! every book is made of the letter that *killeth*. Of every sound ethical system one may say, and say without hesitation, that it is precisely that sort of system which refuses to go into a book. What goes into the book may be systematic but it cannot be ethical. And contrariwise we may say of every book which professes to contain an ethical system that it is not sound. It is in regard to

Morals most of all that book-erudition is apt to become *obstructive* and to illustrate the terrible saying that "the world by wisdom knew not God." Let us tear the veil for one instant from our book-bewildered eyes. A "Moral Text-book" is not the essential equipment of a moral teacher. Stowed away somewhere with the rest of his impedimenta it may come in useful now and then; but if he leans upon it he is lost. Nor need we be greatly daunted when the world denies us the credentials of moral teachers because we are unable, and confess ourselves unable, to write our moral system on a sheet of paper, to hang it on the walls, to print it in a book. So placed, we reply, the system is out of place; so expressed it is mis-expressed; so used it is abused. Fear not him, therefore, who says "There is no moral system in your book." Fear him rather who can say "There is no moral system in your life." By nothing short of the Good-will can the Good-will be expressed. Morals have no language short of personality, and that, we venture to think, in spite of the overwhelming prejudice of this book-ridden age, can never be re-translated into the language of any book.

On these grounds, then, we plead for the man who, at the present day, declines to put his moral system into a book. For our own part we would as soon try to put it into a bottle. It remains to point out, however, that the person who renounces this attempt does not become thereby of no account in the service of morality. Condemned for his want of the recognised credentials he may be; but there are analogies from a closely related sphere which may enable him to take his condemnation standing up. Pheidias, Titian, Beethoven, Turner, and others too numerous to name,

did great things in the world of Art, by which they
have helped, enriched, and permanently lifted up the
life of man. But none of them put his work in a
book. Other men have tried to do this for them—
with doubtful success. There is, it is true, a putative
Science of Art (Æsthetic) to which great artists like
Sir Joshua Reynolds occasionally make a contribution,
though by most of them it is not unhappily ignored.
Nobody contends that this science is the backbone of
Art. Nobody makes it the basis of the artist's education. That it helps in maintaining a certain dull
mediocrity of performance need not be denied; at the
same time it may repress originality, and, if greatly
emphasised, would undoubtedly have this effect. Certain it is that no man's service to the cause of Art is
to be measured by the amount of his contribution to
this science. May we not ask to be put on the same
footing in regard to morality? Believing as we do
that conduct is essentially a Fine Art, is it too much
to claim that no man can live the Good Life without
a touch of genius? And may it not be that this kind
of genius is the common possession of all men to a
degree which we are only prevented from acknowledg-
ing by our scientific obsessions? Is it not possible that
the moral genius of men is being repressed, as well as
ignored, by all those obstinate mental habits of ours
which thrust the scientific character of morality to the
front, which compel others to think of it scientifically,
and which lead us, with highly questionable wisdom, to
force it in the scientific form down the helpless throats
of the young? Would not a parallel procedure in Art
be the death of all great performance? Is it inconceiv-
able that what morality needs most at the present day

is a just measure of contempt for all systems that are merely "in books"; the moral decadence we see around us being due in no small measure to that very standard which would condemn us as incompetent because of our confessed, nay, our boasted, failure in this respect? To those who deny these possibilities we can only repeat the words of Cromwell to the Scotch divines: "I beseech you in the bowels of Christ, think it possible that ye may be mistaken."

But morality by the card, even though it be a contradiction in terms, may have its uses; and there is no denying that a purpose is served by verbal treatment of the Moral Fact, whether by precept, exhortation, or philosophical discourse. Perhaps we shall not greatly err in construing its value to the moral life as that of a tonic, but not of a food. Taken in excessive doses, or used in place of food, such morality is a deadly poison. One may even hazard a guess that many of us who know, or think we know, a great deal about morality are actually taking the tonic in poisonous quantities. Fortunately the taste for it is acquired; to the unspoiled palate of youth it is nauseous—and for that we may be thankful.

Nor must we overlook that well-worn and highly respectable argument which regards the Law as a schoolmaster leading us on to something higher. The use of precept, we are told, is in conducting the pupil to the point at which his moral originality will break out into its own forms, without which propædeutic of the Law, conscience would never pass under the rule of any principle higher than Law.

But it makes a great difference whether we regard this view as the statement of an historical fact or as the

proposal of a working policy. As historical fact it is
true beyond question ; as working policy it is highly
dangerous.

By St Paul it was propounded as historical fact, not
as working policy. St Paul stated that the Law had
been a necessary preparation for the Gospel *in the
past* ; he did not propose that the same order should
be maintained in the future. His working policy for
human education henceforth was not *first* a course of
the Law and *then* a course of Christianity—but Christianity straight away for every man.

St Paul showed himself wiser than some of his would-
be imitators in our own time. One more curious
instance is here supplied of the way in which the
wisdom of the wise confounds itself. None so slow as
the wise in observing that the value of a fact may be
completely altered by the very explanation they give of
its meaning. It is so in the present instance. There
was a time when the Jews thought the Law was final
and its power over the will lay in its assumed finality ;
it was reverenced and obeyed accordingly. Then came
the discovery of its temporary character—the secret
escaped that it was only a schoolmaster. Henceforth,
therefore, the Law is not merely a temporary expedient, but a temporary expedient known to be such.
That makes all the difference — a difference which
deprives the Law of the authority it had over the
will in the times when we knew not that it was a
schoolmaster, but thought it final. If, therefore, we
are to maintain the function of the Law as a propædeutic
we must carefully conceal the truth that it is only this ;
we must encourage the pupil to think of it as final, even
as the Jews did of old. That is difficult, not to say

dangerous. The Law found out to be a temporary expedient is obviously a very inferior kind of propæ-deutic compared with the Law thought to be final, and there is no doubt that concealment of the true state of the case is essential if the power of this propædeutic is to be kept up to its former level. But how conceal it? Children, of course, need not know—perhaps they could not understand. So far so good. But what about the teacher? He presumably *knows*. And is moral teaching on those terms likely to succeed? Must there not be of necessity an element of make-believe in the attitude of the teacher towards his subject which is likely in the long-run to take the heart out of his business? Certainly the teacher, possessed of the school-master-secret, is making a great mistake if he thinks he is repeating the conditions under which the Law was taught and reverenced in ancient Israel. To say the least of it, he is working in a very different atmosphere —an atmosphere wholly uncongenial to the project he has in hand. May he not be reasonably asked to be extremely cautious, and to earnestly consider whether he is not preparing the way for a grave moral disaster? Nor must he suppose that he has a warrant from St Paul. Nothing, we imagine, could have been more abhorrent to the mind of this great moral genius than the notion of making history repeat itself by a forced reproduction of the two stages in the past moral history of the Jews. Such a proceeding would have appeared to him profane. "The times of that ignorance God winked at." But God can hardly be expected to wink at *this*.

XII.—THE QUEST FOR SAFE-CONDUCT

In the science of Political Economy a gradual revolution has been brought about by increased attention given to the interests of the *Consumer*. When wealth is studied exclusively from the point of view of those engaged in its *production*, or when the economic agent is treated as producer only and not consumer as well, we end in some purely abstract result for which no place can be found in the actual economy of the world. The early periods of economic theory were marked, as is well known, by this one-sided emphasis on the interests of the producer, and it was in consequence of the results so reached that Political Economy earned the name of the Dismal Science. Later on, in accordance with the rule that obvious truths are the last to be considered, economists began to discuss the importance of consumption ; and by constructing their science more and more and more from the consumer's point of view they reversed, or greatly modified, the conclusions of their predecessors, presenting these in such a form that they could no longer be fairly described as showing "how the rich become richer and the poor poorer."

The revolution which has been thus happily accomplished or set forward, in Political Economy, is much less advanced on the field of ethics ; in some quarters it has scarcely begun. But here also it is obvious that man lives his life not merely in producing actions of his own, but, so to say, in "consuming" the results of actions done by other people, as well as by himself. His interests as ethical producer are equalled if not outranked in importance by his interests as ethical consumer, *i.e.* as the recipient of other men's offices, the patient of *their* deeds, the re-acting object of *their* wills. And it is not often that one encounters a treatise on morals in which man's interests as Ethical Consumer are adequately recognised.[1] On the other hand, there are many in which Morality is considered exclusively, or almost exclusively, from the Producer's end. Surely Ethics so studied is the most "dismal" of the sciences.

There is a story about David which illustrates the change in an ethical situation when the Consumer's interest comes into play. We read that David, in the midst of a campaign, cried out one day, "O that I might drink of the well of Bethlehem that is by the gate." The cry was overheard, and three daring fellows resolved that the chief should have his wish. At the risk of their lives they brake through the host of the Philistines, got the water, and brought it to David. But David would not drink it. "God forbid," says he, "that I should drink it. This is the blood of the three mighty men who went in jeopardy of their lives." So David poured it out unto the Lord.

And alongside of this one can hardly refrain from recalling the well-worn story about Sir Philip Sidney and the wounded soldier on the field of Zutphen. It is characteristic of our one-sided ethics that this story is almost invariably introduced as an illustration of the

---

[1] They are recognised—perhaps over-emphasised—in the Sermon on the Mount. But the Sermon on the Mount is not a treatise.

magnanimity of Sidney.   But the present writer well
remembers the startled look on the face of a certain
venerable person when, having told this story to his
class and asked them what they thought of it, a spirited
little figure sprang to its feet in the middle of the room
and cried out, " The fellow who took the water was a
cad."   Once more it was the consumer's point of view.

Perhaps the highest duty we owe to "others" is to
remember what kind of "others" they are, viz. that
they are other *men*, other *wills*, other *self-conscious beings*;
not mere "others," empty, abstract, passive, dead; not
tesseræ to be arranged in a mosaic of our contriving;
not open mouths waiting to swallow our wonder-
working dose.   A political cartoon recently exhibited
seemed to show that the artist had been pondering
this aspect of the moral life.   The cartoon represented
a veterinary surgeon in the act of administering a pill
to a horse by the method of blowing it through a
tube down the animal's throat.   But unfortunately
the horse blew first.

This may serve to remind us of a besetting danger.
I refer to the ease with which we may overlook the truth
that the moral relation is never to be understood by
considering the action of a self-contained or isolated
will operating *in vacuo*.   The moral fact is constituted
by the action and reaction of a plurality of wills; and
until we consider it in that character we do not so
much as enter the province of morality.   My decision
to do my neighbour good is never the end of the
matter; nothing can happen until his will consents to
my decision by accepting the good I offer him.   The
verdict of my conscience that I ought to give him a

sovereign in no way binds his conscience to affirm that he ought to receive a sovereign from me. Until his will and mine are at one in the matter nothing can be done.

It is no uncommon thing, for example, to find the virtue of Benevolence discussed with reference only to one side of the benevolent transaction. In order that Benevolence may have free course, some writers seem to assume the existence of a sufficient number of persons whose office is that of lay figures or blocks. That A may have the conditions he needs for the practice of this virtue, B and C must consent to be his targets, they must stand up to be shot at by A's benevolent gun. Until B and C consent to be so treated, A cannot get to business. But will B and C consent? Or, what is far more important, *ought* they to consent? How will *their* reputation for Benevolence be affected by lending themselves too readily as objects for A's benevolent designs? These questions are seldom asked with sufficient emphasis, and it is with no little shock of surprise that the student notes the ease with which they are sometimes passed over altogether. Again and again an argument is presented for making the happiness or well-being of " others " the end of my actions ; little heed being given to the fact that the very arguments which require me to seek the good of " others " would, in many instances, forbid these " others " to suffer their good to be sought by me. These unfortunate " others " are apparently all *dead*, or, at all events, not sufficiently alive to cry out, as any man of honour would, " Stop there, my friend ! Many thanks for your benevolent desire to sacrifice yourself in my behalf. But before heaven, and in the

18

name of your own principles, you shall do no such thing ! "

It is to the habit of overlooking the reciprocity of ethical relations, through failing to give the "others" their full value as self-conscious agents, that we must attribute the hopeless deadlock which seems to be the result of so much ethical discussion. Standing at one end of the moral relation the thinker vaguely feels at the other end the presence of a factor whose influence cannot be gauged, and is compelled in consequence to hold his conclusions subject to reversal by that of which he cannot take account. Perpetual hesitation is the result. For example, if any person, anxious to guide his steps aright in the matter of Benevolence, should turn to the chapter in Mr Sidgwick's *Methods of Ethics* [1] in which this virtue is discussed, he will be bitterly disappointed. With all the respect due to this great moralist it can hardly be doubted that the effect of this chapter is to add enormously to the difficulties of practising Benevolence. Assuredly it is a good thing to pause and think over what you are doing; but it is an extremely bad thing when the process of reflection is so indecisive that the "pause" extends itself beyond the opportunity for action and becomes practically endless, as it always must be in the presence of an incalculable factor at the other end of the line. Nothing, indeed, is so destructive of morality as an attitude of reflective pause indefinitely prolonged; and such an attitude, we cannot refrain from thinking, is the most likely result of attempting to solve the "problem" of Benevolence (or any particular virtue) by such methods as Mr Sidgwick here employs.

[1] *Methods of Ethics,* Book III., Chap. IV.

What we are promised, and led to hope for, is guiding principles; what we really receive is added perplexities; and these are piled up to a degree which threatens a total paralysis of the will. On the one hand, the reader's hopes are continually raised by such a proposal as this, " We have therefore to inquire on what principle these [duties] can be determined" (p. 255); on the other, they are continually dashed by the statement, " It seems that delicate questions of this kind are more naturally referred to canons of good taste and refined feeling than of morality proper" (p. 257); or, " Something between the two seems to suit our moral taste; but I find no self-evident principle upon which the amount can be decided"; or, " Here, again, there seems a doubt how far this feeling ought to be fostered"; and finally, " We must admit that while we find a number of broad and more or less indefinite rules unhesitatingly laid down by Common Sense in this department of Duty, it is difficult or impossible to extract from them, so far as they are commonly accepted, any clear or precise principles for determining the extent of the duty in any case."[1]

There need be no hesitation in saying that this kind of thing, which is typical of what one may find in many ethical treatises, is apt to be demoralising. Were it offered by way of suggesting that what is called the moral "problem" is not a problem in the ordinary

---

[1] In justice to Mr Sidgwick it must be stated that in this chapter it is not always easy to say whether he is stating his own views or criticising views held by other people. But there is nothing in other portions of the book to help us further with the " problems " here left unsolved.

sense of the term, and is obstinately insoluble by the
methods to which other problems yield, then it might
be welcomed; but offered as an *aid* to the solution of
our moral difficulties, it can only be described as falling
disastrously wide of the mark; for it misses the goal
of the intellect and strikes the will with a paralysing
blow. If the reader attentively considers he will find
that his moral difficulties invariably begin at the very
point where this hesitating and indecisive analysis
leaves off; that what these thinkers call "morality
proper" is not morality at all; whereas what they hand
over to the "canons of good taste and refined feeling"
is precisely that moral difficulty which the reader is
asking them to resolve. Were one reduced to the
simple alternative of having to decide a course of action
either by the method of reflective pause required for
Mr Sidgwick's analysis *or* by prompt and unreflective
appeal to instinctive feelings of "good taste," there
cannot be a doubt that it would be well to choose the
latter. For whatever mistakes might result from the
latter method, persistence in the former would involve
the destruction of the will.

At the threshold of ethics stands the truth that the
moral situation is constituted not by the action of a
single will but by the action and reaction of many.
"Solving a moral problem" means, if it means anything,
arriving at a just estimate of the results of action—no
matter whether those results are measured in terms of
Happiness, Moral Perfection, Self-realisation, Peace of
Conscience, or what not. And it is obvious that the
only intelligence which could solve the problem *in that
sense*—the only sense in which the word "problem"

is strictly used—would be an intelligence which had access to all the minds and all the wills involved in the transaction. Undertaken, therefore, by any merely finite intelligence, such an attempt is condemned to failure from the outset. To study the action of an isolated will and apply the results so obtained as determining what will or will not happen, what ought or ought not to happen, in the co-operating system of all the wills involved, is the sheerest fatuity. We are here dealing with a type of action which, as previously pointed out, differs essentially from the action which physical science handles in the field of inanimate Nature ; the difference being that whereas the forces of Nature are *determined*, and act therefore under laws considered as already *made*, the forces of the will, being self-determined, act under laws which *are to be made in and by the action which is taking place*. Hence the notion of "solubility" as applied to the problems of physical science is utterly out of place when applied to the "problems" of morality, and the search for a "solution" of that kind is perhaps the vainest enterprise ever undertaken by the intelligence of man. Unless we suppose in ourselves some faculty which reflects the knowledge and the counsels of Omniscience, the attempt to solve moral "problems" in this way must be frankly given up. Tentative, risky, probable answers may, and are, obtainable by intellectual methods ; but to parade these as scientific "solutions" is certainly misleading. It were far better to confess from the outset what has to be confessed in the long-run—*e.g.*, by Mr Sidgwick's appeal to "the canons of good taste and refined feeling"—that the *moral* character which attaches to the problems of the will involves their insolubility by the methods of the intellect. A *moral* problem might be defined as a problem handed over to the rational will for a kind of solution which the scientific intellect is incompetent to provide. Until, therefore, the problem has passed out of the hands of formal science, it is not a *moral* problem.

When once this transference has been effected it cannot be undone. Its consequences must be accepted. Among these is the impossibility of producing any kind of logical rule of thumb for defining moral distinctions —for separating the sheep from the goats. In admitting the problem as *moral* the intellect has also admitted its own incapacity to provide a " solution," and all attempts to go back on this admission serve merely to embroil us deeper in the Sidgwickian bewilderment and to disqualify the will for playing its part. Plausible as are the reasons which urge reflection on the moral issue, we cannot remind ourselves too often that the process of reflection, no matter how prolonged, will never effect the conclusion of the moral business; will never discharge us from facing that difficult moment when the will must act, and take the risk. To overlook this—to overlook it to the extent of letting our moral interest become absorbed in reflection on moral issues—is to cultivate weakness of character, which, after all, is only another name for immorality. Sooner or later an intellectual risk will have to be faced, and it is better to face it too early than not to face it at all. Paradoxical as it may sound, the *safest* policy in morals is to face your danger, and the most dangerous is to run away from it. " Skulkers," said one of Nelson's captains, " always get the worst of it "; and it may be truly said that the greatest mistakes in conduct are made by those persons who hope by means of pondering on the event to find some course, or some corner, where they will be demonstrably safe. Where a genuine moral issue is involved, no such course, no such corner, can be found. The conception of the will as having nothing to do but to travel in first-class comfort towards points marked out in advance, and along roads securely engineered, by the intellect, is of course a contradiction in terms, depriving the will of every quality which makes it what it is. In a world where all moral courses were thus plotted out in advance like the lines on a railway map it is hard to see how what we call morality could exist. And though the holders of this view will always be taunted, perhaps condemned, for their inability to produce a rule of thumb for moral distinctions, they may nevertheless console themselves by reflecting that their opponents are in the same condition as themselves. Contend as these may that an indisputable rule is forthcoming, they have not produced it, and there are good reasons for believing they never will.

Those to whom the conviction has come that the universe itself is something other than an intellectual problem will not be troubled by these taunts. They will see no reason why in such a world they should force themselves to make a " problem," and nothing but a " problem," of their own lives. Moreover, the actual results of excessive devotion to the problem-fetish are even less encouraging on the field of morality than they are elsewhere; at least they are by no means such as to suggest that the devotees are worshipping the true God. Morality, so far as observation goes, gains singularly little by these exercises. Their fruits are vacillation and weakness of character. Just as the artist, waiting for a rule of thumb which is to guide him in the creation of a successful work of art, produces no art, so the Will, waiting for a scientific canon of moral distinction, *does no Good*. At most it refrains from doing harm.

All attempts to escape from the intellectual *difficulties* of the Moral Life are, ultimately, attempts to escape from the Moral Life itself. These attempts take the form of a search for some final authority which by declaring infallibly what ought to be done provides the will with an indefeasible safe-conduct through all perplexities and dangers. It makes little difference to the value of this safe-conduct whether, in the last resort, it be countersigned by Church, Bible, Exact Science or Conscience. Its supposed value lies in its *demonstrative certainty*, and so long as it carries this on its face, the particular origin of the certainty is a matter of secondary importance.

It is not possible to discuss here the various forms of authoritative guidance thus offered. In what remains to be said we confine ourselves to that form of Authority which is claimed for the individual conscience. In principle it is typical of them all, and it is only as typical that it is here discussed.

If Authority means any kind of inerrant legislation which gives us definite and detailed guidance as to what is and what is not our duty to do in specific cases, then for reasons already given the quest for that authority is necessarily vain from the nature of the case. If, on the other hand, reference is made to some entirely general proposition, as that all actions are subject to the law of right, or that Duty is supreme, then indeed there is no serious objection to our saying

that such universal truths have supreme authority over
the human will. But though this, or something very
like it, was the view held by Kant and his successors,
it bears little resemblance to the current intuitionist
theory of an authoritative conscience. According to
this, the intuitions of the conscience are definite *ad hoc*
pronouncements, not in the universal form that duty
must be done, but in the particular form which declares
this and not that to be your duty and straightway
enjoins you to do it. Further, these *ad hoc* pronouncements of the conscience—do this, don't do that—are to
be regarded (if only you can get them) as infallible in
precisely the same sense as the Vatican decrees are
regarded as infallible by the devout Romanist. They
represent the voice of God speaking in the soul, and
as such are to be accepted with unreserved submission.
Morality is just the life of submission to this divine
voice, and we must submit to it without reserve just
because it is divine. In this respect the final attitude
demanded of the soul is the same whether we take for
our guide Luther, Newman, Martineau; it is the
attitude of absolute obedience to an indefeasible
authority. Taking this theory as a whole I do not
think it possible that it should mean anything less than
this: viz. that each man carries in his breast a divine
oracle revealing to him, with infallible authority, the
right and the wrong of every crisis his will has to face.
Just because that oracle is divine we can, in obeying
its commands, make no mistakes.[1]

---

[1] Martineau fully admits the difficulty of extracting a clear pronouncement from this oracle in concrete cases, and proposes a method for dealing
with complications. But when once the pronouncement is extracted it is
to be regarded as oracular. See *Types of Ethical Theory*, ii. p. 255, ed. 1.

We need not linger over the host of objections that have been brought against this theory. Many of them have been valiantly met by its defenders. Chief among them is, of course, the obvious difficulty of accepting the conscience as the voice of God in face of the extraordinary diversity and conflict of judgments to which it gives rise. This is a difficulty which can be met; though, in order to do so, a monistic conception of the universe seems to be required.

More serious, however, is the difficulty which arises from a fact already noted. There is a large class of actions, by far the most significant with which conscience has to deal, which cannot be performed by any single will, but require the co-operation of several. This is the case, broadly speaking, with the whole class of our duties to one another. My will cannot do its duty by you (except when you are helpless) unless your will is a consenting party. My act in rendering you a service is apt to appear as unitary and entirely under *my* control. But the act is really *double*, and is no more under my control than it is under yours. Unless you take I cannot give, and your taking is as essential to the completion of the act as my giving. Nor can the significance of this be turned aside by referring to the motives involved. In all such cases our moral concern is with the whole *opus operatum*, and there can be no *opus operatum* unless your will co-operates with mine. What I will is not that a certain benevolent motive shall express itself by the offer of a service, but that something should be *done*, viz. the sovereign (say) transferred from my pocket to yours. That is impossible unless you consent. Now what I want my conscience

to tell me is not whether it is right for me to have
certain generous impulses towards you, but whether it
is right *to do this thing* ; and I am at once stopped
short by the reflection that unless your conscience
concurs the thing simply cannot be done at all. My
conscience, therefore, in its isolation is unable to solve
the question I want answered. Nothing could be more
futile than to go on reiterating the fatuous maxim that
each man has control over his own actions. The fact is
that, in the field we are now considering—the field of
social relations—there are no actions which a man can
call exclusively *his own*. The action is a joint affair :
it takes two or more to perform it. *The other* is always
implicated in the control. The notion that your buying
and my selling are two separate actions which make the
transaction by mechanical addition ; that being thus
separate each of them is susceptible of moral valuation
on its own account—this notion is the source of a whole
progeny of pernicious mistakes. My buying and your
selling are inseparable and meaningless if you take
them apart ; each is then a pure abstraction devoid of
content. My selling is simply your buying looked
at from my end ; your buying is my selling looked
at from your end. This will be found to hold good
throughout the entire system of moral relationships.
Every action is a *transaction*, or interaction, and it is
always as a concrete transaction, and not as an abstract
action, that the thing is either right or wrong. It
follows that the conscience of the abstract individual
has no power of dealing with the concrete situation ;
and the fact that we do deal with it every hour of our
lives is proof enough that we are not abstract individuals,
not separate and independent agents, and shows that

the theory which treats us as such can never account for moral judgment.

If, however, you still persist in dividing conduct into two halves, yours and mine, which by mere juxtaposition make up the total deed; if you say that each of these halves is a real action and that I am solely responsible for my half and you for yours; if you affirm that your authority or your science dictates infallibly how you are to conduct your half of the operation and mine renders the same service for me, then you must state precisely what this half action is for which each of us is severally responsible. Certainly it is not my selling, for that involves your buying. Certainly not your buying, for that involves my selling. Each of these is the whole, regarded from different ends, the whole transaction in which we are both involved and not a half for which either can be separately responsible. What, then, is my half, and what yours? Assuming a correct distribution made, observe what follows. You assign my half to me and make me solely responsible for that; you take your own and repudiate all responsibility for mine. Good; but on whom rests responsibility for the total transaction, the *opus operatum*, the actual deed that is done? Nobody. Were I responsible for the deed, I should get involved in your responsibilities; were you responsible you would get involved in mine, which is the very position that individual ethics must avoid. The method of halving responsibilities works out to this: each of us is responsible for something which is *not done*; while for the thing that is done, the *opus operatum*, neither of us is responsible. The isolated judgment, torn from its context, misses the issue;

it tells us what we do not want to know—something about a part that is never played; about the part that is to be played, about the deed that is to be done, it can tell us nothing.

For these reasons, and for many others which need not be stated here, it seems likely that the attempt to place the Seat of Authority in the individual con-science, *regarded, of course, as merely individual,* must go the way of all the other attempts that have been made to find for man a rule of definite, detailed, and infallible guidance through the dangers of his mortal lot. This failure, again, we may regard without the least dismay. The notion of infallibility, even in the form here assigned it, far from being needed by the moral consciousness, is one for which the moral life has actually no place. Morality is a wider enterprise than anything involved in mere submission to a rule known to be indefeasible and inerrant. It contains an element of faith, of courage, of daring, of willing-ness to face the risk which cannot be avoided in any finite dealing with infinite and eternal things.

To the intuitionist school, however, is due the high honour of having treated the so-called moral "problem" by a method distinct from that which is applicable to the problems of the scientific intellect. The intuitionist has discerned that *moral* action is not the mere result of any calculation whatsoever, no matter whether the calculation be in terms of Happiness, Self-realisation, or anything else. *What ought to be done* can never be demonstrated in the sense in which we can demon-strate the answer to any scientific problem, the essence of morality being, not the mere registration in action of a demonstrated result, but the willingness to go beyond the proof and to take risks in a realm where no proof is to be had. Those who delay moral action until a scientific justification is forthcoming of what they are about to do will wait for ever; they will do nothing. This the intuitionist has seen. To him, more than to any others, we owe a just estimate of the moral dangers of allowing our wills to dance attendance on a spurious "science of ethics." In such a "science" there is and can be no conclusiveness, and the habit of waiting for its conclusions, fostered by the mere use of the word "science" in this connection, prevents the will from grappling with that element of inconclusiveness which is present in every genuinely moral situation.

It may be that while rejecting the authority of "science" the intuitionist has repeated the error of his opponents by setting up the authority of conscience. Wherever the latter authority is represented as indefeasible, as infallible *ad hoc*, we are prone to think that the intuitionist has indeed fallen into the very error from which he would escape. Nevertheless, the appeal to conscience, when it carries no expectation of an *infallible* answer, betokens the attitude of mind which is, of all, most favourable to the moral life. This appeal may not end in the avoidance of mistakes; but it is more likely than any other to end in the doing of moral deeds. Speaking broadly, it is hardly too much to say that in the moral world the appeal to conscience is the surest way to get things done. It leads to action —just as mere "science" leads to inaction. For conscience rightly understood is no faculty of abstract judgment laying down propositions as to what ought and ought not to be done; it is not a "voice," though

we often name it such, bidding us do this or that ; it
is rather an *élan vital*, an impulse, an active principle,
nay, the good *Will* itself.   In submitting to conscience,
therefore, we are doing more than appealing to a
tribunal for judgment ; we are calling up our moral
powers, we are opening the way for those dynamic
instincts which are the vital principles of our self-
conscious being.

Is it necessary to further define this principle of conscience ? Does the will need to know the formula of its
action before it can act ? We think not.   This is a case
in which action fathers knowledge and not knowledge
action.   Whatever definition the intelligence may offer
of that absolute obligation which is said to be *felt*—and
this word is a warning against too rigid definition—
will be found on examination to have been revealed by
the action of the will itself, and not prescribed *for* the
will in advance of performance.   Nothing less than
the good will—and be it remembered that the good will
exists only in action—can ever reveal what the nature
of the good will is.   It must be left to tell its own
story in its own way ; and the story it tells of itself
is expressed in the form of moral actions ; its language
is the language of deeds, not of ethical theories alone.
All that science can do here is to follow after, while
the will leads the way.   There is, indeed, no surer
means of degrading the conscience than to treat it as
a problem requiring an answer.   A man who allows
the challenge of conscience to fall primarily upon his
intellect, whose first business with conscience is to
formulate the principle of its action—a man, that is,
who delays the use of his conscience until he can
wholly understand and define the nature of that impulse

which bids him act—such a man, we do not hesitate to say, is approaching that point of immoral neutrality, that dead centre of the will at which he will cease to have any conscience at all.

In the world of problems and appended solutions conscience has no natural place. It is only as living in a wider world than that which is handled by the problem-solving intellect, it is only as holding converse with Reality on sides other than those which address the speculative Reason, that man has need for such a faculty. However much the conscience of to-day may owe to past reflection on moral issues, we can easily satisfy ourselves that the understanding of its own nature, the formulation of its own principle, was never the first thing that conscience asked for but always the last. Love has always been the fulfilling of the law, and love is ahead of all definitions and independent of all formal guarantees.

Suppose a man to say, " There are wrongs to be redressed. As to the remedy we can only dimly guess at this and that. No infallible guidance is obtainable. Any remedy now proposed may ultimately do more harm than good. It remains either to make an experiment or do nothing. I will make an experiment based on the fullest knowledge I can obtain, but on a clear understanding with myself that this knowledge is fallible. I will lay down my life to carry this experiment through, even though I may be told on the Judgment Day that the enterprise is vain. For the sake of the right I will run the risk of being *ad hoc* in the wrong." Such language would, I think, express the voice of the moral consciousness in its moment of deepest insight and most heroic resolution. It is by men who have

thus argued that the moral progress of the world has
been accomplished.   And in paying these the honour
they deserve we must not forget that many a Columbus
has sailed into the West and never come back.   History
for the most part keeps a record only of such moral
experiments as turn out well ; but there are thousands
that fail—fail, I mean, in respect of their intended
results, fail from the point of view of " science," though
in a deeper sense they may illustrate the most splendid
triumphs of the Moral Ideal.

It may be argued that there are certain precepts of
morality about which every sane man is absolutely sure.
We are absolutely sure that it is wrong to practise
polygamy or to eat human flesh.   Any portion of the
Moral Code that can be regarded as permanently established is virtually infallible.   And here, of course, no
infallible guidance is needed.   A conscience which can
only declare that cannibalism is wrong, and such like,
is obviously an otiose faculty among people who have
outgrown the desire to eat their fellow-men.   It were
well, too, that we should remember the history of these
infallible rules.   Like everything else they have grown
to be what they are.   Every accepted rule had a beginning in the example of some daring pioneer who took
his moral life in his hands in the effort to find out a
better way.   Stealing was considered a virtue in primitive
societies.   There is a tribe in the Khyber Pass whose
children are ceremonially admitted into the sacred
communion of thieves.   The child is passed by its
parents through a magic hoop, and the priest who
stands by calls out, " Now he is a good thief."   From
such beginnings as this has the virtue of honesty been
evolved, and every step of that evolution has been the

19

work of men who would be condemned by the existing morality of their times. So with Benevolence in all its forms. It is one thing, as we have seen, to copy the example of the Good Samaritan; it was another thing for the Good Samaritan to set that example in face of a moral code which declared that the Jews and the Samaritans were to have no dealings.

Moreover, as each accepted rule has grown to be what it is, so the whole body of established morality is even now growing into higher forms. Every detail of it is continually calling for pioneers to extend its applications into the hinterland of human life and adapt its requirements to new conditions. The meaning of moral terms is continually changing with the evolution of society. This very notion of stealing is an instance. The characteristic thief of modern society is not the burglar or the highwayman, but quite a different sort of person, who at present hardly realises that he is a thief. There is no man living in society to-day who is not an accessory either before or after the fact in many a complicated process by which extensive harm is done to his fellow-men, and there is no doubt that posterity will judge this complicity by a standard quite out of keeping with the epitaphs we now engrave on the tombs of our most respected relatives and friends. A man who receives an income he has not earned may do so in good conscience; but his conscience will be all the better if he clearly understands that he runs the risk of standing before the morality of the future precisely as the moss-troopers and pirates of the sixteenth century stand before the morality of to-day. There is a host of questions of this kind which awake in fresh forms with every change in the ever-changing complex of human society. It is here, on the frontier line, where we stand facing those new regions into which the voice of authority has not yet penetrated, that the burden, the responsibility, and the splendour of the moral life exist for us all.

Let us remember also that the sanctity of established morality can be maintained only so long as we are continually developing the implications of the Moral Ideal. In vain do we try to persuade Bill Sykes to give up his profession in a society where worse forms of malpractice than his are, I do not say condoned, but not even recognised for what they are. We should be well advised to deal gently with Bill Sykes in this matter. At all events, we can easily avoid the mistake of superimposing our conscience on his, or of thinking that his moral "problem" in the presence of an unguarded cash-box is the same as our own. If we would judge Bill fairly we should think, not of what we should feel and do in regard to the cash-box, but of what we should feel and do on realising that the money in our pockets represented another man's labour rather than our own—and in regard to many other matters of the same sort about which we are not altogether comfortable in mind. Few of us dare claim an infallible scientific authority for what we do in these matters, stoutly as we may argue in defence of the action we take; and it is for that very reason that these disputable and disputed situations afford an opportunity for displaying the moral, or immoral, bias of our wills.

We may ask, in conclusion, what actual effects on human character are likely to be produced by a theory which makes the moral life consist in submission to an indefeasible authority, no matter whether that authority be "external" or "internal." A person holding this view will naturally tend to limit his sphere of moral action to that type of performance in which the safe-conduct of science or conscience is actually forthcoming. Believing that duty lies in submission to a definite command, his conception of duty will tend to stop at the point beyond which the definite command is no longer heard, and to include only such performance as represents an equally definite act of submission to the commanding voice. The sphere marked out for the development of his character is the sphere of established morality, the conduct which is approved by enlightened public opinion, and explicitly enjoined in whatever code he may regard as highest. Such a character will tend to be correct, but unprogressive; irreproachable, but limited. Its history will contain few tragedies, but also few triumphs. The society where the type prevails will be conspicuously clean; but it will be weak on the side of courage, faith, and enterprise; having inherited a certain level of moral excellence it will remain stationary at that level; its temper will be essentially legal and conservative and perhaps timid; it will occasionally degenerate towards a Pharisaic pride; it will discourage originality and be afraid of it; it will produce no new types: out of its bosom no Columbus will set sail into the West—perhaps to be heard of no more. It will honour those who have set great examples in the past, but it will fail of high deeds through not perceiving that the only way to morally imitate an old example is to set a new one.

Such a type of character is likely to be common wherever the idea of fixed rule is the centre of moral teaching. We cannot deny its value. In a society which not only tolerates but requires a great variety of moral types for its healthy development, the type before us stands for the element of stability so essential to ordered progress and helps to preserve an unbroken line of communications with the past. It corresponds in the moral world to the House of Lords in the British Constitution. At the same time we may well doubt whether this type, lofty as it may be in some respects, is the one for which there is the widest use and the most urgent need at the present stage of social evolution; and we may confidently say that elevation to this kind of ethical peerage is not the highest ambition to place before a young and ardent soul. The world needs, as it has never needed before, a spirit of ethical experiment which the clinging to safe-conduct is likely to suppress. We may admit, indeed we must anxiously consider, the dangers attendant upon such enterprises, always subject to the principle that without danger the work of the Moral Will cannot be done; and never forgetting that all we now securely hold in morality was at the beginning the doing of pioneers—of men who took their lives in their hands. We need to recognise that with every step in the organisation of society questions of morality assume more and more of a social character and become less and less matters of private and individual concern. The high walls which formerly secluded the lives of different classes from each other's knowledge have disappeared. We all live in the light of our neighbours' eyes. We who judge others to be sinners are being judged as sinners by them. Bill Sykes thinks meanly of us—not without reasons. The consequence is that the action of example is much more rapid than formerly, the influence of different men and different classes upon one another much more potent and immediate.   Applying this to the question of the moral reformation of those whom we choose to call "bad men," we get the answer that the only form of society under which the worst men will become good is that in which the best men are becoming better.   In modern life, with all its closeness of interaction and mutual intimacy of knowledge, this is the first condition needed for the reformation of the vicious.   Now the tendency of authoritative ethics is always to concentrate attention on the case of the wicked and to overlook what is equally needed, namely, the improvement of the good.   For a good man, who has kept all the commandments from his youth up, is apt to ask himself with a certain self-complacency, "What more remains for me to do?" The answer is that everything yet remains for him to do by which his righteousness is to exceed that of the scribes and Pharisees.   His moral development, arrested at the line where the voice of authority ceases to speak, contributes no vital energy to the life of a rapidly developing society.   Beyond this line there lies a whole host of tremendous moral tasks roughly indicated by the hint given to the rich ruler, "that he should sell all that he had and give to the poor."   In this group of tasks, which constitute the life-business of every man who "is perfect in the works of the law," the safe-conduct of scientific guidance is not to be had.   And it is through the habit of seeking for safe-conduct that we become both blind to the existence of such tasks and incompetent to deal with them when discovered by others.   What is now required is imagination, creativeness, initiative, and that heroic willingness to trust oneself to the unknown which is seldom to be found among the painstaking and meticulous observers of the law. The needed change in moral teaching would therefore take the form of less insistence on submission to authority, and more insistence on the fundamental virtues of courage and faith.

XIII.—MORAL EDUCATION

It is one thing to maintain that virtue can be taught; it is another thing to assume that the way to teach it is by set lessons in virtue. These two positions are commonly confused. We may assent to the first and deny the second.

While admitting that the education of character is the most important function of the teacher, I cannot repress the belief that to teach morals departmentally, as a subject among subjects, at set hours, as a formal exercise, and by the aid of some elementary " Moral Science," is an undertaking which in spite of its good intentions may end in disaster. It will create expectations that cannot be fulfilled; will teach the pupil to lean on a staff that breaks under pressure; and will provoke a hostile reaction against the idea of morality.

For whereas the pupil will find that every other science does help him to solve the problems to which it is addressed, moral science does not solve the moral problem but merely gives to it a new and a more difficult form. This we have already endeavoured to make clear. It remains to consider its bearing on the moral education of the young.

To illustrate our point we will recur to the former example of the Good Samaritan and suppose him to have received instruction according to the programme of some moral science extant in his day. Lesson 1 will have taught him that his duty is to succour those in distress. Lesson 37—under a remote section, or perhaps in the Appendix—will also have taught him that it is contrary to duty to have dealings with the Jews. Equipped with this teaching he now faces the actual situation, and finds to his great perplexity that the person on the road is *both* a wounded man, whom Lesson 1 says he ought to succour, *and* a Jew, whom Lesson 37 says he ought to leave alone. Thus the point at which his problem begins is precisely that at which his science deserts him. To be more exact, his science creates the perplexity, and leaves him to resolve it as best he may. Or, if this seem unfair, let us say that it defines, or helps to define, the problem that has to be solved. But is there any other science which merely defines a problem? Could we claim, for instance, that the teaching of Physics consisted in defining the problems with which Physics has to deal?

The example cited merely serves, of course, to illustrate the commonplace that morality has to do with a "conflict of duties." Virtue is a "mean"; its office being, not obedience to rules taken one by one, but the adjustment of their conflicting claims. So long as we are contemplating an isolated moral rule — as that "Truth ought to be told"—we are not in sight of any moral problem; this comes into view only when, over against the reasons for telling the truth, other reasons appear which seem to justify, or call for, the telling of a lie. This needs only to be stated to make it abundantly clear that whatever else we may be doing in teaching the rule that "truth ought to be told," we are not teaching virtue. For virtue, we repeat, lies not in the blind acceptance of the rule as valid for all occasions, but in the moral skill which directs its application or its abandonment in a given case. About this, which is the crux of the whole matter, no information is or can be given by any moral text-book; for the necessary adjustments of every rule to every other rule would run out to infinity, and even if attempted could be given only in general forms which would always miss the *nuances* of their particular application. No doubt it may be said, and said with perfect truth, that virtue cannot do its work of adjustment unless we know what it is we have to adjust, and this knowledge is precisely what the moral educator gives, and what it is so important he should give, by the teaching of particular moral rules. But then we must ask, By what right is this kind of education called "moral"? So regarded, the rule "Tell the truth" differs in no essential character from the rule "Keep your powder dry," or "Wait till the train has passed before crossing the line," or "Be on your guard against tuberculous milk." By calling it "moral," occasion is given to the mistaken belief that we are teaching *virtue*; the truth being that by imparting this kind of information we get no nearer the teaching of virtue than if we were engaged in spreading any other kind of scientific knowledge.

And lest this should be treated as a mere quibble about words, let us hasten to point out the supreme importance of guarding ourselves from illusion in these matters. We are all too ready to believe that anything and everything can be bought for money—or provided by the State. We have only to set up some system of teaching and call it "moral education," and parents will begin to flatter themselves that they are relieved from the responsibility of training the characters of their children. Is not the State or the schoolmaster doing the business as a *quid pro quo*? Are not daily lessons being given in honesty, purity, charity, and the rest? What, then, remains for us to do? The answer is that so far as virtue or character is concerned everything remains to do. Virtue is precisely one of those human accomplishments which cannot be taught by machinery of this kind, no matter how cunningly contrived; and it is infinitely important for all of us, and for parents especially, to escape from the illusion that it can. This disastrous illusion is fostered by exhibiting as "moral education" what after all may be nothing more than a slight addition to the child's general knowledge of the world in which he lives. Extend his knowledge in these directions as far as you may, it will always be found that "virtue" depends on something which lies outside, though perhaps only *just* outside, the line which the information given him has reached. What a community may have to pay for overlooking this none too obvious truth is illustrated at the present moment in France, where an alarming increase in the statistics of child-criminality—which reveal an extraordinary prevalence of suicidal mania among boys and girls—and a rapidly diminishing birth-rate have been synchronous with a period of universal "moral" education in schools.[1]

---

[1] I am far from saying that those lamentable results must be attributed wholly to the system of moral education adopted in France. Enough that it has not prevented them. In the light of these events it is interesting to read the words of M. Gambetta spoken in 1881: "They (our children) will understand nothing of these old-fashioned fears; for they will not have to make for themselves their code of free conscience and free thought; they will have imbibed it in their

There are, indeed, good reasons to fear that the children themselves may suffer direct and serious harm from the attempt to treat morality as a "department" of education. Some of these reasons are well known; some, on the other hand, have been overlooked. Among the first, it is generally admitted that the perfunctory teaching of morals is worse than no teaching at all. And yet it is hard to imagine any general system of dealing with this subject which would not become sooner or later the merest routine. Competence for the training of character is a rare gift; and of all the blunders into which men may be led by their faith in machinery, we cannot conceive of anything more disastrous than the issue of a general order to all teachers—or even to all head-masters—to carry out some cut-and-dried system of moral education. It needs but little imagination to picture the result—the formality of the process, the half-heartedness of the teacher, the apathy and repugnance of the taught. To save such a system from rapid degeneration into a means of producing effects the very opposite of those intended would be beyond the wit of man. It were unfortunate even that morality should be enveloped in the atmosphere of a school lesson. The duties of life are hard enough; no need to make them harder by recollections of tedious half hours. The skill which would overcome these difficulties is precisely the kind of skill that cannot be procured to order; nor can

mother's milk and in the teaching of their schoolmaster." M. Paul Bert, speaking on the same subject, said: "We are laying the foundation of solid consciences which will bear in themselves their own sanction." M. Bert's idea of morality appears, from these words, to have been different from M. Gambetta's; but the "system" adopted seems to have been a failure from both points of view.

it, if procured, be regulated as to its operations by a code. To estimate the effects of moral education reduced to a "system," one has to imagine that system in the hands of the relatively unskilled. And the prospect does not allure us.

But there is a deeper and less noticed reason for fearing the results of treating morality as an item in an educational curriculum. It is that such treatment gives rise to a false impression in the pupil's mind of what morality is and means. Accustomed to encounter this subject at a fixed point in a routine, and as one among many things he has to learn, he naturally comes to think of morality as a special department of life, as a particular interest among others, as a thing which is on and off like drawing, music, or mathematics, according to the requirements of the hour. It is hardly possible to avoid creating this impression, whatever formal means may be taken to guard against it. Need it be pointed out that such a conception of morality will more than undo any good that may be otherwise achieved? One might truly say that the prime object of moral education is to extirpate, or at all events preclude, the idea of morality as a sectional interest of life. Unless it can be taught in its universal character, it cannot be taught at all; for morality is universal or nothing. And though these are terms that cannot be introduced to children, they are yet of vital importance to the teacher, who will soon find that the attempt to teach departmentally what by its innermost nature is not departmental but universal, is a self-defeating enterprise from the outset. It is bad enough that duty should carry the associations of a formal lesson, or wake the memories of dull exercises and weary hours; it is still worse when continual admonitions act—and they often do so act—as suggestions of the very evil they are intended to prevent; but the worst is reached when, in addition to all this, the idea of morality as an item in the school programme is translated by the pupil into the idea of morality as an item in the business of life. Any system of moral education which does not guard against this danger is to be condemned. And it is difficult to imagine a safeguard that would be sufficient. Whatever might be *said* to the pupil about the matter, the fact that morality was treated departmentally, that it came on and went off like other things, would inevitably tend to a similar conception concerning moral practice. And if it be answered that morality (and religion) have always been taught at set times and places, as items in the programme of the week's business, I can only reply that the objector is here pointing, not to the strongest, but to the weakest feature in moral and religious instruction as hitherto carried on. It is only when we turn to the case of the young that the peculiar evils of this method become manifest. Certainly, were one asked to lay out a set of psychological conditions from which moral failure is likely to result one could hardly do it better than by drawing the character of a boy who has enjoyed in all their fulness the doubtful advantages of some wooden or mechanical system of moral education.[1]

Now if we are to deal with moral education at all—and of course it has to be dealt with—it were well to understand from the outset that there is here no

---

[1] Butler has drawn this character in *The Way of all Flesh*—one of the great novels of the world.

question of introducing a new subject, namely, morals, into an existing curriculum, but only of introducing a better method into what is already taught. It is a question as to the scope and principles of education as a whole. Putting the matter on the broadest ground, may we not say that all education is moral which helps or incites the pupil to fulfil a definite purpose in life? If that statement seems premature, we may be content for the present with this: that all education is immoral which has no bearing on a definite life-purpose. There is nothing so dangerous as knowledge, because there is nothing so powerful; and any knowledge imparted otherwise than as a means of helping the taught to live and let live is a menace to the safety and well-being of the human race. When once this principle has been grasped it will be seen that any subject may be taught morally, and that every subject is ill taught which lacks a moral direction as defined. Thus a boy who is being taught engineering in such a way as to make him a "good" engineer is being morally educated; whereas another who is merely being drilled in set lessons on the virtues, the application of which cannot be defined, is not only getting no moral education, but is being exposed to dangers which bid fair to make him an immoral man. The engineer who builds a crazy bridge or a rotten embankment, and thereby causes a railway accident or an inundation, does no credit to his moral education even though he has kept all the "commandments" from his youth up; and if that is all that moral education can produce, then the less we have of it the better. Or, to put the same point otherwise. A wise man, eager that his children should develop the noblest type of character, would probably prefer to send them to a school where history and geography were being taught in such a way as to make them proud of their country and eager to play a part in the building of the Empire, rather than to another where an artificial scheme of moral instruction was in vogue and well-meant efforts were being made to imbue young minds with the virtues one by one. From the first type of teaching he would expect what we call character; and character in which the gentler virtues were as prominent as any other. The second type, he would fear, might result in the production of prigs or possibly of scoundrels.

It is only on large lines of that kind, which embrace the whole scope of education, that the training of character can be carried on; while any process which starts from the assumption that the pupil is a pathological subject to be dosed with tonics and fed on previously digested food, or which perverts moral training into a *local treatment of the conscience*, is certain to end badly. Disaster is what we should also expect from every attempt to enforce a rigid pattern of virtue or a set of duties. Such methods invariably give the impression to the pupil that another will is being imposed on his own; and this is resented, not because the pupil is corrupt, but because his own moral nature, being healthy, demands autonomy. Nor do I think the case is mended one whit when the will imposed on the pupil is represented as "higher" than his own. This is apt to accentuate the resentment and to make the reaction against morality more destructive.

As against all this, I would submit that the moral

educator is doing his work whenever he is presenting the truth of the human environment in its bearing on the definite life-purpose of his pupil. He should remember that every fact has a moral meaning, because it contains an implicit command to be something or do something. Thus history is not well presented until we hear it commanding us to be good citizens; geography commands us to be wide-minded, mathematics to be accurate, and so on without end. The teacher who has grasped this principle will unconsciously handle every subject in such a way as to invigorate the moral nature of the taught. Making the least use possible of the mere terminology of virtue, he will turn the whole environment of the pupils' intelligence into a field for the exercise of the virtues. Remembering that language is always an inadequate vehicle for the expression of morality, he will prefer to leave facts and events and persons to tell their own story, cunningly setting them in such a light that the indicative of what is or has been is inevitably translated by the pupil into the imperative of what ought to be. He will inculcate no virtue for which he cannot provide an immediate field of exercise; he will be careful not to create temptations to lying by the excessive admonition that truth ought to be told; nor to impurity by continually imploring his pupils to be pure.

This is nothing else than to say that all education which is definitely controlled by a human life-purpose is moral; all that lacks it, immoral. Intensification of the *human* purpose in education is the way to make education moral. And here one must confess that the outstanding feature of so much that passes for education is its appalling lack of purpose. There are many elements

20

in our educational system which in their origin had a definite relation to life-purpose. They have survived into an age when the life-purpose they once served has perished, or survives only in partial and limited forms. They have now become purposeless, and to that extent they are demoralising. It is true that "culture" has been defined in a way which makes it an aimless acquisition. Some even find its value in its very aimlessness; and this seems to underlie certain current theories about the functions of Universities. Instances are alleged, though I think they are not genuine, in which this view seems to produce good results. What its defenders are pleading for is not, in truth, the elimination of purpose from teaching, but the introduction of higher and wider purpose than that which is recognised as valid by common minds. Nevertheless it is to be greatly feared that the average result of a one-sided emphasis on the higher purpose of culture is not a Matthew Arnold or a Jowett, but the type of public school boy or undergraduate who looks upon this world merely as a place to sprawl round in.

It is not possible to exaggerate the value of *definite* life-purpose as the controlling principle of moral education. By laying stress on the word definite we are enabled to meet the chief difficulty which such a statement seems to involve. "What!" it will be said, "are all purposes equally good? Are not some distinctly bad?" To this we may answer that life-purpose becomes good in proportion as the pupil makes it definite, and bad in proportion as he leaves it vague. Suppose, then, a man were to say, "My purpose is to make myself the biggest blackguard under the sun." What would the moral educator do with him? If he were wise he would accept the purpose as stated, but challenge the man to make it definite. Let him define all the forms of blackguardism he means to cultivate, let him unfold their implications, and before the process is half through the man will have to acknowledge that his alleged life-purpose is nothing but a mass of absurd contradictions and therefore not a purpose at all. It has only to be defined to be dismissed. The act of defining life-purpose is the most wholesome moral exercise any man can undertake ; for in so doing, whatever is bad will surely get itself sifted out as something which no rational being can really mean to aim at. Therefore we need not hesitate to accept any purpose which is genuinely definite, in the sense of being the object the man really means to pursue as the aim of his life, as being sufficiently sound to provide the basis of moral education. Let it be remembered, however, that he must define it for himself; no science can define it for him. On the other hand, we cannot build morality on the foundation of *ill-defined* purpose, even though it clothe itself in the most highly respectable form of words. If, for example, the subject were to state that he wanted to be a gentleman, or a Christian, or to spend his life in doing good to others, this of itself would offer no means of guiding his moral education, and the fear would be well grounded that vague aims of this sort would produce at best but a feeble and mediocre type of character. But suppose he were to define his purpose thus : " I want to do good by helping the Charity Organisation Society "—then the instructor would be in a position to begin. And his business would be, not to teach charity as an abstract virtue, but to teach charity *organisation*, with a view to making his pupil the sanest, most level-headed, best-informed and most efficient charity organiser.   And that would be the only kind of moral education that really met the needs of the case.

Or, if the question were whether the Humanities, or the technical sciences, provide the best means of educating character, again the answer would depend on the definite relation to human purpose with which these subjects may be severally taught.   In spite of the high reputation the Humanities bear in this respect, there can be little doubt that the purposeless teaching of the Humanities is a demoralising form of education ; and that as between new universities where electricity and brewing are taught for the purpose of making good electricians and good brewers, and old universities (if there are any such) where the Humanities are taught for no purpose in particular, the new universities are likely to turn out better men.   Of course there is no reason why the Humanities should be taught without purpose ; though they do seem to lend themselves very readily to that sort of teaching.   They can be taught as an essential instrument to the making of good citizens, and probably no finer instrument for the purpose was ever devised.   But when one observes how often they are taught in another manner, one can hardly refrain from joining the outcry of those who would sweep them away.

Finally, if it be true that conduct is the greatest of the Fine Arts, let us remember all that this involves for the teacher of morals.   In the Fine Arts there is only one effective way of showing how the thing ought to be done—and that is by doing it.   And the aim of the moral educator, after all, is to get things done and

not merely to impart information about morals.
The building of character is a very different enterprise from the building of machines, and demands
in those who attempt it qualifications which are not
easily acquired.

XIV.—RELIGION

RELIGION is the consciousness of a spirit which knows itself to be one with the Highest. In Religion there is and must be something dogmatic, authoritative, irrevocable, even defiant. What Religion announces is a final decision, which may not be withdrawn, modified, or made the subject of negotiation under any circumstances whatever. It is the soul's ultimatum. If in one sense Religion is the humblest of attitudes, in a deeper sense it is the most exalted. It claims to overcome the world and to put all things under its feet. Religion is content with nothing less than the absolute submission of the entire range of human experience to itself. Opposition only quickens it into completer self-assertion, and the hour when its foes are most active is the hour of its firmest carriage. When the highest interests of the soul are being threatened, and the foundations of life are on the point of being swept away, Religion rises up with an answering menace, and delivers its ultimatum in the teeth of the facts. "For this cause," it cries, "came I unto this hour. Yea, though He slay me, yet will I trust Him." It is the pillar of fire which burns at its brightest in the blackest night. It is the trumpet-call of man's unconquerable soul breathing a challenge to the armies of doubt, sorrow, and sin.

The majesty of Religion is self-supported, and her

authority is never merged in that of her ambassadors. Her splendours are unadorned, and she needs no devices of man's wit to make her acceptable. She has no *alter ego*, and refuses to be identified with that which is voted good by the majority. She is no member of the Grand Committee of Human Interests. To pass off Religion as Morality, Art, Science, singly or together, is to mistake the viceroy for the monarch and to ignore the hiding-place of Power. She will not be harnessed to the yoke of any human purpose whatsoever, and suffers no man to commend her as a thing that is likely to please.

Religion has no fellowship with idols; is never disguised; cannot be hidden under a phrase, nor revealed by a dance of thin abstractions. Of all the idols that usurp her place, those are the vainest that are built up out of *words*. The vainest—but the most eagerly run after in every age that boasts enlightenment. They are set up in the market-place; they deck the shop-windows of Eloquence; men sell them for money in the House of God. Religion weeps over these things as Christ wept over Jerusalem; and again she drives them from the Temple with a whip of small cords.

Before the overwhelming immensities of the universe, Religion alone remains unabashed. The doom of earth is written in the sky; human life, through uncounted generations, is but a breath breathed forth into voids of endless time; the sun and the planets short-lived as a dance of fireflies on a summer night. All is as nothing. To an imagination like Carlyle's which has opened its arms to the terrors of Time and Space, or looked upon the littleness of man, as Dante's did, from the empyrean height, there comes a moment when Hope and Faith shrivel out of being and the very will to live expires.

The soul is on the point of total collapse beneath the weight of the everlasting No.

Then it is, when all seems lost, that the mighty heart of Religion begins to beat. She knows that her hour has come: "Out of the deep, O Lord, I cried unto Thee, and Thou heardest me." None save a being infinitely greater than the world would be aware of his own infinite littleness within the world. Religion is the soul of that being. It is the shock of the entire universe of sense that has to be met; the deeps of immensity have poured out their legions, clad in the iron raiment of inexorable law; armies of negation are encamped beneath the walls and battering at the gates. This is the challenge; and well may we say that *all* of it is needed, and nothing less would suffice, to stir the soul of man into that final act of self-expression which we call Religion.

Unbroken by the cosmic challenge, Religion runs no risk of succumbing to any lesser strain. Summoned to action by the evils of the human lot, she gathers enthusiasm from the magnitude of her task. Just because she is the spirit of the Best she rises to her greatest when she knows and faces the Worst. Undisguised in her own majesty, she penetrates every disguise that is used to cover the malignancy of her foe. That evil should be extenuated or proved not to be; that black should be painted white; that the groaning and travailing of creation should be hushed up or put out of sight —this is no prayer of hers. Things are as they are; new names do not alter them; evil is evil, pain is pain, death is death; and it is only by accepting them in their naked reality that Religion can be true to herself. Let them be what they are, and she will deal with

them. Let the sinner be a sinner and she will put her
arms round him; let the sheep be veritably lost and she
will recover them; let evil come armed to the battle
and she will draw her sword; let the gloom thicken
and her radiance shall glow like the noonday; let life be
tragic and she will lift it up among the stars.

"When thou hearest the fool rejoicing, and he saith, 'It is over and
past,
And the wrong was better than right, and hate turns into love at
the last,
And we strove for nothing at all, and the gods are fallen asleep;
For so good is the world agrowing that the evil good shall reap':—
Then loosen thy sword in the scabbard and settle the helm on thine
head,
For men betrayed are mighty, and great are the wrongfully dead." [1]

It follows that Religion is the deepest principle of
unity among men. The challenge she answers, the
burden she lifts, the shock she encounters and repels, is
one and the same for all men everywhere. Wherever
her authentic voice is heard, no matter what its language,
we feel that it speaks for us *all*; the answer it makes is
the answer we fain would give, the battle it announces
is the battle we are yearning to win. Religion may
speak in propositions to which we cannot assent; may
practise rites we cannot join; may build altars where
we can lay no offering. But let it once appear that
these things represent the self-assertion of a soul that is
winning the victory over the world—fearless of Nature,
of Death, of Evil, of Immensity—and who will not
thankfully proclaim that *his own* cause is being pleaded
before high heaven? who will not acknowledge that
these brave ones are holding the fort where his own soul
standeth in jeopardy? Shall there not be deepest
blood-brotherhood between them and us? Shall not

[1] *The Song of Sigurd the Volsung.*

love go forth, unfeigned and entire, towards these masters of the fate that threaten us all? Is it not enough for unity that all men have one terror to face, one shock to encounter, one world to overcome, one death to endure? Are not the ultimate terms of the human compact wholly fulfilled by any soul of man that shows us the way in bearing up against these things? Need we inquire into the secret of his endurance and refuse to accept him until he has answered— when once we have seen that he endures?

The spirit that is in Religion is that of uncompromising loyalty to the Highest. Its fealty is entire and requires no confirmation by an oath. It lives in the whole, loves the whole with a patriot's devotion, and passes into utterance, or into action, "with the felt strength of the universe at its back." Religion stands by a Cause; but this rests on no reasoning, for it is the Cause of Reason itself. Religion is not afraid of its future, suffers from no sense of insecurity, and speaks in language that is both triumphant and serene.

Religion, therefore, does not apologise for itself, does not stand on the defensive, does not justify its presence in the world. If theorists would vindicate Religion, they may do so; but Religion comes forth in the majesty of silence, like a mountain amid the lifting mists.[1] All the strong things of the world are its children; and whatever strength is summoned to its support is the strength which its own spirit has called into being. Religion never excuses its attitude, and when at last a Voice is lifted up it simply chants the Faith, until the deaf ears are unstopped and the dead

[1] "The rest may reason, and welcome; 'tis we musicians know."
—*Abt Vogler.*

in spirit come out of their graves to listen. There is
nothing so masterful; and it speaks as one who has a
right to the mastery. It is the major control of thought,
to which all systems whatsoever bear witness, either
silent or confessed. Authority is not what it requires,
but what it confers. Its voice is peremptory but not
violent, convincing but not tyrannical, and every truth
that it announces passes insensibly into a command.
Its indicatives are veiled imperatives; and no hypothetical proposition ever escapes from its lips. So that,
unless a man is overborne by his religion, we may truly
say his religion is vain.

Religion depends on no favourable conditions. It is
a vain thing when we say one to another: "Go to,
now; let us make a garden in a sunny spot; let us
create a soft atmosphere of happiness such as Religion
loves; let us build a mighty hedge of argument to
shield this tender plant from the ravages of the east
wind." To argue thus is to look at life from the
wrong end. It is not in man to make Religion
what he would have her be, but only to be what
Religion is making him. As weak, she makes him
strong; as defeated, victorious; as naked, she clothes
him; as exposed to every desolating wind, she wraps
her mantle around him and he is safe. Were it easy
for the natural man to believe in God there would be
no such thing as Religion; were even the argument
for morality a mere conclusion from premises there
would be no such thing as doing right. Unless the
soul were greater than its arguments it would never
see the gaps in its own logic; unless it were mightier
than its deeds it would never be aware of imperfection;
and it is only as conscious in himself of a Rational Will

which is fully expressed in none of his achievements, either of logic or of life, that man is able to assert himself above his failures, and bridge the gaps between the actual and the ideal. "The righteous man," says Kant, "may say: I *will* that there should be a God; I *will* that, though *in* this world of natural necessity, I should not be *of* it, but should also belong to a purely intelligible world of freedom; finally I *will* that my duration should be endless. On this faith I insist and will not let it be taken from me."

To many who have inherited the Christian temper it may seem at first sight that statements such as these are at variance with the essential character of the spiritual life. That life is, before all else, meek and lowly, gentle and peaceable; it vaunteth not itself, is not puffed up, is not easily provoked. Its note is self-repression, not self-assertion. The humble, the contrite, the broken-hearted are its chief exponents, and the most perfect symbol of its spirit is the little child. It does not strive nor cry, nor smite with the sword; its language is a prayer of submission and not a challenge; its deeds are the healing acts of love.

Such a rejoinder is true in all that it affirms, and false in all that it denies. Every one of the qualities here affirmed is truly predicated of Religion, and Christianity in particular bases on them its claim to represent the highest stage in the evolution of the religious life. But these finer qualities are often commended in language and illustrated by examples which suggest that they have their original spring in some weakness of the soul. They are, rather, the most perfect fruit of the soul's strength, daring, and energy. Forgetfulness of this has, perhaps, done more than all

other causes put together to discredit Christianity in
the modern world. Among other damage it has given
occasion to the invective of Nietzsche, and to the whole
literature of the self-assertion of unconverted Man.
The summit-truths are always the easiest to pervert.
And the doctrine which makes Religion the refuge of
the weak, and declares that only failures are ever
beaten to their knees, is precisely such a perversion.
For what is self-repression? Is it merely the turning
of one's back on each particular object of desire, or
the shutting of one's ear to every voice which cries
"Lo here, lo there"? Were it only this, there would
be no denying that in Nietzsche's philosophy Christianity
has met its overthrow. But self-repression means infinitely more. Its essence is not the negative abandonment of the particular, but the dynamic grasp of the
universal; not the mere forsaking of the husks, but
the rising up in the total strength of manhood and
the arduous climbing of the path which was so easy
in descent. Self-repression is self-assertion—or it is
nothing. It represents the developing attack of the
spirit on the Object of supreme desire, wherein the
beggarly elements are not destroyed but transmuted—
first compelled into unconditional surrender and then
enlisted and taken up as the working forces of the
great design. The fruits of the spirit in all their mild-
ness and sweet reasonableness are thus the fruits of
the world that has been overcome; and the world is not
overcome by running away from its perishing shows.
In Goethe's well-known lines there is one word that
seems to bear the emphasis of this pleading:

"Im Ganzen, Guten, Schönen,
    Resolut zu leben."

The great-heartedness of Religion craves expression and must be expressed. There is a moment in the act of worship when neither the prayer of contrition nor the hymn of adoration will satisfy, when the Will breaks the leash of constraint with which the understanding has held it back, and launches itself in triumphant affirmation, and with the full force of its argument within it, against all that is irrational, dark, or terrible in the world. The precautions of apology and self-defence are now abandoned; the baggage train is emptied and left behind; the soul ceases to parley with Principalities and Powers, and, in a joy that is free from all fetters, lifts on high the battle-hymn of its faith with its deep refrain of "I believe." This moment is the very consummation of worship, gathering into itself the meaning of all that has gone before, and precluding a yet greater moment when faith passes into action and truth becomes a deed. When sincere, there is nothing which so stirs the pulses of the spiritual life, nothing which puts such power into the arm of the Good. Religion, no longer entrenched behind bulwarks, is now seen marching into the open like an army with banners, the Ark of the Covenant in the midst, and the trumpeters going on before.

Isaiah and Jesus had no other conception of Religion than this. They spake with authority, and the note of triumph was in their voices. When they argued it was unto conviction. The sense of power, dependent on no temporal suffrages whatsoever, rings out in every prophet's cry. The attitude of self-defence is foreign to the prophet; he must always attack, must always

be of good cheer; must always go forth conquering
and to conquer.

> " Gladness be with thee, Helper of the World !
> I think this is the authentic sign and seal
> Of Godship, that it ever waxes glad,
> And more glad, until gladness blossoms, bursts
> Into a rage to suffer for mankind
> And recommence at sorrow."

The attitude of self-defence is foreign even to the
makers of the ancient Creeds. Their creeds have been
found inadequate to the expanding reason of mankind,
but their spirit has been fatally misunderstood. They
have been treated as having no aim save that of laying
down articles of agreement for the Church of God,
signed, sealed, and delivered. Were that all, we might
truly say that the labour was vain. But they sought
to satisfy a deeper need. Then as now a word was
wanted to sustain the courage and confirm the loyalty
of the marching host. In the stress and difficulty of
life, which were more insistent for them than they
now seem to us, Religion could not be suffered to
lose confidence in itself. Over and over again the
issue must be frankly faced, for it is the issue of
life or death; the soul must be reminded, and again
reminded, that its ultimatum has been delivered; the
final decision must be recalled and reaffirmed; the
soul's covenant with God must be displayed, and the
will of man recommitted to its clauses one by one.
Such was the deeper intention of the ancient Creeds.
Would any lesser aim have secured their survival
into an age which has grown beyond them; or
made it possible that many good and enlightened
men should still chant them in a voice of triumph
when, by their own confession, they can give an

unqualified assent to scarcely a single one of the propositions they utter?

Theirs was not the spirit of spurious open-mindedness, so much in fashion nowadays, which worships a note of interrogation—the timidity which dare commit itself to nothing; the half-hearted religion which negotiates for its status and proposes a perpetual parley with Doubt, Sin, and Death. "Such, my friends, are the principal objections which Christianity has to encounter at the present day, but I venture to think we need not despair." *Retro Satanas!* The lines have indeed fallen unto us in a highly apologetic age. We apologise for the highest things; we introduce them tentatively— often with a veiled implication that their opposites are almost as good. But if the dogmatism of the Creeds is bad, this other extreme is infinitely worse. How can the world fail to despise a religion which is accompanied by a perpetual excuse for its own existence? The world knows well that the thing so offered is not Religion at all. Whatsoever comes before man with the airs of a suppliant cannot be the Spirit of the Highest. It is the devil who is the prince of apologists, and even he is not always fawning for the suffrages of his constituents. The Good, however lowly its form, does not apologise for itself, nor creep into the world with an abashed countenance and an air of "I hope I don't intrude?" It stands on its rights.

Is there, then, no need of the Apologist, no service which he can perform? Most assuredly there is. Does not Faith, even when most confident, demand a base secure within Experience, and a line of communications kept open in History? Nevertheless a time may come,

indeed has come, when the base is so distant and
indistinct, and the lines of communication so long,
numerous, and confused, that their maintenance drains
the best energies of the host. When these conditions arrive, the whole position becomes insecure,
Faith loses heart, and the Light ceases to invade
the Darkness. And weakness passes into decadence
when, in addition, there falls upon the Church
the task of protecting a huge baggage-train, packed
with obsolete munitions and a mixed assortment of
worldly goods. What ought to be subordinate now
becomes supreme. The priest drives out the prophet;
Religion gives no lead to life; laboured explanation
displaces the word of command; the objective is lost
sight of; the front is forgotten; force is scattered;
loyalty perishes; demoralisation spreads; the host
loses momentum and impact; strong men linger in the
rear and quarrel over the spoils of ancient victories.
The exclusion of Defence from the business of the
Church is not indeed to be thought of; but let the
things defended be worth defending, and such as are
really assailed. Religion conserves nothing that it
cannot use, for it is, before all else, a creative principle,
an active Good, an invasive Ideal.

The loss of this central conception is the recurrent
misfortune of every organised Church, and much of
the theological literature of the present time shows
little trace of its presence. The science of Christian
Apologetics has grown to enormous dimensions, its
convincingness inversely proportional to its mass. Sects
even have arisen which devote no small part of the
resources at their command to discovering a reason why
they should exist — the characteristic occupation of

sectarianism all the world over. The literature thus produced, whether in defence of doctrine or of denomination, is not inspiring though it seems to be popular. Many go to church for the purpose of hearing Religion defended, and explained, and placed on some perilous footing of accommodation with alien things in which they really believe. There is a strong disposition to meet doubt half way, discuss the matter as an open question, and effect some kind of feeble compromise. The Churches have laid themselves out to meet the demand, and the weakest of them all are the most apologetic.

XV.—IS THE MORAL SUPREMACY OF CHRISTENDOM IN DANGER?[1]

IF there is any considerable number of Christian thinkers who habitually take due account of the meaning of the great non-Christian religions, I must confess that the fact has escaped my observation.[2] That the extent to which these religions prevail has been accurately measured by Foreign Missionary Societies I do not doubt; but that their accuracy of measurement has always been accompanied by intelligent comprehension of the thing measured is not so clear. Nor do I overlook the splendid labours of Oriental scholars —Max Müller, Rhys Davids, Legge, Estlin Carpenter, and others in this country alone: they leave us all with no excuse for ignorance. But although the work of these thinkers deserves to be ranked among the great achievements of modern science, and although, as it seems to me, they have a close bearing on the problems of the Christian consciousness, the fact remains that in modifying the general form of Christianity they have effected next to nothing.[3]

[1] This essay was published in *The Hibbert Journal* at the conclusion of the Russo-Japanese war. As the question to which it relates has lost none of its importance in the interval, the essay is here republished.

[2] M. Loisy, and the Modernists generally, form a conspicuous exception.

[3] They have at least made incredible the doctrine of exclusive salvation, though this, to the scandal of Christendom, still remains in the formularies.

In its earliest stages Christianity displayed a wonderful power of assimilating elements from the various pagan religions, Greek, Roman, and Gothic, with which the new teaching came in contact, and this power of assimilation in early days has been upheld by some as one of the surest proofs of the divine mission of the Gospel. But how much has modern Christianity assimilated from Buddhism, either through actual contact in the countries where this religion prevails, or through the efforts of our own scholars to make its teachings intelligible to the Western minds? I question indeed if many of us could honestly claim to have adjusted the perspective of our Christian thinking to the elementary fact that there are five hundred million Buddhists in the world,[1] and that the followers of Buddha greatly outnumber the followers of Christ.

Not even yet has the truth of the Copernican astronomy become thoroughly soaked into the substance of Christian thought. When Milton wrote *Paradise Lost* he found it inconvenient to work that theory into the framework of his poem, and accordingly he did not make the attempt. To-day we may observe a similar attitude in the minds of Christian thinkers towards the stupendous facts of the non-Christian religions. Those facts cannot be fitted in with the scenic framework of popular Christianity; and many of our theologians seem content, like Milton in the other case, to simply leave them out of the account. They do so not in wilful blindness, but from a defect of

[1] This is the reckoning of Dr Rhys Davids. It is questioned by Dr Legge; on grounds, however, which do not convince me. See Legge, *Fâ-hien*, Preface.

imagination. The facts in question, like the truths of Copernican astronomy, are on a scale so vast as to baffle the mind. Their meaning is so subversive of prejudice, and so little in keeping with our customary environment, that the human mind is unable to grasp their significance all at once; and thus they remain unnoticed, because the sweep of our thought is not wide enough to compass them.

Even those Christian thinkers who not only know of the existence of these religions—this we all may be supposed to do — but are acquainted with their history and doctrines, are none too eager to bring this knowledge into relation with current beliefs. In consequence of this oversight it is hardly too much to say that the larger half of Christian Apologetic needs to be re-written. How many of our current arguments require modification, in view of the existence of the non-Christian religions; how often is one tempted to say that such and such a theory of human salvation would be flagrantly untrue if the five hundred million Buddhists were allowed to be human; and how often does this criticism provoke answers which show that the minds of apologists are unprepared for the reference —so unprepared, indeed, as to find it superfluous or even irritating. This again is no cause for surprise. For centuries past there has been so little foreign interference in the course of Christian thought that the mere possibility of its occurrence has passed out of sight. What wonder, then, if Christian thinkers regard the reference to Buddhism as a needlessly disturbing element,—an impertinent intrusion of the foreigner, of which they are in no sense bound to take account? That men should refuse to recognise plain truth until the thunder of cannon has dinned it into their heads is, indeed, no new thing.

The early history of Christianity was largely determined, as every student knows, by causes external to Christendom. The fall of Jerusalem before the Roman arms, the contact of dispersed Judaism with the thought of Greece, the break-up of the Roman empire, the southward march of the Goths, the pressure of the Saracenic hosts from the East, the rediscovery of Aristotle's philosophy—who shall say how much both of the doctrine and polity of Christendom is due to these causes? One has only to open the pages of Justin and Tertullian, or, in modern literature, to read the story of the Holy Roman Empire, as told by Mr Bryce, to realise at once how the main lines for the development of Christendom were formed by its action and reaction with forces external and foreign to itself. It is, however, a remarkable fact, and one which, so far as I know, has not been sufficiently weighed, that this process of interaction with foreign elements has for several centuries almost entirely ceased. Since the armed aggressions of Islâm were finally checked, Christendom has lived secure within her own borders; there has been no development through the reaction of non-Christian forces; there has been no assimilation of non-Christian ideas; there has been no challenge from the outside world; there has been no external standard by which the Church could measure either her faith or her works. Herself the judge of others, she has been judged by none. We may survey a longer period, and say that for more than eight hundred years Christianity has been unaffected by any event in the world's history the consequences of which to the Church can for a moment be compared with those which followed the fall of Jerusalem, or the invasion of the Goths, or the rediscovery of the teachings of Aristotle. Her evolution during this time has been rapid, but it has been self-contained. Political changes no doubt have played a large part in shaping her fortunes, but these changes took place among races she had already conquered and in territory that was already her own. Science, classical learning, and biblical criticism have thrown doubt upon many of her formulas, but it was science, learning, and criticism to which her own deeper spirit had given birth : action and reaction among her own component elements has been incessant, and productive of extraordinary results ; this stream of Christian thought has met and mingled with that ; this part of Christendom has won supremacy over others ; but Christianity *as a whole* has been unvisited by any shock from without, and the day seemed passed for ever when, as a whole, she had to give account of herself before the world.

But now, in spite of all our assumptions, it seems likely that Christianity is about to experience a return of the conditions she had to face at the beginning. For the first time in the course of many centuries she has received a series of shocks from without. A new development, outside her own borders, has taken place in the world's history, the peculiar significance of which, for her, lies in this : that it affects not this or that element of her teaching, but her claim to be the universal teacher of mankind. Christendom, as a whole, long accustomed to treat all pagan races as morally inferior to herself, now stands confronted by a non-Christian civilisation, of vast power and splendid promise, whose claim to moral equality, at least, cannot be disregarded, except by those who are morally blind. Through the rise of Japan a fresh term of comparison has come into existence in the presence of which the self-estimates of all Christian nations and of Christianity itself will have to be revised. What the labour of scholars could not effect is thus being brought to accomplishment by the march of events : the religions of the Far East have ceased to be a curious phenomenon in our eyes, and appear as a factor of immense potency in the moral development of the race ; a new era has opened in the comprehension of the East by the West ; a new environment has been created for Christianity as such ; and it is as certain as anything can be in this world, that the evolution of the Christian religion will no longer be self-contained, but will have to adjust its inner relations to the fresh outer relations created by these surprising events.

The hold of Christianity upon the peoples of the Western world is rooted in the conviction that *this is the religion which produces the best men*. To a greater degree than is commonly recognised, each church or sect of Christendom thus derives its confidence from the final court of ethical appeal. Whatever ground be alleged for a given doctrine, whether of Scripture, Authority, or Reason, the argument would instantly lose its force if it were to appear that the ethical result of denying the doctrine was superior to that which followed its acceptance. Unless a man felt that he was ethically better for his belief, he would not—he could not— believe at all ; and no one in his senses would seek to convert another to any form of religion which was known to be morally injurious. Implicit, therefore, in the fact of our being Christians at all, is the conviction that there is no other religion which produces higher character or better men. In support of this it is enough to quote the words of the Bishop of Ripon in the *Hibbert Journal* for April 1905 :—

" Assent to a proposition or belief in a fact may enter into consideration in a discussion on matters of belief . . . . but unless they can ally themselves with some ethical quality or principle they will entirely fail in evolving anything that can rightly be called faith. In other words, the creed, whatever it is, must make an ethical response if it is to become a spiritual power. The only avenue to spiritual conviction is an ethical one ; . . . . without the sanction of the moral nature there is no faith."

Accepting the ethical test in the sense indicated by the Bishop, I submit the following question :—How would the general status of Christianity be affected by the appearance in the world of a religion which should stand the test better than itself ? Or, slightly varying the terms of the problem, let us suppose that a race of non-Christian men should appear who, when judged by accepted standards of character, should be at once pronounced the moral superiors of the Christian races. I am far from asserting that such a thing has happened ; I offer the question in a strictly hypothetical form—how would Christianity stand affected *if* it were to happen ? The answer is that the whole edifice would be shaken to its very foundations. Not the united zeal and ingenuity of all the doctors of Christendom could secure the Church against the shock of the discovery that another religion produced better nations and better men. That we should all hasten to become adherents of this other religion does not follow, but we should at once be compelled to re-examine and perhaps reform our own. All differences among ourselves would be merged in a common insignificance. As the wild creatures of the prairie suspend their wars when they scent the fumes of the oncoming fire—as the pursuer forgets his chase and the victim his flight, as the panther and the hart seek a common hiding-place from destruction—so would it be with us and with our controversies in the day when this thing should come to pass. Reason and Authority, Christian metaphysics and Christian evidence, dogma and apology, Catholic and Protestant, Churchman and Dissenter—of what consequence would these distinctions be in face of the advent of another religion which produced better men? The defence and the propagation of Christianity would alike come to a dead stop. The Church could no longer chant her favourite text about the gates of hell, for she would be stricken utterly dumb.

But—be it said in passing—this dismay would have a short duration. Soon the question would be asked: What has Christ himself to say to these new conditions, and how does He bid us greet their appearance? Then would flash upon the Church the full meaning of those much-neglected words—"neither in this mountain nor yet at Jerusalem." It would be seen that the coming of this new religion was nothing other than a second advent of the Universal Christ himself. Fears would give place to rejoicing; frowns to the look of welcome; the faithful would resume their labours; the spirit of exclusiveness would vanish, and a Christian Religion, worthy of its name—a genuine Open Brotherhood of the children of the Spirit—might at last appear in the world.

The bare supposition that a religion capable of producing higher character than the Christian could ever rise into existence may still seem to some a monstrous, if not a profane, hypothesis. For centuries past nothing has occurred, as we have said, to shake the confidence of Christians in the moral superiority of their own to all other forms of religion. Hence it has come to be regarded as in the nature of things impossible that this confidence should ever be challenged. There are those to whom the propounding of the above hypothesis will be like asking what would happen if the laws of thought were abolished, or the multiplication table found to be untrue. It is difficult indeed to find language which adequately describes the confidence of Christendom in its moral superiority, or the inveteracy with which that confidence has entered into Christian thought. We are here dealing with one of those unconscious habits of mind which are the most difficult to call to account. But, be the assumption true or false, we can at least assure ourselves that it has not been unattended by evil. The easy notion that Christians are necessarily the best sort of men has not helped Christendom to see the eternal necessity to make herself better. That some, perhaps much, of the moral failure which is the disgrace of Western civilisation must be set down to this cause, does not, in my opinion, admit of a moment's doubt. Dreaming on in the unchallenged security of one who has no rival to fear, the mind of Christendom has wandered far from the eternal truth at the fountainhead, and vast energies have been wasted on irrelevance which were sorely needed for the betterment of the world. Meanwhile an enemy has been sowing tares.

Hard, however, as the effort will seem to many, it has now become the duty of Christendom to realise that her hold on the moral supremacy of the world is not so secure as many of us imagine. There is room, nay, opportunity, for a rival candidate. That the Christian ideal of moral excellence is splendid, even unsurpassed, no one doubts. But no less certain, no less striking, is the failure of the West to justify that ideal, both in national and private life. The sense of dissatisfaction which this failure has produced has entered deep into the moral consciousness of Christians all the world over ; and if the impression has been deep in the case of those who profess and call themselves Christians, it has been yet deeper with the multitudes who have turned their backs on the Church. I rate this feeling among the greatest of the forces now moving the minds of men. Other things may create a louder noise, but this works revolutions. The question of theological standards is being merged into that of moral consistency, and we are being summoned, as never before, to find the correspondence between our professions and our lives. Such a state of things exposes Christendom to a rival challenge, and marks the fitting moment for another claimant to appear on the scene. If outside the pale of Christendom there should arise the example of a saner, nobler, more rational, more joyous, more humane, more self-controlled life than the West has so far achieved, the minds of men are prepared to greet its appearance as a divine fulfilment of the urgent needs of mankind.

Nor would such an event be without its parallel in the past. The confidence of Christendom in the inalienable supremacy of its moral position is the repro-

duction on a large scale of that view of their status in
the world's history which the Jews held in the time of
St Paul. Among the many things which Christians
have inherited from Jews is the unquestioning conviction
that they are the chosen people of the Lord. Based on
different assumptions in the two cases, it may perish in
the second from the same cause which destroyed its
logic in the first. It may be cast out in the process
of moral evolution. And certainly there is much in
the present state of the world which might incline
a religious man to regard such an issue as more than
possible. The faithlessness of Christendom to its own
moral ideal has indeed been so obstinate, so long-
continued, so unashamed, that one might well look
for the call and election of a more "faithful nation"
as among the decrees of a just Providence. What
can be more closely applicable to modern Christians
than the words in which St Paul addressed the
Judaizers of Rome?

"There is no respect of persons with God. . . . But if thou
bearest the name of a Jew and restest upon the law and gloriest
in God, and knowest his will, and approvest the things that are
excellent, being instructed out of the law, and art confident that
thou thyself art a guide of the blind, a light of them that are in
darkness, a corrector of the foolish, a teacher of babes, ... thou
therefore that teachest another, teachest thou not thyself? Thou
that preachest a man should not steal, dost thou steal? Thou
that sayest a man should not commit adultery, dost thou commit
adultery? Thou that abhorrest idols, dost thou rob temples?
Thou who gloriest in the law, through thy transgression of the law
dishonourest thou God? For the name of God is blasphemed
among the Gentiles because of you" (Rom. ii. 11-24).

If any reader should conclude from what has been
said that I regard the rise of Japan as the most

important event in religious history since the call of the Gentiles, he will so far correctly understand my drift. But if he takes this as a prophecy that Christianity will fall and Buddhism rise into its place, he will do violence both to the letter and the spirit of the argument. I make no prediction whatever. The contention is that a serious challenge to the moral hegemony of Christendom is not, *a priori*, impossible; that such a challenge has actually been offered; that Buddhism, represented for the moment by Japan, is even now in the field as a claimant for that position which the vast majority of Christians regard as the indisputable birthright of their own religion.[1] What verdict history will finally pass upon this claim no one can tell, no one should try to tell. Enough for the present that the claim has arisen; that it lacks no element of seriousness; that it has been forced on the attention of the world in a fact-language which admits of no mistake.

Since the Russo-Japanese war of 1903–5, the potentates of Europe have found reason to think twice before shaking their mailed fists in the face of the Far East. But not for her guns alone, nor the way she handles them, is Japan to be feared. *The " Yellow Peril" is an ethical phenomenon.* Far more significant than the efficiency of Japanese arms is the advent into the world's history of a people possessed of a disciplined will in combination with the highest order of intelligence. An observer has declared that the greatest brains in all

[1] " If I were asked whether there is any one of the great established religions from which it is possible that a conception of the world-problem could, in our time, come, I should look perhaps to Buddhism." —Graham Wallas, *Religion and Empire*, reported in the *Inquirer*, June 29, 1901.

the world are to be found at this moment in Japan. But
a great brain is no guarantee of efficiency ; isolated from
other gifts, it may even become the ruin of its possessor.
This divorce, however, does not exist in Japan ; her
purpose and her intelligence are one. She has shown
herself great not only in conceiving her ends but in pursuing them ; she has poured her energies into her ideals.
Thus she rises up in possession of all that we mean by
character ; and it is in the strength of character rather
than in the strength of arms that she now challenges
the world.

Praise of Japanese virtue is superfluous. But none
the less a prudent man will not cease to observe the
facts, nor grow weary in his study of their meaning.
He will be quick to notice that Japan has all along
been impressing Europe by qualities higher than those
which pertain to martial valour. To very many persons
—I think to the masses of the people—it appeared that
Japan in her hour of trial showed a degree of calmness,
moderation, self-restraint, and dignity which are strange
to the working moral standards of Europe, and beyond
what we have been accustomed to expect. Her armies
and navies taught the world many lessons in the
making of war, and she won an equal glory by showing
how the people who stay at home should behave themselves while the war is being made. By what she
refrained from doing, no less than by what she did,
she deserved our respect. In no act of that appalling
drama did she allow herself to play to the gallery.
She did not make a spectacle of her fight for life ; she
encouraged no reporters to witness the shedding of
heroic blood ; but, as though some terrible operation
of surgery were in progress, she repulsed the sightseer

and locked the door. In all these respects she did not copy an example previously given, but set a new example to the civilised world.

How deep this impression sunk in the minds of Western peoples, how far it has already compelled an unconscious process of readjustment among inveterate mental habits, has yet to be discovered, but it will scarcely be doubted that the impression went very deep, and that great changes are bound to follow in many of our accepted ways of thought. The working classes of our own country in particular, never prone to rate too highly either the *bona fides* of their religious instructors or the practical value of the instruction given, undoubtedly found here a new reason for distrusting the moral efficacy of the Christian religion. And not among the working classes only, but everywhere, one may observe a growing readiness to compare the respective moral harvests of the East and the West, with the result that Western society sees with cleared vision the scantiness of the domestic crop and the general nakedness of the land. A new point has been given to the arrows of the sceptic: has he not indeed been provided with a new poison for his barbs? The astounding divorce between the ethical ideals of Christendom and its normal practice; the liberty of interpretation with which the first principles of Christian morality are misapplied to our social life; the freedom, amounting to effrontery, with which one thing is professed and the opposite practised; the disgraceful sophisms by which the Christian conscience is taught to be blind to its own faithlessness—these and many other truths of a like nature, once apprehended only by a small and neglected company, were during

those three years revealed in their true colours to tens
of thousands of persons who never thought of them
before. Who can doubt that the crisis which has so
long been in preparation for Christianity has been
brought appreciably nearer by these things—so near,
perhaps, as to be even now at the doors?

To explain the moral character displayed by Japan as
due to the stimulus of a crisis in her history is, at least,
to show an astonishing ignorance of human nature. A
nation unprovided with character to begin with would
be unnerved, distracted, paralysed by such a crisis. No
menace to the life of a people can at a moment's notice
summon into being the qualities with which Japan won
the admiration of mankind—the far-reaching purpose,
the grasp of conditions needed for its fulfilment, the
unswerving pursuit of the goal, the combination of
millions of wills into one, and the readiness to endure
every sacrifice at the call of duty. The explanation lies
deeper—deeper perchance than our analysis can reach.
In offering such an explanation here I make no pretence
to be exhaustive, and am well aware that none of
the reasons I am about to give would have validity if
separated from one another, or even if taken out of
the general context of life in the Far East.

1. *Religion.*—Interpretations of Oriental religions by
Western scholars need, as a rule, to be accepted with
some reserve.[1] The wine of the East is apt to become
water when transferred to the bottles of the West. In

[1] This difficulty no doubt applies to the Western interpretation of
the Bible, which we can never too often remind ourselves is an
Oriental book. But in our attempts to understand the Bible we of
the West have enjoyed an exceptional advantage, from the circumstance that we have always had the Jews at our elbows.

the case of Buddhism, however, there are one or two features of extreme interest which may be described without undue risk of error. Buddhism, unlike our Christianity, is a cosmocentric religion. The universe, instead of being conceived as the theatre or scene of the human drama is itself the one drama, outside of which there is no action, no life, no being. The individual, who constitutes the central concern of Christian thought, is nothing to Buddhism: his individuality is an illusion. Such a view of human life, we have been accustomed to think, must be in the highest degree unfavourable to the development of character, inasmuch as it seems to sap the source of individual endeavour, and to substitute a state of apathy for the spirit of keen interest in the things of the world. The profound error of this conclusion ought now to be manifest to Christendom. The spirit of Buddhism, entering into the life-blood of Japan, has produced an ethical result of a character exactly opposite to that which we have been accustomed to expect. Instead of crippling individual endeavour, *it has checked the operation of personal selfishness*[1]—the chief source of the ugliness, the misery, the wickedness of the civilisation of the West. By so doing Buddhism has not indeed directly produced any virtue, but it has prepared the soil on which many virtues might be cultivated. The citizen, freed from the obstructing vision of his own importance, can discern the meaning of his duty and his ideal, and, surrendering

[1] It is not here forgotten that other elements besides Buddhism enter into the religion of Japan. I count Japan a Buddhist nation for the reasons and with the reservations given by Dr Rhys Davids (*Buddhism*, ch. i. and p. 142), and I attribute to the operation of the Buddhist spirit precisely what is contained in the italicised clause.

himself to that, reach a high level of moral vigour and efficiency.

2. *Education.*—The Japanese system of education has an ethical aim : it is a system which educates character.

" Education is compulsory. Every child on attaining the age of six must attend a common elementary school where instruction is given in morals, reading, writing, arithmetic, the rudiments of technical work, gymnastics, and poetry. If a child after graduating at a common elementary school desires to extend its education, it passes to a common middle school, where training is given for practical pursuits and for admission to higher educational institutions. The ordinary curriculum at a common middle school includes moral philosophy," etc. etc. [1]

But this is by no means all. As everybody now knows—though it was known to few ten years ago—the profession of arms in Japan is controlled by a highly developed ethical code — no mere affair of military etiquette among officers, but a well-understood moral discipline for every man in the army. We are assured by competent witnesses that this system—known as Bushidô—is the controlling influence in the life of the Japanese soldier ; and since military service is compulsory, it becomes directly a factor of the first importance in forming the moral character of the nation. A brief description is as follows :—

" Frugality, fealty, filial piety—these may be called the fundamental virtues of the Samurai. To be swayed in the smallest degree by mercenary motives was despicable in his eyes. [2] He

---

[1] *Ency. Brit.,* article " Japan " (new volumes).

[2] An occasional outbreak of lawlessness does not, I submit, affect the general truth of these statements. The self-restraint of Japan would be meaningless if there were no lower forces to restrain. That some portion of these forces should escape control at a moment of great tension is not surprising.

made self-control the ideal of his existence. . . . The Samurai rose to a remarkable height of moral nobility. . . . The Samurai entertained a high regard for the obligations of truth. 'A Bushi has no second word,' was one of his principal mottoes. . . . A pledge or promise must never be broken, but the duty of veracity did not override the interests or the welfare of others. . . . Lifted high above his surroundings, he [the enlightened hero] is prepared to meet every fate with indifference. The attainment of this state seems to have been a fact in the case both of the Samurai of the military epoch and of the Japanese soldier to-day."[1]

What the fruit of such a system may be in dealing with the problems of international ethics was, at the conclusion of the war, written in letters so large that all the world may read. The action of Japan in waiving her claim to a Russian indemnity can be understood only by assuming that her statesmen acted therein as the representatives of a nation whose moral instincts have been trained to a high level of discernment and vigour. Sordid explanations cannot rob her conduct of its due: beyond all gainsaying she thus rendered the most illustrious service of modern times towards raising the standard by which the nations are to be judged.

Quid adhuc egemus testibus? There may, indeed, be those who, on learning that Japanese ethics square neither with the Sermon on the Mount nor "the greatest happiness of the greatest number," neither with Aristotle, Hobbes, Butler, nor Green, will deny that they are ethics at all. This would be obviously absurd. Nor does it affect the issue that the Japanese ideal of character is not the highest known to mankind —that, for example, the Christian is higher. This is a side issue. The point is that a moral ideal, be it high or low, is the basis of Japanese education. From this

[1] *Ency. Brit.*, article "Japan" (new volumes).

general fact the most important consequences follow. It means that the will-power of the community is undergoing a process of continuous cultivation; that individual selfishness is being checked, that the sense of obligation to some kind of "not-self" is being wrought into the fibre of the race; in a word, that character is being formed, nourished, and inspired.[1]

3. *Art.*—It is no easy matter for Europeans, at all events for Englishmen, to understand what Art has done in building up the virility of this Far Eastern race. The whole situation is strange to our experience, so strange that we even question if the picture can be true.[2] And yet if there is one point on which all competent witnesses agree it is this: that the love of beauty is an active force in the daily life of the whole Japanese nation; that the power to appreciate beauty is developed

---

[1] Mr Harada affirms that Japanese character has four principal qualities. "The first," he says, is "Giri, the Sense of Ought." I may mention the others at this point: (2) Hôon, the Sense of Gratitude. "I remember being frequently taught as a child that to be ungrateful is to be brutish. . . . We have it impressed upon us from our childhood on, that nothing is so base as ingratitude." (3) Renketsu no Sei, the Spirit of Disinterestedness. "We have a saying: 'The true gentleman does not think about his own advantage.' . . . This spirit existed among all classes down to the common day labourer. . . . It is in consequence of this spirit of disinterestedness that there are many who endure hardships and are content to remain poor." (4) Chukô, the Virtue of Loyalty and Filial Piety. This spirit is "essentially the same as that expressed by the Apostle's words, 'none of us liveth to himself, and no man dieth to himself.' Loyalty and filial piety are to-day the greatest inspiration to millions of Japanese."—T. Harada, from an Address on Japanese Character, published in the *Tōkyō Maishu Shinshi,* Aug. 23, 1894.

[2] The case of Ancient Greece, which is sometimes cited, is, of course, far from being a parallel. There is no slave population in Japan.

in every class; that the poor multitudes, no less than the few rich, are by nature at once the lovers and the critics of the beautiful; that they seek it with the instinctive pertinacity of an animal in quest of its food, and rejoice when it is found. With us the beautiful is an adornment and a luxury, with them it is daily meat and drink; with us it is the purchased possession of the rich, with them it is the birthright of the people.[1]

What follows? In the social life of the Japanese there is a marked absence of the spirit of restlessness with which we have become so familiar in the West— the spirit of baffled endeavour and unsatisfied desire, born of distress, on the one hand, and of luxury on the other, which more perhaps than any other single cause disturbs and hinders the best life of men. The Japanese as an individual unit still retains that quality of self-poise which enables him to see life steadily and see it whole. And we do not hesitate to assign the origin of this quality, in large measure, to the national love of beauty, both in nature and art. " He who possesses any one of the virtues," says a modern Aristotelean, " possesses in that measure all the rest "; and it is not hard for us to see how the individual citizen of Japan is made, by his possession of this one gift, into a better man all round. The sense which takes delight in beautiful things saves his life from becoming a process of exhaustion. He knows how to rest, and his leisure is an opportunity for genuine happiness and recuperation. Incessant resort to deceitful stimulants is not necessary. He is under no

[1] I would here refer the reader to Lafcadio Hearn, *Gleanings in Buddha Fields, passim.* See also Mortimer Menpes, *A Study in Colour.*

compulsion to be perpetually running away from himself, for he has resources within. The mood of a man who cannot be anywhere without at once desiring to be somewhere else—the motoritis of character—is not his. He can be content under privations which no European would tolerate; can retain the dignity of a man in the midst of extreme poverty; can find in all conditions a sufficient joy in life. He considers the lilies of the field, and learns that lesson which the Christian nations of the West have set their faces not to learn. He finds his happiness in that which makes others happy also, and the vision of "a joy in widest commonalty spread" is never wholly absent from his mind.

This is the character of Japan—not of a favoured and fortunate few, but of the people. So bred and nurtured, she has accumulated a vast reserve of moral force. Her people are normally self-collected, and the instinct of order is in their blood. The cry of *panem et circenses* has been rarely heard within her borders. Thanks, in part, to her love of beauty, she has *men* for her citizens. Each unit in her ranks is a unit of moral force, and the impetus of their combined movement is moral also. This is higher than Gothic violence and more even than the strenuous life. Here we may see how a love of the beauty of simple things and a care for the Fine Arts, entering as co-efficients into the structure of a nation's character, may so operate as to sharpen the wisdom of the serpent for a finer discernment and to nerve the strength of the tiger for a surer spring. To many persons it may appear incredible that the consistence of Japan's statesmanship and strategy, the far reach of her military plans, the splendid qualities of her soldiers and sailors, the steadiness of nerve, the accuracy of aim, the coolness of advance, the deadliness of attack, the self-immolation of regiments at the word of command, are not unconnected with the fact that she alone among living nations has a truly national art, that her senses are refined and her taste fastidious, that her poor love beauty and seek their pleasure among flowers. This is a hard saying, but the truth is even so.

> "Isles of blest Japan,
> Should your Yamato spirit
> Strangers seek to scan,
> Say, scenting morn's sun-lit air,
> Blows the cherry, wild and fair." [1]

It would be an easy task to exhibit the weak points of Japanese ethics, but this task I shall not undertake. Suffice it to say that I have no intention to represent them as a race of morally perfect beings. Nothing of the kind can be reasonably maintained, nor is it needed for the purpose of this argument. Let this only be granted : that the strength of Japan lies in the existence among the people at large of a disciplined moral will, and in the general diffusion of moral culture ; that Morality and Art — the Good and the Beautiful — are *national* interests ; and it follows that the rise of Japan forebodes the rise of a new and serious claim to the moral supremacy of the world. To appreciate the meaning of this it needs only, in the second place, that we should place in contrast the conditions prevailing among ourselves. We have the Christian ideal ; but we must confess, in sober truth, that the Christian ideal does not control the great tides of Western energy. What, then, does control them ? Shall we fall back on the Gothic qualities of "chivalry and honour," and

---

[1] Translation of a Japanese verse in Nitobe's *Bushidô*.

uphold these as the operative ideal of the West? One could wish indeed that this were possible; but he would be a bold man who should affirm that chivalry and honour were the keynote to, say, the last fifty years of European history. The policy of Bismarck or the story of our Colonial expansion may serve to illustrate the maxims of Rob Roy, but in their broad outlines they have almost as little to do with chivalry and honour as they have with the Sermon on the Mount. The truth is, that if search be made for any conception of social and international ethics which the nations of Christendom are agreed in striving to realise, we are finally forced to confess that such a conception does not exist; for these nations have in practice long turned their backs on the Christian ideal, and they have found no other to take its place. The contrast, then, reduces itself to this: that whereas Japan has both a *national* art and a *national* morality, we have neither. This does not mean, of course, that there may not be tens of thousands of individuals among us who cultivate the loftiest ideals of private character and plead for righteousness in public affairs; it means that the community, as such, can appeal to no common ideal for the moral inspiration of its acts. "Cities," says Plato, "cannot exist if a few only share in the virtues as in the arts."

That we have here a grave weakness in the claim of Christendom to moral supremacy there cannot be the shadow of a doubt, nor will the effect of that weakness be long in making itself felt if it be true that Japan is strong at the precise point where we are so conspicuously weak. The effect indeed has long been manifest in the inner evolution of Western society. The absence of a moral ideal for the community has had its counterpart in the appearance of masses of human beings, grouped chiefly in the great towns, who seem to lack the power of self-guidance, a dangerous and ever-increasing element of the population, whose misfortune is not that of being poor or rich—for they are to be found in both classes—but rather the demoralisation and decay of the Will. This gradual deterioration of will-power is an evil which few social reformers have yet measured in its full extent, and too little is being done to stem its further growth. Perhaps the example of Japan may teach us ere it is too late that one of the highest aims of a community is to maintain the moral vigour of its members, to increase it by discipline, and to provide it with inspirations. Not only have we failed to do this; we have scarcely realised that it needs to be done. It is precisely in respect of moral culture that our educational system—in this country at least— betrays its worst defect. The very faultiness of our methods, on which we have remarked elsewhere, is only a further proof that the intelligence of the nation is not awake to the importance of the subject. A formal alliance exists between the Church and the School; but this alliance, in spite of the inseparable connection between Religion and Ethics, has failed, so far, to be productive of any combined and intelligent endeavour to build up the character of the people. For religion itself has drifted away from its ethical basis; hence "religious teaching" has come to mean anything and everything except the one thing it ought to mean. All kinds of side issues—some of which are none too creditable to the parties concerned—have been suffered to obscure the central purpose of education. We have made idols of our theological jealousies and ecclesiastical

divisions, and in blind devotion to these have trusted to
scraps of doctrinal patter to form the manhood of the
race, and to save us from being as Sodom and Gomorrah
in the day of judgment. Bushidô may be a poor thing
—I do not think so—but what would one give for a
breath of Bushidô among the vicious and anæmic youths
who throng the lighted thoroughfares of our great towns,
among the idle rich, among the drunken thousands of
Glasgow, Liverpool, Birmingham, or the East End?

Hitherto it has been taken for granted that political
as well as moral supremacy belonged of right to the
West. As every people in Europe knows to its bitter
cost, the Great Powers have long been engaged in a
baneful strife as to who should be greatest; and in
speculating upon the outcome of this rivalry, it has
always been assumed that the first place in the dominion
of the whole world must necessarily fall to the successful
competitor. But now Japan has spoilt the game. The
victory of any of the Great Powers over any other,
whether in wealth or war, would decide nothing, so far
as world-dominion was concerned, since Japan—*and all
that lies behind Japan*—would still have to be reckoned
with. For what boots it to strive who shall be greatest
when a possible greater stands outside of the dispute?
Cadit quæstio.

Thus, though nothing can be foreseen, it is not
unreasonable to hope that one indirect result of the
rise of Japan will be to cool the jealousies of the Great
Powers and to establish the prospect of a long-continued
European peace. In view of the fact that by far the
largest part of the energies of Christendom have hitherto
been used up in preparing for mutual destruction, it is

small wonder that these communities have developed internal evils which make their civilisation, if not a failure, at all events a meagre success. Judged by the condition of the masses of the people, there is not one of the great lands of Christendom which can boast itself free from the danger of moral and physical[1] decay. All their energies are needed for the remedy of the mischiefs hence arising; they have none to spare upon the blowing of each other's souls into eternity. The question whether this one shall rise or that one fall is of little moment compared with the greater question whether all are not falling together. The answer to that depends on how long they are content to postpone the interests of manhood to the interests of wealth. To pretend that this is beyond the wit of man is to overlook the fact that the wit of man has never yet been fully employed in the enterprise. When the Christian states of Europe have given as much thought to securing the conditions of a noble manhood for the masses of the population as they have hitherto spent in devising mischief for each other, it will be time to decide whether the higher education of the people is or is not beyond the wit of man. Certain it is, that if the rise of Japan as a moral and political force leads, as we may reasonably hope it will, to the cooling of our Western jealousies and the liberation of some part of the social energies hitherto wasted in their service, we shall have good reasons for regarding her as a benefactor of mankind.

And greater gains should follow. The task of bringing the energies of Western civilisation under the

[1] See the Debate on Physical Deterioration in the House of Lords, 20th July 1905.

actual control of its religious ideal will be brought into a new prominence. Familiar but forgotten truths will rise into remembrance—that for nations, as for individuals, the mere profession of Christianity is a vain thing: that the claim of Christianity to be supreme must assuredly fail unless it finds its exponent in renovated national life. It is good for us thus to realise that our ideals and our practice are at variance, even though it be the finger of a non-Christian race that is pointing to the breach. All our Christian pride will not prevent us from taking heed. It is, indeed, the conviction of the writer that the present hour is the fullest of hope for humanity which the world has seen for long ages. Not the least element of that hope is the prospect of a union between the forces of Christianity and Buddhism for the uplifting of mankind. For these two religions, in their highest expressions, are not estranged. They are approaching each other; and their approach is the dawn of a better age.